P9-DCB-867

Praise for *Pledging Allegiance*

"A valuable sourcebook for those who are uncertain about what patriotism is and, even more, for those who are certain that they know."
—Howard Gardner, Harvard University, author of *Five Minds for the Future*

"By bringing together diverse and often divergent perspectives of patriotism, *Pledging Allegiance* opens to critical scrutiny the very idea of loyalty to a country. In doing so, it not only offers a useful educational resource but also performs a valuable political service. I can't think of many books more likely to stimulate deep reflection and spirited discussion, and these activities, after all, are integral to democracy itself."
—Alfie Kohn, author of *The Schools Our Children Deserve* and *What Does It Mean to Be Well Educated?*

"A powerful and timely account of the struggles between authoritarian and democratic patriotism in the schools."
—David Tyack, Stanford University

"Filled with outrage and hope; brilliance and despair; history and imagined futures; Mohammed Ali, Mark Twain, and the Yankees, this volume is a must-read for educators, organizers, lawyers, youth, activists, and those who have politically fallen asleep in the twenty-first century."
—Michelle Fine, Professor, City University of New York Graduate Center

"Joel Westheimer has brought together a fine and thoughtful collection of essays that probe the perhaps inevitable but nevertheless deeply problematic role of patriotism in a democratic society."
—Frances Fox Piven, author of *The War at Home* and *Challenging Authority*

"Is patriotism compatible with democratic education or citizenship? Taking on civic educators' most enduring questions, *Pledging Allegiance* is a primer in how to enrich civic education for today's youth. What could be more patriotic?"
—Daniel Perlstein, UC Berkeley, author of *Justice, Justice: School Politics and the Eclipse of Liberalism*

"Asks hard questions about what it means to ask the most of our country—and how we can teach this in our schools. Offers strong reflections and perspectives on the fundamental stories about our country that we tell our future citizens."
—Paul Loeb, author of *Soul of a Citizen*

"Everybody in America should read this book, every patriot in support of war should read this book, every patriot opposed to war should read this book. Then we can talk, because then maybe we won't know the answers, but we will know what we should be talking about."
—Terri Camajani, facilitator of the Manalive Violence Prevention Program, George Washington High School, San Francisco

"Reading this splendid book will prevent you from ever taking the pledge of allegiance casually. The rituals and compulsions that bind us to national loyalties have seldom been better dissected."
—Andrew Ross, New York University, author of *Fast Boat to China*

The Teaching for Social Justice Series

William Ayers—Series Editor
Therese Quinn—Associate Series Editor

Pledging Allegiance:
The Politics of Patriotism
in America's Schools
JOEL WESTHEIMER, EDITOR

See You When We Get There:
Teaching for Change in Urban Schools
GREGORY MICHIE

Echoes of Brown:
Youth Documenting and Performing the
Legacy of Brown v. Board of Education
MICHELLE FINE

Writing in the Asylum:
Student Poets in City Schools
JENNIFER MCCORMICK

Teaching the Personal and the Political:
Essays on Hope and Justice
WILLIAM AYERS

Teaching Science for Social Justice
ANGELA CALABRESE BARTON, WITH
JASON L. ERMER, TANAHIA A. BURKETT,
AND MARGERY D. OSBORNE

Putting the Children First: The Changing
Face of Newark's Public Schools
JONATHAN G. SILIN AND
CAROL LIPPMAN, EDITORS

Refusing Racism:
White Allies and the Struggle for Civil
Rights
CYNTHIA STOKES BROWN

A School of Our Own:
Parents, Power, and Community at the
East Harlem Block Schools
TOM RODERICK

The White Architects of Black Education:
Ideology and Power in America,
1865–1954
WILLIAM WATKINS

The Public Assault on America's Children:
Poverty, Violence, and Juvenile Injustice
VALERIE POLAKOW, EDITOR

Construction Sites:
Excavating Race, Class, and Gender
Among Urban Youths
LOIS WEIS AND
MICHELLE FINE, EDITORS

Walking the Color Line:
The Art and Practice of
Anti-Racist Teaching
MARK PERRY

A Simple Justice:
The Challenge of Small Schools
WILLIAM AYERS,
MICHAEL KLONSKY, AND
GABRIELLE H. LYON, EDITORS

Holler If You Hear Me:
The Education of a Teacher
and His Students
GREGORY MICHIE

Pledging Allegiance

★ ★ ★

The Politics of Patriotism in America's Schools

Joel Westheimer, Editor

Foreword by Howard Zinn

Teachers College, Columbia University
New York and London

Pg. x: "Flag Seller" used by permission of Kevin Bubriski. Copyright © 2001 by Kevin Bubriski.

Pg. 5: "Boondocks" cartoon strip used by permission of Aaron McGruder. Copyright © 2001 by Aaron McGruder.

Pg. 37: "God Bless America and Peace," copyright © 2001 by St. Joseph School for the Deaf, Bronx, NY.

Pg. 38: "Do You Wanna Be Adam?" used by permission of Jimmy Holmfeldt. Copyright by Jimmy Holmfeldt.

Pg. 74: "Bleeding Flag" used by permission of Ziva Kronzon. Copyright © 2001 by Ziva Kronzon.

Pg. 98: "No Child Left Behind" used by permission of Christopher C. Kaufman. Copyright by Christopher C. Kaufman.

Pg. 126: Photo of students at University of California Peace Strike used by permission of the Rondal Partridge estate. Copyright © 1940 by Rondal Partridge.

Pg. 152: Photo of students listening to the speaker at the California Student Peace Strike, used by permission of the Rondal Partridge estate. Copyright © 1940 by Rondal Partridge.

Pg. 170: "Patriotism Starts at Home" used by permission of Steven Dana. Copyright © 2001 by Steven Dana.

Pgs. 97, 164, 177, 194, : Photos of protesters at Republican National Convention, copyright © by 2004 Joel Westheimer.

All other photographs used in this book are from the Library of Congress archives and are in the public domain. Credit has been given to the photographers where possible.

Published by Teachers College Press, 1234 Amsterdam Avenue, New York, NY 10027

Copyright © 2007 by Teachers College, Columbia University

Library of Congress Cataloging-in-Publication Data

Pledging allegiance : the politics of patriotism in America's schools /
Joel Westheimer, editor.
    p. cm. — (The teaching for social justice series)
    Includes bibliographical references and index.
    ISBN: 978-0-8077-4750-6 (pbk : alk. paper)
    ISBN: 978-0-8077-4751-3 (cloth : alk. paper)
    1. Education—Political aspects—United States. 2. Patriotism—Study and teaching—United States. 3. Critical pedagogy—United States. 4. Patriotism—United States. I. Westheimer, Joel.
LC1091.P513 2007
379.73--dc22   2006028925

978-0-8077-4750-6 (pbk : alk. paper)
978-0-8077-4751-3 (cloth : alk. paper)

Printed on acid-free paper.
Manufactured in the United States of America.

14   13   12   11   10   09   08   07   8   7   6   5   4   3   2   1

For Michal and Benjamin

★　★　★

History is yours to make.
It is not owned or written by someone else for you to learn.
It is being made by you, right now, reading this page,
thinking and acting on the ideas you will
read about in the pages that follow.
It is your rage, your sympathy, your understanding.[1]

Contents

Pledging Allegiance

★ ★ ★

The Politics of Patriotism in America's Schools

Flag Seller. Photographer: Kevin Bubriski (http://kevinbubriski.com). Copyright © 2001 by Kevin Bubriski. Used with permission.

Foreword

Howard Zinn

Sometime in the 1960s, the folk singer Tom Paxton wrote a song, "What Did You Learn in School Today?," which included the lines:

> I learned that Washington never told a lie,
> I learned that soldiers never die. . . .
> I learned our government must be strong,
> It's always right and never wrong.

The song is amusing. An exaggeration, of course, but not too far off the mark, because all of us who grew up in the United States, as soon as we entered first grade, were taught to have pride in our nation. Our classroom walls were decorated with photos of the Founding Fathers, all wise and benign, and our first heroes were military heroes: George Washington, Nathan Hale, Andrew Jackson.

Even before we knew what the words meant, we were reciting, in unison, the Pledge of Allegiance, "with liberty and justice for all." We sang "The Star Spangled Banner," ending with the words "the land of the free, and the home of the brave."

Did the teacher point out that, at the time the national anthem was written, "the land of the free" was a country that held several million Black people as slaves? Not likely, because while slavery might be mentioned at some point, it would not be juxtaposed with the words about liberty and justice—that might spoil the picture we all had in our heads of a nation unique in its virtues, deserving of pledges and salutes and anthems.

So much of our early education is filled with stories and images that come out of the Revolutionary War: the Boston Massacre, the Boston Tea Party, Paul Revere, the battle of Bunker Hill, Washington crossing the Delaware, the heroism of soldiers at Valley Forge, the making of the Constitution. This is a history suffused with emotional satisfaction, glorying in military victories, proud of our national leaders.

The march across the continent that follows the Revolution is depicted in history books as Westward Expansion. The phrase suggests a kind of natural, almost biological, growth, and neglects to mention the military forays into Spanish Florida, the armed aggression against Mexico, the forced removal of Indians from their land, and the massacres of Indians on the great plains. Instead, classroom maps color and label the different events with benign language, such as "Louisiana Purchase," "Florida Purchase," "Mexican Cession," giving the impression of commercial transactions and generous gifts, rather than military occupation and conquest.

Young people who are learning such history, indeed a "patriotic" history, would easily conclude that, as Tom Paxton's song put it, our government is "always right and never wrong." And if so, it is our duty to support whatever our government does, even to be willing to give our lives in war. But is that patriotism, in the best sense of the word? If patriotism means supporting what your government does without question, is that not a good description of patriotism in a totalitarian state?

Patriotism in a democratic society cannot possibly be unquestioning support of the government. Not if we take seriously the principles of democracy as set forth in the Declaration of Independence, our founding document. The Declaration makes a clear distinction between the government and the people. Governments are artificial creations, the Declaration says, established by the people with the obligation to protect certain ends: the equal right of all to "life, liberty, and the pursuit of happiness." The Declaration also makes clear that "whenever any form of government becomes destructive of these ends, it is the right of the people to alter or abolish it."

Surely, if it is the right of the people to "alter or abolish" their government, it is their right to criticize, even severely, policies they believe to be destructive of the ends for which their government has been established. This principle suggests that a true patriotism lies in supporting the values the country is supposed to cherish: equality, life, liberty, and the pursuit of happiness. So, when a government attacks those values, it is being unpatriotic.

The characterization of governments expressed in the Declaration, as "deriving their just powers from the consent of the governed" has been understood by the most heroic of Americans—not the heroes of war, but the heroes of the long struggle for social justice. Mark Twain was one of many who distinguished between the country and the government. In 1906, after American soldiers had massacred six hundred men, women, and children in the Philippines, he bitingly criticized President Theodore Roosevelt for sending a telegram of congratulations to the general in charge of the military operation.

Several years before that incident, Mark Twain wrote the novel, *A Connecticut Yankee In King Arthur's Court*, and put the following words into the mouth of his main character:

> You see my kind of loyalty was loyalty to one's country, not to its institutions or its officeholders. The country is the real thing, the substantial thing, the eternal thing; it is the thing to watch over, and care for, and be loyal to; institutions are extraneous, they are its mere clothing, and clothing can wear out, become ragged, cease to be comfortable, cease to protect the body from winter, disease and death. To be loyal to rags, to shout for rags, to worship rags, to die for rags—that is a loyalty of unreason, it is pure animal; It belongs to monarchy, was invented by monarchy; let monarchy keep it.

The same distinction between government and country was made in the years before World War I by the anarchist Emma Goldman, who lectured in many cities on the subject of patriotism:

> What is patriotism? Is it love of one's birthplace, the place of childhood's recollections and hopes, dreams and aspirations? Is it the place where, in childlike naivety, we would watch the fleeting clouds, and wonder why we, too, could not run so swiftly? . . . Indeed, conceit, arrogance, and egotism are the essentials of patriotism. Patriotism assumes that our globe is divided into little spots, each one surrounded by an iron gate. Those who have had the fortune of being born on some particular spot, consider themselves better, nobler, grander, more intelligent than the living beings inhabiting any other spot. It is, therefore, the duty of everyone living on that chosen spot to fight, kill, and die in the attempt to impose his superiority upon all the others.

Defining patriotism as obedience to government, as uncritical acceptance of any war the leaders of government decide must be fought, has been disastrous for the American people. Failure to distinguish between the country and the government has led so many young people serving in the military to declare: "I am willing to die for my country." Would not those young people hesitate before enlisting if they considered that they were not risking their lives for their country but for its government, and even for the owners of great wealth and the giant corporations connected to the government?

Obedience to whatever the government decides is founded on the idea that the interests of the government are the same as the interests of its citizens. However, we have a long history of government policy that suggests political leaders have different interests than the people. The men who gathered in Philadelphia in 1787 to draft the Constitution provided for a certain degree of representative government and agreed to a Bill of Rights, but did not represent the interests of the slave, whose enslavement was, indeed, legitimized by the Constitution.

Nor did the authors of the Declaration represent the average White person of that time—the small farmer—for they intended to fashion a government that would be capable of putting down the rebellions of farmers that had taken place all over the country the year before the Constitutional Convention. The very term we use, "Founding Fathers," suggests a family with common interests. But from the founding of the nation to the present day, the government has generally legislated on behalf of the wealthy, has done the bidding of corporations in issues involving working people, and has taken the nation to war in the interests of economic expansion and political ambition.

It is crucial for democracy that we understand this difference of interest between the government and the people, and that we recognize that expressions like "national interest," "national security," and "national defense" attempt to obscure that difference and entice citizens into subservience to power. It becomes important, then, to be wary of those symbols of nationhood which attempt to unite us in a false "patriotism" that works against the interests of the country and its people.

It is not surprising that African Americans, conscious of their status in a White-dominated society, would be more skeptical of such symbols. Frederick Douglass, a former slave who became a leader of the abolitionist movement, was asked in 1852 to speak at a Fourth of July gathering in Rochester, New York. Here is a small sample of what he had to say:

> Fellow citizens, pardon me, allow me to ask, why am I called upon to speak here today? What have I, or those I represent, to do with your national inde-

pendence? Are the great principles of political freedom and of natural justice, embodied in that Declaration of Independence, extended to us? And am I, therefore, called upon to ring our humble offering to the national altar, and to confess the benefits and express devout gratitude for the blessings resulting from your independence to us? . . .

What, to the American slave, is your 4th of July? I answer; a day that reveals to him, more than all other days in the year, the gross injustice and cruelty to which he is the constant victim. To him, your celebration is a sham; your boasted liberty, an unholy license; your national greatness, swelling vanity; . . . your shouts of liberty and equality, hollow mockery; . . . a thin veil to cover up crimes which would disgrace a nation of savages. There is not a nation on the Earth guilty of practices more shocking and bloody than are the people of the United States, at this very hour.

African Americans have always had an ambivalent attitude toward the idea of patriotism. They have wanted to feel patriotic in the best sense of the term—that is, to feel at one with their fellow Americans and to feel part of a greater community. And yet, they have resented the attempt to enmesh them in a false sense of common interest while they have endured slavery, lynching, segregation, humiliation, and economic injustice. Thus, their reaction to the nation's wars has been a troubled one. This complexity is illustrated by the dramatically different reactions of two African American boxing champions in two different wars. There was Joe Louis, who was used by the U.S. government to build Black support for World War II, saying that whatever was wrong in this country, "Hitler won't fix it." And there was Mohammed Ali, who refused to be drafted for the Vietnam War and told a reporter who challenged him on the subject:

No, I'm not going 10,000 miles from home to help murder and burn another poor nation simply to continue the domination of White slave masters of the darker people the world over. . . . The real enemy of my people is here. . . . So I'll go to jail, so what? We've been in jail for 400 years.

As I write this, the United States has been at war for three years in Iraq, and has been continuously at war in Afghanistan since October, 2001. The initial support for what President Bush has called a "war on terrorism" was based to a great extent on the premise of a false patriotism: a faith that the government was acting in the interests of the people of this country. That support has largely dissipated, and it is clear that the premise of a common interest between the government and the people is being challenged by more and more Americans. In doing so, they are redefining patriotism.

In times of war, the definition of patriotism becomes a matter of life or death for people in this country and in the world. The essays in this book, therefore, come at a critical moment, and should be welcomed by anyone who is concerned that the values of peace and of democracy be held high by the coming generation.

Acknowledgments

Some months ago, I sat in the New York City living room of my friends George and Photini talking about U.S. policy in the ongoing war in Iraq. George had just finished reading some of the material for this book, and he said to me, "Of course this book had to be written from Canada rather than from within the United States."

My initial reaction was to shrug off George's comments. After all, I've spent thirty-nine of my forty-three years living in the United States. Although my current position at a Canadian university is fortuitous, considering my terrific colleagues and my Canadian wife, Barbara's, appointment at a nearby university, my job's geographic locale seemed hardly significant for my work on this project.

Yet, as I reflected on George's observation, I thought about what Margaret Mead had said: "If human beings were fish, the last thing we would discover is water." To be sure, there are a number of excellent books, journal and magazine articles, and editorial pieces written about American patriotism, but I perhaps underestimated the value of living outside of the United States while putting together this collection. Sometimes we see most clearly those forces that act on our lives only when we can, at least partially, step outside of their influence. At the same time, residing outside of the United States while producing this collection of essays made my ties to colleagues and friends all the more important.

This book began as a special issue of the education journal *Phi Delta Kappan* on patriotism and education that

I edited in 2003. I am indebted to the tremendously professional and able staff that helped me pull together the essays for that collection. *Kappan* editor Bruce Smith was always ready with thoughtful suggestions and witty exchanges. Risë Koben, Delaine McCullough, and Carol Bucheri also all added their expertise.

At Teachers College Press, I owe special thanks to Carole Saltz and series editor Bill Ayers, both of whom are colleagues extraordinaire as well as friends. Their guidance at every step of the process was invaluable and always went above and beyond what was required. Similarly, Shannon Waite, Leyli Shayegan, and Judy Berman all worked tirelessly to shape and improve the work. I am grateful for their ever-present enthusiasm for the project.

In Canada I have been lucky to have many welcoming and supportive colleagues. Marie Josée Berger stimulated this project not only with material and collegial support but also with Haitian-grown coffee beans. Yves Herry has scaled the highest mountains (both the real kind made of rock and the metaphorical kind within our university) to always ensure that I had the resources—especially time—required to complete both the preceding *Kappan* issue and this book. Martin Barlosky, Sharon Cook, Brad Cousins, Barbara Graves, David Paré, Chris Suurtamm, and Tim Stanley are among the best colleagues one could have, ensuring that my transition from New York University to the University of Ottawa was entirely positive, exciting, and rewarding. Musical interludes were absolutely essential, and so I thank (in addition to Martin and David above) Caleb Lauer, Paul Paré, and Richard Pinet for making sure that bouts of American patriotism were interspersed with music of multinational origins.

I owe a great deal to karen emily suurtamm, not least for the level of patience that must be required to work with someone with a few too many overlapping deadlines. A superb project director for Democratic Dialogue (www.democraticdialogue.com) and an outstanding research assistant, karen's thoughtfulness, thoroughness, and creativity made this book possible. I also received invaluable research assistance for this project from Alessandra Iozzo-Duval and Luz Alison Molina.

Funders provided direct and indirect support to this and related projects. I am indebted to the Social Sciences and Humanities Research Council of Canada, the Center for Information and Research on Civic Learning and Engagement, the University of Ottawa Research Chair program, the Faculty of Education, and the Surdna Foundation for support.

Several friends and colleagues indulged my need to discuss the finer points of patriotic education, read occasional drafts, and offered advice and support: Michael Berkowitz, George Bourozikas, Robby Cohen, Sondra Cuban, Joel Einleger, Danny Factor, Maxine Greene, Joe Kahne, Hillary Kunins, Gloria Ladson-Billings, Gordon Lafer, Ted and Steve Leckie, Pierre Lehu, Nel Noddings, Franny Nudelman, Dan Perlstein, Photini Sinnis, David Tyack, and Miriam Westheimer.

David Holton (www.wordforward.com) created the design for the cover, and Walter Parker provided the perfect title (brazenly borrowed from the title of his essay). Larry Cuban has been my mentor and friend for 18 years, and I thank him for his always tough and probing questions.

My mother, Dr. Ruth Westheimer, came to the United States two decades after she left Germany, alone, at the age of 10 on a kindertransport. Patriotism is palpable in my mother's gratitude for U.S. soldiers' heroic liberation of concentration camps in World War II. She has taught me a great deal about loyalty, gratitude, and *joie de vivre.*

Barbara Leckie is my constant support, a kind critic, and the love of my life.

—Joel Westheimer
17 July 2006

Pledge of allegiance at Raphael Weill Public School. San Francisco, California, April 20, 1942. Photographer: Dorothea Lange. Library of Congress, Prints and Photographs Division. Farm Security Administration and Office of War Information Collection [LC-USZ62-17131].

Introduction

Joel Westheimer

A cartoon published in the *New Yorker* in October 2001 shows a couple in a New York apartment entertaining friends. As the hosts clutch each other's hands, the woman confesses to their guests, "We're still getting used to feeling patriotic." Another *New Yorker* cartoon shows a policeman walking away from a car. Inside, reading the newly issued ticket, the driver asks his passenger incredulously, "Flagless in a patriotic zone?" In a third cartoon, an elegantly dressed woman hands a pile of expensive dresses, a fur coat, and her credit card to a sales clerk and says, "This isn't for me—it's for the economy."

New Yorker cartoons are hardly a barometer of national sentiment about patriotism following 9/11, but the magazine has a distribution of over 800,000—a large percentage of which are subscriptions in the city where the Twin Towers fell—and its authors, cartoonists, and even advertisers have reflected a mélange of conflicted feelings about loyalty, solidarity, and the right to dissent in a democracy. Editor David Remnick was initially criticized for censoring authors and capitulating to pressure from the Bush Administration to lend support to military operations in Afghanistan and elsewhere, but the magazine also was where Susan Sontag furiously observed that "the unanimity of the sanctimonious, reality-concealing rhetoric spouted by American officials and media commentators in recent days seems, well, unworthy of a mature democracy." Perhaps the contributor who most plainly captured the confusion of the months to come was cartoonist Victoria Roberts, who drew a middle-aged husband and wife sitting down to dinner. Both look slightly per-plexed as the husband says simply, "Who ever thought patriotism could be so complicated?"

The complexity of patriotism is further reflected in the great many ways it has been represented by politicians, the media, authors, critics, and religious leaders. Each has shaped various ideas about patriotism and its importance to national unity and sought to advance particular notions of patriotism over others. Nowhere are the debates around these vari-ous visions of patriotic attachment more pointed, more protracted, and more consequential than in our nation's schools. In Madison, Wisconsin, the parent community erupted in fierce debate over a new law requiring schools to post American flags in each classroom and to lead students in either pledging allegiance each day or playing the national anthem. In Detroit, Michigan, a student was repeatedly suspended, first for wearing a t-shirt with an upside-down American flag, and then for wearing a sweat-shirt with an anti-war quotation by Albert Einstein, before the ACLU filed a civil liberties suit resulting in the student's reinstatement. And in Virgin-ia, House Bill 1912, which would have required schools to notify parents any time a child declined to recite or stand for the Pledge of Allegiance, passed the House of Delegates with a 93–4 vote. (The bill was ultimately defeated in the State Senate.) As these and many other such stories make clear, patriotism is highly contested territory, especially when it comes to the daily activities of the nation's schoolchildren.

This book explores the relationship between patriotism and educa-tion, and it does so from a variety of perspectives. It is also a deeply per-sonal undertaking. On the morning of September 11, 2001, I stood with my wife and daughter on a street corner 18 city blocks away from the World Trade Center and watched as the second plane hit the South tower. Soon after, both buildings collapsed into the impossibly dense financial district streets below. No written description can capture the haunting silence, shock, and grief that spread across our fellow New Yorkers—who stood with us on that corner and on countless other corners, in cafés, and in living rooms throughout the city—in the minutes that followed. It was not long after the second tower fell that the first office workers arrived at our corner covered in dust and debris and carrying first-hand accounts of what had happened. As rumors of gas explosions spread and as the enor-mity of the events slowly revealed themselves, we raced home to fetch bicycles and pedal uptown to Washington Heights, the northern Manhattan community where my mother lives—still close by but removed from the noxious air that ensued for months after the attacks. We spent the next few days, like most New Yorkers, communing with others on the streets, in local restaurants, and in parks, trying to make sense of the unthinkable.

Given the still-contentious debates over the teaching of the events of September 11 and of patriotic civic duties more generally, I should explain, then, what some readers may perceive as bias in the content of this book. To be sure there are views contained herein that span a broad spectrum of political positions and ideological perspectives on patriotism and education, but the careful reader will no doubt note a gentle advocacy for a form of patriotism that embodies dissent more than unquestioned loyalty and government support.

Here's why: Following the morning of September 11, the outpouring of support and solidarity from across the United States and the world was breathtaking—which is what made the subsequent inexplicable news blackouts all the more curious and hurtful. Every week for months following September 11, thousands of New Yorkers gathered in Union Square and Times Square and marched up Fifth Avenue, Sixth Avenue, and Broadway to warn against hasty military acts of vengeance. It was in these weekly gatherings and marches that many New Yorkers who had lost family members, colleagues, and friends expressed their heartfelt belief that national grieving should take place immediately, but that foreign policy decisions should emerge from reasoned deliberation and debate and not from rushed emotions or political grandstanding. These weekly, sometimes massive, outpourings were summarily ignored by all mainstream media outlets. To be sure, periods of *mourning* at these gatherings were covered exhaustively. The entire nation is familiar with the images of burning candles, photographs of missing relatives, and pro-war banners. But five weeks after September 11, New York's own Channel One news, a part of Time Warner, seemed to offer the first meager coverage of just one of the protest gatherings. The coverage lasted for fourteen seconds on their evening news broadcast and reached New York City–based Time-Warner cable TV subscribers only.

In the past five years, despite a few significant outliers, mainstream news, media coverage, and school curriculum and activities about the September 11 attacks, the wars in Afghanistan and Iraq, and the larger and more elusive "war on terrorism" have been overwhelmingly in support of no-questions-asked civic policy towards government actions. Indeed, until recently, a "wanted-dead-or-alive" bravado pervaded newspapers, television, and classrooms throughout the country.[1] Even the massive protests that immediately preceded the Republican National Convention in New York City in August 2004 were strangely ignored or diminished by most media outlets. I know many people who reported the eerie sensation of marching among tens of thousands of protesters up Sixth Avenue beneath the enormous live-screen TV for Fox News. Above the throngs, for hours on end, Fox News steadily broadcast a repeating video clip of workers inside Madison Square Garden unfolding empty chairs in preparation for the following day's convention. There was no mention of the tens of thousands of protesters walking literally right outside of Fox's New York headquarters for virtually the entire day. It was like the protesters didn't even exist.

In short, there are plenty of sources from which to find represented arguments for the kind of patriotic allegiance to government that borders on what I call (in Chapter 13) "authoritarian patriotism." In fact, there is little need to rehearse the arguments that follow this position because the perspective is so well represented in our daily exposure to news, television, advertising, and other manifestations of popular culture. This book predominantly and unapologetically emphasizes the other side—a kind of patriotism that goes by many names: *cosmopolitan patriotism, real patriotism, progressive patriotism,* and *democratic patriotism,* to name a few.[2] For those readers already familiar with these perspectives, you will find in this volume a detailed articulation of the inherent complexity in forging a critical kind of patriotism that allows—indeed encourages—healthy democratic dissent, especially as it relates to schools. For those readers who are more inclined to assert the need to teach children to have pride and loyal adherence to the United States without distraction or confusion from dissenting accounts, I encourage you to read this book with an open mind. There are a great variety of perspectives represented inside, many of which you are sure to find engaging and challenging.

Before I describe the chapters that follow, let me return momentarily to the realm of comics, since they capture so well the mix of public sentiment around deeply complex political issues. A high school social studies teacher I know developed a curriculum for her students that would engage the full complexity of issues that arose following the U.S.-led war in Iraq. Frustrated with the lack of curricular resource materials available, she found, through the *Rethinking Schools* website, a suggestion to use political cartoons in order to examine the contentious issues arising from the war. Enthusiastically, she put together several lessons that would allow her students to examine critically all sides of the debates about the war by culling cartoons from across the political spectrum. But when two of the cartoons she used raised the ire of a parent of one of her students, her principal requested that she discontinue the lessons.

The two offending cartoons both came from the controversial comic strip "Boondocks," the brainchild of twenty-eight-year-old cartoonist Aaron McGruder. The strip stars Huey Freeman, a little African American kid living in suburbia who has attracted more than his share of controversy. The first cartoon the teacher used (shown below) was originally published on Thanksgiving Day 2001, when polls suggested that President Bush's approval ratings were higher than 90% and when popular support for the war on terror was widespread. Huey is leading the Thanksgiving prayer: "Ahem," he begins. "In this time of war against Osama bin Laden and the oppressive Taliban regime, we are thankful that our leader isn't the spoiled son of a powerful politician from a wealthy oil family who is supported by religious fundamentalists, operates through clandestine organizations, has no respect for the democratic electoral process, bombs innocents, and uses war to deny people their civil liberties. Amen." The second strip the teacher used shows Huey calling the FBI's antiterrorist hotline to report that he has the names of Americans who helped train and finance Osama bin Laden. "Okay, give me some names," the FBI agent says. And Huey responds: "All right, let's see, the first one is Reagan. That's R-E-A-G . . ."

© 2001 by Aaron McGruder. Distributed by Universal Press Syndicate. Used by permission.

Students responded to these and the other cartoons used with an enthusiasm for debate that the teacher reported she had rarely witnessed in her classroom. She was careful to ensure that students received exposure to the broad spectrum of political perspectives, and, she noted, a vast majority of her students sported a plethora of patriotic symbols on their clothes and schoolbags during the weeks following 9/11.

Schools, of course, did not invent the brand of patriotism that involves stifling democratic debate. The same fear of dissenting viewpoints sometimes witnessed in schools can also be seen outside. It was not only the sixteen- and seventeen-year-old students of this teacher who were prohibited from debating McGruder's critique of the war. Some of the 250 newspapers that run the "Boondocks" strip pulled it either selectively or in its entirety after September 11. Many noted that it was "too political." In what could arguably be a successful alignment, the school curriculum may actually prepare students well for the adult world they are soon to enter—one in which, as McGruder observes, the media have "become so conglomerated that there are really very few avenues left for people to express dissent."

Indeed, there is some evidence that many are learning the lessons of my-country-right-or-wrong patriotism very well. In response to a "Doonesbury" strip that was critical of Bush Administration policies, some readers posted notes on the "Doonesbury" website. A reader from Maurepas, Louisiana, wrote: "Your . . . biased state of mind has no place for a patriotic thinking America. Grow up. . . . We are at War!" A reader from Melbourne, Florida, wrote: "Your disloyalty to our society and our country shine through quite clearly." Apparently confusing former Canadian Prime Minister Pierre Trudeau with "Doonesbury" creator Gary Trudeau, one reader from Arkansas echoed the xenophobic sentiments so often part and parcel of jingoistic patriotism: "Why don't you go back to Canada, or even better France?" But perhaps Virginia Beach resident Stuart Schwartz best captured the attitude toward dissent shared by those who favor what I describe in Chapter 13 as "authoritarian patriotism": "Please do the public a service and die."

A Pew Research Center poll in 2003 found that 92% of respondents agreed either completely or mostly with the statement "I am very patriotic."[3] However, as will become clear when reading this book, what it means to be patriotic is a matter of considerable debate. And it always has been. As far back as the 1890s, policy makers realized that public schools could serve as a "mighty engine for the inculcation of patriotism."[4] One hundred and sixteen years later, patriotism and its role in the school curriculum remain disputed territory.

A Map of the Book

In Chapter 1, Gloria Ladson-Billings shares a deeply personal exploration of what it means to be a patriotic African American woman in the United States. "I am a patriot," she flatly declares, adding, "To most people who know me that statement probably comes as a surprise." Ladson-Billings, who is past president of the American Educational Research Association, takes readers through her experiences growing up as an African American in the 1950s and 1960s and deftly examines the effects of those experiences on her thinking about the United States and about her patriotic attachments. How are we to understand patriotism, she asks, in a country where African Americans could be excluded from attending schools that White children attended or where "a fourteen-year-old boy from Chicago could be killed (beaten, lynched, castrated, and drowned) for whistling at a White woman"? Many members of Ladson-Billings's family served proudly in the military—in segregated units. Criticizing the "vacuous speeches" and "empty rhetoric" that politicians employ when they talk about what it means to be patriotic, Ladson-Billings reclaims the noble call to patriotic action on behalf of all U.S. citizens and those who are powerless around the globe.

In Chapter 2, Pedro Noguera and Robby Cohen ask readers to think about what educators' responsibilities are in wartime. Digging deep into the nation's past, they present provocative historical examples that do not lend themselves to facile analysis or good-guy/bad-guy stories. They ask whether, in an era of educational accountability, educators are ignoring their responsibility to students to present clear and accurate information on varying viewpoints about the "war on terrorism." "Given that our nation is at war in at least two countries," they ask, "shouldn't educators be accountable for ensuring that all students have some understanding of why we are fighting, of whom we are at war with, and of what is at stake?"

In Chapter 3, clinical psychologist Michael Bader asks readers to consider the psychological needs served by various expressions of patriotic fervor. From a psychologist's perspective, he examines the collective responses both to 9/11 and to the devastation wrought by Hurricane Katrina. In a compelling analysis of the links between our need for security and protection and our early life experiences at home, Bader suggests that patriotism can be a force for good or evil, but that the key to understanding our own motivations is to understand their emotional and psychological roots in the universal need for attachment and affiliation. He draws on twenty-five years of clinical experience to show that patriotism often offers a symbolic resolution to longings we all experience for both safety and relatedness. Bader shows how both the political Left and the political Right "seek to link their partisan agendas to the evocation and satisfaction of these frustrated longings."

Deborah Meier, school reform activist and founder of Central Park East schools, examines the connection between her vision of patriotism and her loyalty to the New York Yankees in Chapter 4. Detailing her experience growing up in the 1940s when "good and evil seemed so clear," Meier deftly dissects the multiple and sometimes conflicting forces influencing first, second, and third generation immigrants to the United States. At the same time, in comparing fandom for a sports team and unquestioning patriotic allegiance to a government, Meier raises important distinctions and challenging questions.

"In most schools and colleges today," writes Gerald Graff in Chapter 5, "students typically go from one classroom in which the openness and fairness of our system is the default assumption to another in which the system is viewed as unfairly rigged." Graff argues for a third way: *Teach the debate about patriotism itself.* Present students with multiple and opposing positions and ask them to form their own opinions. Avoiding both political indoctrination and "spurious neutrality" (mindless reinforcement of the status quo), Graff's method explicitly brings controversial questions into the classroom. Graff's essay also makes clear the nexus between the structure of the one-teacher classroom found in most schools, colleges, and universities, and "pedagogical authoritarianism," in which only one side of the issues gets airtime.

In Chapter 6, Robert Jensen makes a strong case for abandoning the notion of patriotism altogether. "I am against nationalism, and I am against patriotism," he writes. In his cogent and provocative essay, Jensen first dismisses the idea that patriotism in a democracy obliges all citizens to support the nation as it goes to war. But he goes on to question the competing idea, argued by some anti-war organizers, that "dissent and critique of an immoral, illegal, and counterproductive war" are also expressions of patriotism. Drawing on his extensive experience as a journalist, Jensen questions whether the word *patriotism* is worth redefining and explores journalists' response to the conundrum.

In Chapter 7, Diane Ravitch challenges us to think about what schools actually do to encourage students' appreciation of U.S. culture. She points out that educators stand strong in their belief that children's self-esteem is linked to knowledge and appreciation of their ancestral culture but not to the culture of the United States, where they live and will one day vote and raise children. "How strange," Ravitch muses, "to teach a student born in this country to be proud of his parents' or grandparents' land of birth but not of his or her own. Or to teach a student whose family fled to this country from a tyrannical regime or from dire poverty to identify with that nation rather than with the one that gave the family refuge." Critical of jingoistic conceptions of patriotism, Ravitch nonetheless calls attention to the need to respect and celebrate the nation's heritage and democratic principles and ideals.

Patriotism and war have been intertwined in complex ways since the dawn of the nation-state. Many readers may know that the No Child Left Behind Act includes a provision that requires high schools to turn over students' personal information to military recruiters. In addition, the Pentagon now maintains a database of some 30 million sixteen- to twenty-five-year-olds, including their names, ethnicities, addresses, cell phone numbers, family information, extracurricular activities, and areas of study (for more information, watch the eleven-minute video at www.LeaveMyChildAlone.org). In Chapter 8, "Hearts and Minds: Military Recruitment and the High School Battlefield," William Ayers tracks the recent explosion of military presence in U.S. schools and classrooms, paying special attention to Chicago. Ayers notes that Chicago has the largest JROTC program in the country and, according to some, the "most militarized" school system in America. His powerful stories of recruits, veterans, and Purple Heart recipients are as emotionally wrenching as they are deeply hopeful. What's more, his topic has important historical antecedents. For example, in 1911, Katherine Devereux Blake, a New York City elementary school principal, predicted an upcoming struggle in public education between those who advocate a greater military presence in schools and those who want students to learn peace. "They are organized for war," Blake proclaimed. "We must be organized for peace."[5] In this essay, Ayers details the heavy incursions those who are "organized for war" have made.

In Chapter 9, Joseph Kahne and Ellen Middaugh provide a systematic and sobering examination of high school students' attitudes toward patriotism. They surveyed over two thousand seniors in twelve California high schools and conducted fifty focus groups to learn about students' patriotic commitments. Regardless of your beliefs about the importance of teaching patriotism in schools, it's reasonable to ask what should be taught, and what students already think and know, about patriotism. Kahne and Middaugh's findings are likely to challenge your assumptions. For example, although a majority of high school seniors believe that "if you love America, you should notice its problems and work to correct them," only 16% of high school seniors express consistent support for what the authors see as a democratic vision of patriotism. Moreover, most students do not necessarily see any connection between patriotism and civic participation.

Diana Hess and Louis Ganzler describe, in Chapter 10, a study of ideological diversity among students in U.S. classrooms. After an extensive study of over nine hundred and fifty students in twenty schools, they assert that having a diversity of opinions and perspectives within any classroom is the surest way to ensure the strength of our democratic institutions and our democratic polity. Teachers who aim to develop young patriots, they argue, should encourage students to "learn that a diversity of views is to be cultivated, not repressed." Vigorous discussions of political issues in classrooms with a diversity of political opinions, they note, is sadly too rare in the nation's public schools.

In "Patriotism, Eh?" (Chapter 11), Sharon Cook adds a Canadian perspective on patriotism and education. This contribution from the north proves what anthropologists know so well: One's understanding of one's own culture is greatly improved by the study of another. My (and Cook's) country of residence, Canada, offers a starkly different perspective on American notions of patriotism. Canadians, Cook argues, have pride in peacefulness, in welcoming new immigrants (at a higher per-capita rate than virtually any Western nation), and in caring for the nation's citizens and other residents. By analyzing key historical events, Cook plumbs the significance of Canada's relationships to England and the United States. She explains that national patriotism in Canada (though it too has had its excesses) is generally of a mild-mannered kind, perhaps because a more jingoistic form "seems unnecessary if one already finds inclusion in the family of a respected imperial power."

In Chapter 12, Cecilia O'Leary details the history of patriotism in American schooling and shows that the Patriot Act and the school and civic policies that followed are only a continuation of long-standing historical trends in patriotic fervor and the nation's schools. A historical overview of the twentieth century, O'Leary suggests, reveals a reoccurrence of a militarist form of patriotism, often in response to war and periods of increased immigration. Moreover, she argues, this form of patriotism has "more often than not undermined the very ideals it purports to protect."

Finally, my essay, "Politics and Patriotism in Education" (Chapter 13), explores the ideological and political battles that are being waged in the name of patriotism in U.S. classrooms. I suggest categories that can help educators examine the politics of patriotism in schools. Like Kahne and Middaugh, I argue that patriotism and democratic ideals are not inherently at odds with one another but that a democratic form of patriotism is far from inevitable. To the contrary, there is much cause for concern over a far more dangerous brand of patriotic sentiment that is better described as "authoritarian" and that is widely on the rise. I detail examples of these worrisome developments from classrooms across the country and describe alternative models for teaching democratic patriotism to the nation's schoolchildren and young adults.

Between chapters, this book also features a series of point of view opinion pieces in which fourteen prominent educators and public figures from a wide range of backgrounds and perspectives provide short responses to the question "What should children learn in school about patriotism?" The answers are as diverse and fascinating as the contributing authors. After reading responses from Studs Terkel, James W. Loewen, Cindy Sheehan, Maxine Greene, Bill Bigelow, Walter Parker, Charles Payne, Peter Dreier and Dick Flacks, Héctor Calderón, Joan Kent Kvitka, Chester Finn, Denise Walsh, karen emily suurtamm and Edwin Darden, and Delaine Eastin, you are unlikely to think about patriotism and education in precisely the same way as you did before.

This book sets out to capture the controversies surrounding patriotism and education. Like the teacher who wanted to show a range of controversial opinions using cartoons, the contributors to this volume express a healthy variety of viewpoints and approaches to the topic. In *Spheres of Justice*, Michael Walzer argues that the democratic citizen must be "ready and able, when the time comes," to engage in dialogue and "to deliberate with fellow [citizens], listen and be listened to."[6] The authors of this book write in that spirit.

Black woman by building with Georgia and United States flags, near White Plains, GA. 1941. Photographer: Marion Post Wolcott, Jack Delano. Library of Congress Prints and Photographs Division, Farm Security Administration—Office of War Information Collection [LC-DIG-fsac-1a33897].

Chapter 1

Once Upon a Time When Patriotism Was What You Did

Gloria Ladson-Billings

I love America more than any other country in this world, and, exactly for this reason, I insist on the right to criticize her perpetually.

—*James Baldwin*

I am a patriot. To most people who know me that statement probably comes as a surprise. Critical, yes. Radical, perhaps. But patriot? Not her. Yet I make this statement with the same vehemence as Cornel West when he asserts that he is a Christian (and I am one of those, too).[1] The reason this declaration seems so strange to most people is that, like many words in the English language, the term *patriot* has been hijacked by an increasingly narrow and undemocratic sector of society. Other words that have fallen into this category include *Christian, liberal, multicultural,* and *religious.*

George Lakoff asserts that progressives have to learn to recapture the public discourse by reframing the debate.[2] I believe we are in a much worse place than simply lacking the ability to frame the debate. Indeed, I argue that there is no debate to frame. Instead there are shouting matches. Everything is already settled, and if you do not subscribe to the current dominant orthodoxy you are unpatriotic and godless. Your very presence is a threat to society. According to conservative pundit Ann Coulter, you are a traitor.[3]

In this chapter, I hope to address the challenge of patriotism in this current age. I want to challenge those who are patriotic enough to criticize common discourses about the nation and national policies to work on re-capturing the language so that real debate is not only possible but valued. I make my argument in a time when this kind of bold patriotism is being eroded in favor of a "new patriotism" that is more akin to indoctrination than critical, analytic citizenship and civic discourse.

My thinking about patriotism is deeply autobiographical. As an Afri-can American who grew up in the 1950s and 1960s, I have clear memories of what being an American meant in that era. For one thing, it meant par-ticipating in regular air raid drills in schools—huddling under our desks, away from windows, in anticipation of an attack by the Communists. It meant recognizing Communism as the worst evil that could happen to the nation and identifying and rooting out Communist influences wher-ever they appeared. It meant that, after the Soviets successfully launched Sputnik, it was part of my duty to be a good student, and that when I became one I was participating in the national defense. Indeed, when I made my way to college I was eligible to borrow money for tuition and fees at extraordinarily low interest rates and would not have had to pay the money back at all if I had decided to teach in a low-income commu-nity, thanks to the National Defense Education Act. It also meant that some people had to be excluded and persecuted for their collaboration with Communism either through party affiliation or through association with known Communists. Thus, people like Paul Robeson and W. E. B. Du Bois—heroes in my eyes—could not be spoken of in open conversation. It meant a war hero like Dwight Eisenhower was a more valuable national leader than an intellectual like Adlai Stevenson.

My vision of patriotism, the nation, and my role in it was also shaped by the race relations of this period. In the early 1950s, African Americans could legally be excluded from attending schools that White children attended. A fourteen-year-old Black boy from Chicago could be killed (beaten, lynched, castrated, and drowned) for whistling at a White woman. Children could not go to school with members of racial groups and social classes different from their own, even if it meant they had to go miles outside of their neighborhoods to a school with inferior resources. In short, racial and ethnic encapsulation was a way of life, and we could be "Americans" only within our own groups.

I knew that we were Americans because there were photos of my dad and the other adult men in my family—uncles and cousins—on display throughout our home, smiling out at me in their military uniforms. I did not know that these proud soldiers had served in segregated units and did the most menial and dangerous work the military required. They had been cooks, launderers, and ammunition handlers, but all I knew was that they had been soldiers—American soldiers—and I was very proud of them.

Being an African American at this time also meant that adults in my house spoke in hushed tones about a change that was afoot in the nation. Names such as A. Philip Randolph, Bayard Rustin, Martin Luther King, Jr., and Malcolm X were regularly uttered. Black people were mobilizing to change their lot, and with it they were going to change America. It was a time of fear and terror, but, paradoxically, it was also a time of hope and social transformation. I was learning that African Americans could work together to form a social movement that could transform the nation and force it to live up to its democratic promise for all of its citizens.

One of the tangible—and perhaps silliest—signs for me that we had hope in America is that on every national holiday my brother and I would fight over whose turn it was to place our American flag in the flag stand attached to the main pillar on our front porch. In our largely African American neighborhood (there were also a few Irish Catholic families), one could look down the block and see American flags waving from almost every porch. Segregation and ongoing racism notwithstanding, we were Americans and were proud to display the flag. America was flawed, but it was working on being better. And the struggle for racial equality was a clear indicator of its willingness to live up to its promise.

The Loss of Hope

Fast forward to September 2001. The nation is traumatized by an attack of three airplanes (and the foiled attempt of a fourth) on New York's World Trade Center and the Pentagon. Soon my neighbors in the predominantly White neighborhood of my "progressive" college town are placing flags out on their lawns, doors, mailboxes, front porches, and any other place where they can prominently display them. It strikes me that I do not own a flag. I have nothing with which to display my "patriotism." Why don't I have a flag?

This is not a simple question. It involves a series of sociohistorical events that made my belief in the hoped-for possibilities of America seem unreasonable. By the time I reached adulthood, I had suffered hundreds of what critical race theorists refer to as "microaggressions."[4] The dailiness of racism had worn on me, and I felt thwarted at every turn. School deseg-regation was the law, but nearly every major city was working actively to subvert it. Civil rights leaders lived in constant terror of assassination and the fire bombing of their homes. And African American people remained disproportionately poor in the land of opportunity.

But it was not these big challenges that bothered me directly. It was the thousand tiny cuts: being passed over by teachers in my integrated ju-nior high school, being excluded from study groups by White classmates, being misled by my college guidance counselor, being second-guessed about my academic ability. These are just a few examples of the way issues of race were trumping my ability to lay claim to my Americanness.

Despite these challenges, I entered the late 1960s attempting to push democratic possibilities in America. The antiwar movement, the civil rights movement, and the women's movement were all surging ahead, and in my mind the real American patriots were busy organizing, pro-testing, demonstrating, and pushing for social change. Unfortunately, the older generation (remember "Don't trust anyone over 30"?) insisted that we were destroying America. Why couldn't we just cut our hair and get jobs? My own college career was book-ended by the assassinations of Malcolm X and Martin Luther King, Jr. Before the strains of "Pomp and Circumstance" had faded from my memory, Robert Kennedy lay dying in a hotel restaurant in Los Angeles. What message was America sending me? That if you want change, you will die for it?

The cynicism that these events engendered in me did not overwhelm the small victories that emerged. The passage of the Voting Rights Act, the endorsement of affirmative action as a remedy for past social and eco-nomic wrongs, the growing number of people of color and women seek-ing election to and serving in local and state offices—all of these made the continuing struggle worthwhile. Little by little, institutions such as universities, schools, corporate boardrooms, and portions of government were responding to the voices of people on the ground. But at the highest seats of power, things seemed intractable. After the 1968 Presidential elec-tion (the first I voted in), the country began its drift to the Right. Despite President Nixon's self-destruction over the Watergate affair, no credible voices were emerging from the Left. Jimmy Carter's appeal to the moral high ground was drowned out by corporate interests, and the election of

Ronald Reagan marked the beginning of a conservative restoration that continues to this day.[5]

Today, the impact of conservative rhetoric and policy is not only visible in federal politics but is also increasingly evident in our schools. After the attacks of September 11, schools were directed to step up their patriotic rhetoric. In my state, schools were mandated to display the flag in every classroom (a previously passed but rarely enforced law), and all schools were directed to lead students in either the Pledge of Allegiance or the playing of the national anthem. One of the schools in my local district in Madison, Wisconsin, serves a large number of international students who come from families in which at least one of the parents is completing graduate studies at the nearby university. Many of these parents were understandably troubled by the idea that their children would be expected to pledge their allegiance to what, for them, was a foreign nation. A group of the parents approached the school board and asked that their children be excluded from such an activity.

After hearing the parents' plea, the school board voted to allow schools to choose the "playing of the national anthem" option allowed by the state law. Before the end of the week, conservative talk show hosts on both national radio and television were labeling Madison both Communist and anti-American. The school board members who had voted for substituting the national anthem for the pledge were being attacked and threatened with recall, and another school board meeting was hastily called. The number of people who signed up to speak at that meeting exceeded the capacity of the district's regular auditorium, and the meeting was moved to the largest high school auditorium. On the evening of the meeting, the auditorium was filled with more than two thousand people, a sizable number of whom did not reside in or send their children to the district's schools. The meeting lasted well past midnight and was regularly interrupted by spontaneous recitations of the Pledge of Allegiance and the singing of "God Bless America." One school board member of Southeast Asian ancestry was told to "go back to Vietnam." (He is from Laos.) Two of the school board members rescinded their vote. A third refused, saying, "Patriotism is what you do, not what you say!" As a result of his dogged democratic stand, he became the target of a recall effort.

In the midst of the recall campaign, the local newspaper decided to do a "profile" (read: investigation) of this school board member. To its surprise, the community learned that this board member and former teacher had spent much of his retirement teaching new immigrants how to read, write, and speak English so that they could prepare for the citizenship examination. Indeed, patriotism *was* something he was *doing*, not something he said. The recall effort failed, primarily because many of its instigators lived outside the district, and this courageous school board member continues to serve. The entire incident took place in what is allegedly one of the most liberal communities in the United States.

Where Is My Country When I Need It Most?

I began writing this in late August 2005 when the major stories in U.S. newspapers were about the continuing war in Iraq, the protest of Cindy Sheehan, and the President's nomination of John Roberts to the Supreme Court. Eight short days after I began the essay, Hurricane Katrina devastated the Gulf Coast region. But the real story of Katrina was not the story of a natural disaster, but rather the social, civic, economic, and cultural disaster that its devastation exposed.

When the hurricane first hit, I was at a conference in London. I watched the BBC and CNN World broadcasts in stunned silence in my hotel room. Londoners approached me, asking "What kind of nation is the U.S.? How can people be living like that?" My initial thought was that the only difference between what Londoners were seeing on television and the situation of the people two weeks before the hurricane hit is that the people were wet! Before the hurricane, far too many lived in substandard housing, far too many were either unemployed or underemployed, far too many lacked health care and resources, and, yes, far too many had received or were receiving a substandard education.

Following the hurricane and slow disaster response, some of the news magazines and tabloid headlines referred to the "Shame of America" and called for a redoubled effort to eradicate poverty and racism. Even President Bush was forced to utter the words "history of racial discrimination" when referring to the condition of so many people who were victimized by both the hurricane and their government's response. How ironic that the "No Child Left Behind" President got a firsthand look at what it means to be "left behind" and could see the results of a series of conservative policies dating back to 1980 that had steadily eroded the infrastructure of the Gulf Coast region.

The slow response to Hurricane Katrina raised a number of questions about priorities and privilege. While it was clear that elected officials on every level failed, there was an interesting set of coincidences. The Democratic mayor of New Orleans and governor of Louisiana could not get a satisfactory response from federal agencies. The Republican governor of Mississippi (and former chair of the Republican National Committee) was able to dial the White House directly. I am not faulting Governor Barbour for using any connections he had to get the aid his people needed: I am questioning my government's poor preparation and allocation of resources based on those connections.

The height of absurdity in the aftermath of the hurricane was that a substantial portion of the Louisiana National Guard had been deployed in Iraq and thus had to be redeployed to their own home state to do search and rescue and to try and restore order. It is hard to remain patriotic when confronted with a government that cannot be counted on in the face of a disaster. As I write this essay, some seven months after the storm, thousands of Gulf Coast residents remain essentially homeless, thousands of students are without schools, and few of the neediest residents have been employed in what will be a lucrative rebuilding effort. The television news cameras have turned their gaze elsewhere.

If there was any upside to the Katrina disaster, it was that it stripped away the veneer of equity and justice in which American society regularly cloaks itself. Another "positive" was the genuine charity and compassion shown to the hurricane victims by millions of Americans and by people throughout the world. But where was my government when those citizens needed it most? Why were news anchors and correspondents calling storm victims "refugees"? Why were people who were desperate for water, diapers, and medicine called "looters"? Why were the fabrications about murder and rape in the Superdome left unchallenged? How can one remain patriotic in the face of such utter collapse? How can one muster a sense of loyalty when it is apparent that circumstances of race, class, and gender can easily leave one stranded on a rooftop or a freeway overpass?

The vacuous speeches and empty rhetoric of politicians about what it means to be patriotic have no place in the real lives of people who have been regularly and consistently disappointed by their government. We cannot legislate or bully people into patriotic submission. Rather, we must inspire people to patriotic action. Patriotism is not what you say; patriotism is what you do.

Civil rights march on Washington, D.C., August 28, 1963. A procession of African Americans carrying signs for equal rights, integrated schools, decent housing, and an end to bias. Photographer: Warren K. Leffler. Library of Congress Prints and Photographs Division, U.S. News & World Report Magazine Photograph Collection [LC-U9-10364-37].

No Black in the Union Jack

The Ambivalent Patriotism of Black Americans

Charles M. Payne

In one of our rambling discussions about the differences between Black life in the States and Black life in Britain, Gary Younge, the Black British journalist, commented on how struck he was by the patriotism of African Americans. I was so shocked—and insulted—at hearing Black people accused of patriotism, that I could only sputter my denial. He was adamant, arguing that he sometimes saw African Americans displaying the American flag at picnics or on holidays. That kind of thing would be unthinkable among Blacks in Great Britain. I had to admit that there are Black Americans who celebrate the flag, though many of them are older, many of them are Southern, and many of them are veterans. On the other hand, many Black Americans were displaying flag decals in the wake of 9/11 and this seemed to be a more representative group.

My annoyance at the idea of Blacks as patriotic caught me off-guard. It was not something I had ever given any thought to. I had simply taken it for granted that Blacks were less patriotic and that this was a good thing. My feelings about patriotism are common among those who graduated high school in the mid-1960s, when the country was in the throes of the Vietnam conflict. For many of us, patriotism connotes mindless support for an out-of-control government; it means disregard for the lives, the rights, and the dignity of non-Americans; and it means casual contempt for people who look or talk differently. Too many of the people blathering about the Stars and

Stripes are entirely too comfortable with the stars and bars of the Confederate battle flag. Patriotism, imperialism, racism, and sheer stupidity all seem joined at the hip. Being called patriotic is hardly a compliment in my book.

Nevertheless, Blacks do much better than average on one traditional measure of patriotism: Since the integration of the Armed Forces in 1948, Blacks have been more likely to enlist in the military than Whites, substantially more likely to reenlist, and more likely to volunteer for the most dangerous units (which typically offer a higher rate of pay, as well as conferring a certain degree of prestige). For much of that time, the proportion of Blacks in the Army has been roughly twice that of their proportion in the general population. In 1995, Blacks made up 27% of active-duty personnel in the Army, a full 35% of non-commissioned officers (the professionals who, in the end, have to make a military work), and 12% of commissioned officers. Seven percent of generals were Black, the kind of fact that allows military boosters to describe the military as the country's most successfully desegregated institution. In what other area of American life do Blacks constitute 7% of the highest level of leadership? Surveys of Black troops make it clear that they see a plentitude of discrimination inside the military but that they still generally think they have a better chance for fair play and personal advancement inside than out.

The Iraq conflict is helping to put an end to all that. In 2004, despite record recruitment bonuses, African Americans represented just 15.9% of Army recruits. According to a March 15, 2005 *St. Louis Post-Dispatch* article by Ron Harris:

> At the root of the decline among Blacks is a deep philosophical difference between African Americans and much of the rest of the nation regarding the war in Iraq. And that difference has been passed on to African American adolescents, who, according to the military, are much more inclined than White youth to be influenced by their parents, their clergy and coaches.

A kind of tacit compact between Black Americans and the Armed Forces may be ending after more than half a century—a compact which said, in effect, that Blacks would stick with the military establishment and the military establishment would provide a more open mobility system than existed outside the military. "And, oh yeah, every once in a while, some of you will get shot." (One is reminded of the mocking song of some White Civil War soldiers, responding to the debates about whether Blacks were men enough to be allowed to wear the uniform of their country: "So liberal are we here, we'll let

Sambo die in place of meself, on every day of the year.") Some of the military recruiters who use to swarm over inner city Black high schools are switching their attentions to Hispanics.

The history of Black over-participation in the military is something that we should be teaching in schools. The idea that Blacks are leeches on society, always asking, never contributing, remains pervasive and is delivered to young people in many subtle and blunt ways. The history of Black military service counters that part of the racial narrative. It is also important to underscore the fact that American military power is dependent on the exploitation of those least well-served by the country. This contrasts with Britain, say, where the children of social elites are much more likely to see military service than are their American elite counterparts. It would be interesting to lay the facts before American high school students and ask them to think about what these facts say about our country.

Let us note, too, that the "deep philosophical differences" the *St. Louis Post-Dispatch* article found between Blacks and others also seems to operate among those Blacks who *do* go into the service. Black troops abroad certainly have not been immune to picking up the usual Ugly American attitudes toward their host countries, but one might say that race does seem to give some of them a degree of inoculation against xenophobia. In his book on the American enlisted man, military sociologist Charles Moskos notes that Black troops abroad seem less likely to accept stereotypes about other people and show more interest in the host cultures, even to the point of showing more interest in learning the native language. (Moskos notes, too, that during the Korean conflict, Black troops were more difficult to brainwash than Whites, a fact worth pondering.) Wallace Terry's oral history of Black troops in Vietnam contains several interviews with soldiers who came to feel a kind of kinship with the people they were fighting against, even though some of them started their tours talking about "chinks" and "gooks."[1] Obviously, many Black troops in Vietnam developed a sharp critique of the war, a critique built in part on their understanding of race in America. To whatever degree Black military service represents anything one could reasonably call "patriotism," there is reason to believe it may be a different kind of patriotism, a patriotism not so strongly predisposed to Othering, a patriotism that remains critical of the claims of the powerful. That is a patriotism I can lay claim to without embarrassment, a patriotism worth teaching. It is a kind of critical citizenship, to borrow a phrase from my colleague, Adam Green, that on more than one occasion has called the country back to its higher principles.

Poster promoting patriotism and suggesting that careless communication may be harmful to the war effort. Thomas A. Byrne, artist. WPA War Services of La., circa 1941–1943. Library of Congress Prints and Photographs Division, Work Projects Administration Poster Collection [LC-USZC2-5581].

Chapter 2

Educators in the War on Terrorism

Pedro Noguera and Robby Cohen

What are the responsibilities of educators while our nation is at war? This is not a question that comes up at most conferences or workshops on education, even though anyone familiar with our work as educators knows that it is nearly impossible to avoid taking a stance on the issue.

Should educators be expected to promote patriotism and support for the military effort in Iraq or Afghanistan? If our students seek our advice and counsel, should we encourage them to enlist? Or should we tell them that the decision is theirs to make? What about the Patriot Act? Should we urge our students to accept curtailments of our civil liberties as a necessary sacrifice in the "war on terrorism," a war against a stateless enemy that is not confined to a particular territory? Or should we warn them of the potential dangers that may arise when any government is allowed to invade the privacy of its citizens?

Ignoring these questions does not allow one to escape taking a stand. Even if you are uncomfortable speaking out for or against the war, it is important to understand that in times such as these we cannot pretend that education is apolitical work. Particularly now, when accountability has become a national mantra, we believe that educators must hold themselves accountable for ensuring that students acquire an intellectual grounding in history, civics, and culture that will enable them to develop informed opinions about the war, about U.S. foreign policy toward the Middle East, and about the implications of the war for civil liberties in American society.

Silence and inaction are nothing more than a form of complicity with the status quo. The war is raging now, and those who do not express opposition are in effect demonstrating complicity if not support. People—Iraqis, Afghanis, and Americans—are dying, and decisions are being made in Washington that will affect our future. Our schools are being used as recruiting grounds for the military because No Child Left Behind (NCLB) requires schools to provide military recruiters with access to schools and student records.[1] Our schools are not required to provide antiwar groups with equal access, so it seems clear that our education system is tilted toward war rather than peace.

During the 1960s, universities and colleges were the sites of demonstrations and sit-ins when campus administrators provided the federal government with access to student records for the military draft during the Vietnam War. Today, the use of student records for military recruitment provokes relatively little protest. Fear of terrorist attack, fear of being perceived as sympathizing with terrorists or enemies of the United States, and the undocumented but enduring belief that the war in Iraq will prevent terrorists from attacking us here—all combine to make it increasingly difficult for individuals to take public positions against the war. Sensitivities are also heightened whenever American men and women (actually a large number of those serving in our armed forces in Iraq and Afghanistan are not U.S. citizens) are deployed to fight in a foreign land, and this too contributes to the chilling effect on domestic dissent. However, as educators, we have a special responsibility to encourage critical thinking among our students. Indeed, citizens who think critically are essential for the functioning of our democracy. We ought not to allow our nation's schools to remain cogs in a war machine, nor should we allow ourselves to become unwitting supporters.

Linking Accountability and Patriotism

Over the past decade there has been a new emphasis on accountability in our nation's schools. NCLB has required schools to produce evidence that students are learning (as measured by performance on standardized tests) and that when they graduate from school they possess basic competencies in math and literacy. While many educators (including both of us) applaud certain aspects of NCLB, federal education policy under President Bush has been increasingly linked to other Administration initiatives, including the war. Thus educators are being held accountable in new ways. As a result of this linkage, the stakes are increasingly high for teachers, administrators, and students.

Educators who support the war, the President, and the policies of the Administration may experience little difficulty doing what they can to embrace the military effort and NCLB with patriotic enthusiasm. They may do so either because they trust the President and his policies or because they believe that obedience and loyalty are essential when the nation is at war. They may have no qualms about promoting a similar brand of patriotism among their students and encouraging them to enlist in the military, even if they do not encourage their own children to do the same.

Others may secretly oppose the war and the policies of the Administration but fear making their opposition known. Perhaps they fear being accused of disloyalty or being seen as a troublemaker. Or perhaps they are concerned that if they speak out they will be censured, fired, or worse.

It is not surprising that many who oppose the war (and polls show that a majority of Americans no longer support it[2]), who question the rationale and logic used to justify the military occupation of Iraq and Afghanistan, and who regard NCLB as a threat to the integrity of public education may be reluctant to express their views openly. In some parts of the country, critics of the war, including prominent politicians, journalists, and celebrities, have been castigated for being "soft" on terrorism, and their patriotism has been questioned. Just before launching the war in Afghanistan, the President declared, "You are either with us or with the terrorists." When the lines of debate are drawn so starkly, even passive neutrality may give rise to suspicion.

Yet educators who prefer to avoid controversy and who would rather remain silent on these polarizing issues may find a stance of neutrality difficult to maintain during these tense times. When the National Education Association is called a terrorist organization by one secretary of education and when the state superintendent of Connecticut is described as "un-American" by another, simply because both have been critical of NCLB and other aspects of federal education policy, it is clear that a link between war and education has been forged. It may seem odd—and even unfair—for one's attitudes and positions toward the war to be linked to one's position on NCLB and federal education policy, but these are not ordinary times.

While no one wants to risk being questioned by the FBI, blacklisted, or detained (or even deported if one is not a U.S. citizen) for taking public positions that are regarded as unpatriotic, it is important for us to remember that the right to dissent is an essential part of our democracy. It is also important to remember that, as educators, we have been given the great responsibility of imparting knowledge that will prepare our students to become citizens in this democracy. This is not a responsibility that can be taken lightly.

Accountability and Democratic Citizenship

As accountability has become the leading policy fixation in education, it might be helpful for educators to think of patriotism and citizenship in terms of accountability as well. Given that our nation is at war in at least two countries, shouldn't educators be accountable for ensuring that all students have some understanding of why we are fighting, of whom we are at war with, and of what is at stake?

Citizenship education is important in every society, but there is no place where it is more vital than in the United States, the world's preeminent military power. Our government spends far more on the military than does any other nation. We have military bases and troops deployed in more than one hundred foreign countries and hundreds of nuclear warheads ready to be launched on the order of the President. A nation with so strong a military and so vast a military presence must have an education system that is equally strong in teaching its future citizens to think critically and independently about the uses of American power and about the role of the American military in the world.

Unlike most military superpowers of the past, the United States is a democracy, and the results of our elections can influence the global policies we pursue. Since the rest of the world cannot vote in our elections, even though their fate may be determined by the outcomes, it is up to us, as citizens and as educators, to ensure that our teaching fosters the kind of informed debate and discussion that is necessary for the functioning of a healthy democracy.

Such an approach to teaching must include a willingness to discuss controversial issues, such as the nature and implications of American imperialism, our role as a global power, and our ongoing desire to intervene in the affairs of other nations. Every student in our nation's secondary schools should be exposed to both sides of the debate about how the United States uses its power in the world. All students should be able to understand the rationale given for American troop deployments and military actions abroad, and, before graduating, they should be able to write a coherent essay exploring the merits of various courses of action and putting forward their own perspective on the ethics of U.S. foreign policy.

To acquire this form of political literacy, our students must have an understanding of American and world history that goes far beyond regurgitating facts and dates or passing state history exams. They must also understand the complexity of politics in ways that exceed the typical offerings of the mainstream media. In short, they must learn, as Paulo Freire once admonished, to "read the world" so that they might have a clearer understanding of the forces shaping their lives.

Let us use the concept of imperialism to illustrate how these educational goals might be pursued. The American Heritage Dictionary defines imperialism as "the policy of extending a nation's authority by territorial acquisition or by the establishment of economic and political hegemony over other nations." To determine whether it is appropriate to apply this term to the actions of the United States, students would need to be exposed to a thematic approach to the history of America's territorial expansion, its ascendance to global power after the Spanish-Cuban-American War, and its emergence as the world's foremost superpower in the aftermath of World War II.

Such an approach to history would compel students to grapple with the meaning and significance of economic and political changes rather than merely to recall a chronology of isolated facts. It would also enable students to comprehend the significance of blatant contradictions in U.S. foreign policy. For example, many Americans do not realize that the United States once supported many of the groups that now are part of al Qaeda (including Osama bin Laden himself) when these individuals and groups were carrying out acts of terrorism in Afghanistan in opposition to the Soviet occupation of that country. They also may not know that Saddam Hussein was once a U.S. ally and that we supported him in his war against Iran, even when we knew he was using chemical weapons against the Kurds.[3]

We should teach history in ways that make it possible for students to make sense of contradictions such as these. Indeed, we must do so if our students are to appreciate the complex social processes that led to America's rise as an imperial power. This does not mean that we should engage in an unfair bashing of the United States. One way to avoid this is to provide readings that offer a variety of points of view on the same subject. However, even as we strive for balance and fairness, we should provide our students with the analytical skills to critique and evaluate the information they are exposed to so that they can develop a logical and historically grounded framework for comprehending present conflicts and foreign engagements.

To have a context for understanding the present war in Iraq, every student should know that war and violence were central to the founding and early development of the United States. What began as thirteen states on the East Coast of North America eventually expanded from sea to sea through a process of conquest and conflict. Students should understand that, while some historians view this expansion in positive terms, as the growth of a liberty-loving republic, others see it as having been achieved by the near genocide of Native Americans and by the seizure of immense western territories from Mexico.[4]

Similarly, to appreciate the significance of President Bush's assertion that Saddam Hussein had weapons of mass destruction as a pretext for taking the nation to war, it would help students to know that similar tactics have been used in the past. The 1846 clash of U.S. and Mexican troops on lands that historically had belonged to Mexico; the sinking of the battleship Maine off the coast of Cuba in 1898, which Americans, without evidence, blamed on Spain; and the alleged but never confirmed second North Vietnamese attack on U.S. vessels in the Gulf of Tonkin in 1964 are all examples of controversial rationales that were used to take the nation to war. Understanding the nature of these historical controversies—namely, who wanted the war, who opposed it, and why—would help students to appreciate the significance of the ongoing debate over how and why the United States entered the war with Iraq.

Accountability in teaching should also include ensuring that students have the ability to process the news and information they are exposed to each day so that they can understand how the war is being conducted and develop informed opinions about it. To be intelligent citizens today, students should be able to use the daily reporting from Iraq—from mainstream and alternative sources—to question and critique the claims of the Administration, such as Vice President Cheney's recent assertion that the insurgency in Iraq is in its "last throes." The parallels between such claims and the equally misleading claims made by the Johnson Administration during the Vietnam War are worth exploring, as they offer historical precedent as well as evidence that the Republicans have no monopoly on this kind of spin. As the saying goes, "In war, truth is the first casualty."

Students should understand both the risks involved if the U.S. leaves Iraq before peace and democracy are established and those involved in staying longer. Again, the parallels to Vietnam are haunting. Making sense of such issues and arriving at an intelligent, well-thought-out point of view requires an ability to critique arguments and opinions that are presented as facts and to recognize misleading statements.

In a recent essay titled "War and the American Constitutional Order," Mark Brandon asserts that, as of 2004, Americans had been involved in wars or military actions in 182 of the 228 years since the colonies declared independence in 1776.[5] He also points out that U.S. military actions became much more frequent in the twentieth century. Remarkably, from 1900 to 2000 there were only six years in which the United States was not engaged in some form of military action. Today, we are pursuing an open-ended commitment to a global war on terrorism that knows no national or temporal boundaries.

Critics such as Andrew Bacevich write of a "new American militarism" whereby the nation's political elite, infatuated with the capabilities of high-tech weaponry and emboldened by the collapse of the Soviet Union and the lack of a countervailing superpower, has embraced military action as a first rather than a last resort to advance U.S. interests.[6] Our students need not accept Bacevich's arguments, but they do need to know enough about American history to be able to critique and debate them. Why has the United States been so reliant on military force for so much of its history? Do other nations have similar histories? What rationales have Americans used in the past to justify going to war? How do we reconcile this long history of U.S. warfare with the fact that U.S. territory has so rarely come under attack from foreign powers? Our students need to engage questions such as these with an understanding of history and with a critical frame of mind.

It is also well past time for U.S. schools to confront what is new about this latest U.S. war: This is the nation's first preemptive war. By conventional standards, the United States could well be seen as the aggressor in this war, since it invaded a far weaker state not in response to any *immediate* threat or attack on Americans but in response to a *presumed* threat (Iraq's alleged possession of weapons of mass destruction) that later proved to be nonexistent. Students need to grapple with the whole idea of preemptive war and its international implications. If the United States is entitled to wage such a war, attacking weaker nations whenever it construes a potential threat from them, then do we accord this same right to other major powers? Can China, for example, be given a green light to invade Taiwan if China's leaders believe that this smaller nation poses a threat to its security?

Our efforts to ensure that our students understand the war we are fighting should also include discussion of how our troops conduct themselves during the war. We must help our students to understand how it was possible for prisoners of war to be abused and tortured by American forces in Iraq and why it is that Amnesty International has referred to the prison at the Guantánamo military base in Cuba as the "Gulag of our times." Here the linkages between past and present can be made by simply asking why it is that the United States owns this naval base in Cuba.

We should encourage our students to debate who should be held accountable when atrocities such as these come to light. Those who torture, those who supervise and command them, both? They should know why the Geneva Conventions for the treatment of prisoners during war were adopted and why America's designation of certain prisoners as "unlawful combatants" represents a threat to Americans who may be captured. Likewise, similar kinds of questions must be asked of the Iraqi insurgents and of the terrorist groups whose suicide bombings and attacks on civilians have created the worst horrors of the war.

The extent to which our civil liberties should be curtailed as a result of the war on terrorism is yet another topic that should be fully explored. Is the Patriot Act fundamentally different from Senator McCarthy's search for Communists during the Cold War years? Was President Roosevelt's decision to intern Japanese Americans during World War II similar to or different from the mass detentions of Muslims who are still being held without trial or legal representation throughout America today? With police searching bags at airports and security agencies possessing new powers to order wiretaps on Americans, students need to assess whether the national security rationales for these acts can stand up under critical scrutiny.

The Middle Eastern focus of much of the war on terrorism poses a serious challenge to our schools, because most students—indeed, most of our citizens—lack the kind of understanding of the history and culture of the region that would be needed to understand the complex issues. Not many public schools teach Arabic or have teachers with expertise in the history of Islam. With such educational deficiencies being the norm in the United States, it is little wonder that the American electorate was unable to sort out the secular tyranny of Saddam Hussein and the violent religious fanaticism of Osama bin Laden. Educators need to do better than politicians have in grappling with the complexities of the Middle East, and they need to make distinctions among those we regard as our enemies.

Perhaps the most provocative area of inquiry our students can explore as they reflect on their nation's international impact and posture is at the macrohistorical level. What is it that motivates the United States to act as it does internationally? Is American foreign policy and war-making driven by democratic altruism? Or do economics and the search for markets, cheap labor, and raw materials shape the American agenda? Should the United States work with and support the United Nations, the international body we helped to create, or should we denounce the UN as an anti-American institution and reject the idea of allowing outsiders to debate questions pertinent to our defense and security?

While many of the topics we have highlighted are most easily dealt with in social studies and English classes, teachers in other subject areas should not shy away from participating in the process of citizenship education. American students need to understand how the rest of the world perceives us and why so many people who sympathized with the United States after September 11th no longer do. Teachers of all kinds should raise these issues with their students, not to dictate what they should think, but simply to encourage them to think. Too much is at stake for citizenship education to be treated as an isolated unit to be covered solely in a social studies class.

My Country Right or Wrong?

If we are honest in our approach to teaching history and getting our students to think critically about the war, we will point out that there is a tension between flag-waving nationalism and a willingness to confront the ugly side of American history. For example, American nationalism impels us to think of 9/11 not merely as a day of U.S. suffering or as an act of brutal violence, but as a rallying cry for a global war on terror. If we can put aside our nationalist lenses for a moment, we might seek to understand why many developing countries regard us as an international bully, a nation motivated more by power and greed than by altruism and a sincere commitment to human rights and democracy.

Chilean writer Ariel Dorfman reminds us that there is "more than one America and more than one September 11th."[7] Dorfman and millions of others remember another September 11, this one in 1973, as a day of mourning. That was the day that a U.S.-backed coup overthrew the democratically elected socialist president of Chile, Salvador Allende, and replaced his government with a military junta led by General Augusto Pinochet. Dorfman asks Americans to recognize that their suffering is neither unique nor exclusive. He challenges us as educators to see that, when we push beyond the boundaries of a narrow patriotism, we see a world in which the United States plays a complex and contradictory role—sometimes as victim, sometimes as perpetrator, of antidemocratic violence.

Criticizing Islamic fundamentalists and rabid nationalists in other countries is easy. It is far more difficult to challenge the patriotic assumptions and biases of one's own country, especially during wartime.

The pioneers of the idea of public education—Thomas Jefferson, Horace Mann, and John Dewey—argued that schools were essential to the health and well-being of our republic. They understood that an uneducated citizenry would doom the republic because ignorant citizens would be incapable of electing good leaders or voting out of office those who abused their power. As educators, it is our democratic responsibility to foster critical thinking among our students.

Those who deem taking up such challenges as unpatriotic would do well to heed the warning of English writer G. K. Chesterton: "My country right or wrong is a thing that no patriot would think of saying except in a desperate case. It is like saying, 'My mother, drunk or sober.'"[8]

With NCLB seeing to it that our schools become sites of military recruitment, educators have an even stronger obligation to ensure that their students are able to make informed decisions about their future. They must be exposed to all sides of the debates over America's role as a superpower. They must be able to draw lessons from the past so that they will be more informed about the present. In short, they must be made to understand what they may be putting their young lives on the line for. To do anything less is irresponsible and a willful neglect of our professional duties as educators.

"Children Are the Living Message We Send to a Time We Will Not See"

Delaine Eastin

I believe the genius of America is that it is founded on the notion that all are created equal and that the way to achieve the greatest possible life for all is through liberty, justice, and a great education.

I believe that coming out of the depression and World War II, the Greatest Generation gave us the most extraordinary gifts of educational opportunity possible, despite the debts and hardships associated with their early lives. America became wealthy as a result. Why are we so stingy with the education of the next generation when we have been so richly rewarded with better educations than our ill-schooled forbearers?

Indeed, in the dark first year of the Civil War, President Lincoln began the Land Grant Colleges and dreamed of greater educational opportunities for future generations.

In the difficult days of World War II, President Franklin Roosevelt did not say we cannot afford education because we are at war. Instead, he called for a GI Bill of Rights and doubled the number of students attending college.

In the immediate aftermath of World War II, in 1946, President Truman was stunned to find that record numbers of nineteen-year-old draftees were rejected by the military because of malnourishment in their formative years, which happened to be during the Great Depression. To fix this problem, Truman proposed the National School Lunch Act, which says the school lunch program is a matter of "national security."

In the Cold War, when American resources were stretched by a massive defense budget, and later on, after Sputnik, President Eisenhower (a Republican) did not say that we could not afford to improve education. Instead, he called for an ambitious program to encourage more students to attend college and to become scientists, engineers, and teachers. He called it the National Defense Education Act.

By contrast, the most recent federal budget proposal seeks to cut education spending by more than $3 billion. Much of the cuts would come from eliminating more than 40 education programs totaling $3.5 billion, including programs for the arts, state grants for vocational education, Perkins loans for low-income college students, and the Even Start literacy program for poor families. The largest source of federal education aid to states, the $12.7 billion Title I program for low-income students, would receive no new funding under the proposed 2007 fiscal year budget now under review by Congress.

Politicians who cut education betray both our past and our future.

Great American patriots of all political parties believe that, in the immortal words of John Adams, "Laws for the liberal education of youth are so extremely wise and useful that to a humane and generous mind, no expense for this purpose should be thought extravagant."[1] I believe that the value of investing in education at all levels from preschool to graduate school should be as obvious as saving Yosemite, digging the Panama Canal, building the Golden Gate Bridge, or going to the moon.

In a global economy, America's stinginess toward its children's education is a formula for disaster. Instead of educating them, we are larding them up with our debt. That is a double disaster for the future of our great country. I believe Neil Postman was right when he said, "Children are the living message we send to a time we will not see."[2]

I believe my parents' generation should be revered for their many sacrifices. Sadly, I also believe that my generation has been a disappointment when it comes to education and being honest with our children. Every dollar we borrow for tax cuts is a debt our children carry for decades. Every failure to invest in education is a formula for America's decline. I believe real patriots must stand up for America's children.

"God Bless America and Peace," Copyright © 2001. St.
Joseph School for the Deaf, Bronx, NY. Library of Congress
Prints and Photographs Division, Exit Art's "Reactions"
Exhibition Collection [LC-DIG-ppmsca-01696].

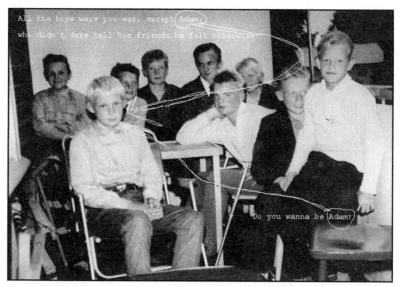

"All the boys were pro-war, except Adam, who didn't dare tell his friends he felt otherwise. Do You Wanna Be Adam?" Poster, flyer, postcard, sticker. Copyright Jimmy Holmfeldt, Norrkšpiing, Sweden. Used with permission.

Chapter 3

The Psychology of Patriotism

Michael J. Bader

Patriotism can be a force for good or evil. American patriotism helped vanquish fascism; German patriotism helped create and sustain it. Wars of national liberation depend on patriotic fervor to oppose colonial rule; unfortunately, ethnic cleansing draws on this same fervor. Appeals to the transcendent value of the nation-state can be progressive or regressive.

Regardless of the purpose to which patriotism is harnessed, all forms of it share similar psychological dynamics. Patriotic symbols such as the "nation"—including its manifestations in images like the flag or the Founding Fathers—represent the fulfillment of our longings for connectedness and safety. In this sense, the nation is a metaphor for a family. Families serve the function of providing psychic security and attachment. We project onto ever-expanding forms of social authority the longings originally satisfied by parents in childhood.

It's easy to see the workings of these two needs in our collective responses to the attack of 9/11 and to the devastation visited on New Orleans and the Gulf Coast by Hurricane Katrina. In the first instance, people looked to government to provide security and defense, including a muscular retaliation against our enemies. On a symbolic level, we looked to our leaders to provide the protection and strength usually associated with fathers. In the second instance, people looked to government to provide care and nurturance, a safety net— qualities associated in our culture with mothers.

While patriotism draws a great deal of its energy from the unconscious mind, it is not reducible to it. That is, social attitudes and behaviors are the products of a complex interplay between the rational and irrational, conscious and unconscious, private and public factors. Nevertheless, one of the reasons that patriotic fervor can be so passionate—and, as a result, so vulnerable to manipulation and exploitation—is that its roots lie in the deep levels of the psyche.

Patriotism is a container for a range of psychological needs that originally play themselves out in the family. Over fifty years of psychological research have established that human beings have an innate need for attachment and recognition and that not only is the satisfaction of this need essential for our psychological and physical survival, but its frustration is one of the primary sources of mental suffering.[1] I see such suffering every day in my consulting room—families in which parents can't empathize with their children or each other, or narcissistically use their children, or neglect them altogether. I see children who grow up taking care of others instead of themselves and who retreat from intimacy because of fears of rejection and abandonment.

The helplessness of the human infant and its absolute dependence on adult caregivers for survival generates a powerful need for protection and an idealization of the power and authority of these caregivers. When parents are protective and reasonable, children grow up with a basic sense of security and an ability to rely on others. When parents fail to protect children and exercise their authority in arbitrary, frightening, or inconsistent ways, children grow up with a basic sense of insecurity and have difficulty trusting others. Unfortunately, this latter scenario is all too common.

However, the fact that our needs for connection and security are often thwarted does not mean that they go away. We continue to long for recognition and reciprocal relationships even as we suffer from loneliness. And we continue to seek security even as we feel unsafe and unprotected.

In this context, it's easy to understand the powerful psychic meaning of patriotism. To feel like an "American" and to identify with the "United States of America" is to feel at once safe and connected. Patriotism establishes a "we" that satisfies the longings for connectedness and affiliation that are so often frustrated in our private lives. And it offers an image of a strong and fair authority in whose arms we can feel safe and secure.

The powerful satisfactions provided by patriotism become even more compelling when we consider how imperiled or absent they are in everyday social life. A great many sociologists, psychologists, and philosophers have written about the ways that a market economy based on an ethos of selfish individualism undermines communities, atomizes social life, alienates work, and tends to make relationships increasingly instrumental. From David Riesman's 1950 masterpiece *The Lonely Crowd,* to Paulo Freire's *Pedagogy of the Oppressed* in 1970, to Robert Putnam's 2001 sensation *Bowling Alone,* social critics have argued that the decline of traditional communities of meaning in contemporary society has had disastrous consequences for the psychological well-being of citizens.

Thus the unfulfilled longings for attachment, recognition, and security first manifested and frustrated in early family life get further blocked in our everyday lives as citizens and workers. The suffering that results is often unconscious. As children, we invest our families with an awesome power to define the way things are and the way they're supposed to be. We experience our frustrations and psychological pain as *normal,* as somehow wired into the fabric of reality, fate, or our genes. Similarly, in a culture based on individualism, need for community can seem foolish. We grow up and become cynical about the possibility that things could really be different, and so we conclude that our suffering is illegitimate and unworthy of articulation. Our loneliness and collective insecurity become problems with no names.

Patriotism, appeals to national pride, invocations of historical purpose, and symbols of collective unity (the flag, the Constitution, and so forth) all offer a symbolic resolution to unspoken and inchoate longings for relatedness and safety. For as much as there are powerful forces in our familial and cultural lives that create alienation and apprehension, there are forces acting as an undertow against the prevailing waves. To the extent that people continue to need to feel safe and connected, they will make do with whatever they can find to satisfy these needs.

Political movements on both the Left and the Right seek to link their partisan agendas to the evocation and satisfaction of these frustrated longings. For example, in his book *Moral Politics: How Liberals and Conservatives Think,* linguist George Lakoff argued that liberals speak to values arising from a conceptual paradigm that he calls the "nurturant parent"—including the values of empathy and responsibility for others—while conservatives appeal to a mental metaphor involving discipline and self-reliance that he terms the "strict parent." Both models seek to address needs for connectedness and security, albeit in radically different ways.

Thus the political exploitation of our collective passions and distress is rampant in our public lives. The passions evoked by politics must, of necessity, involve an encounter with deep-seated human longings. Whether people are marching against abortion or against the war in Iraq, intense emotions—and not simply cognitive beliefs—are on parade.

Sometimes, in fact, a movement or institution can use the power generated by its success in satisfying the psychic needs of its members to promote both liberal and conservative agendas. For example, the hugely successful fundamentalist megachurch run by Rick Warren in Orange County, California, manages its rapid growth by encouraging the formation of small prayer groups that function to provide social and emotional support and affiliation, as well as spiritual development. And Warren's Saddleback Church simultaneously supports a conservative social agenda and has invested heavily in creating a safety net for the homeless in Orange County.[2]

However, while both Left and Right seek to take advantage of the frustrated longings for community and safety, the conservative side has done so more successfully of late. In the post-9/11 climate, conservative and neoconservative ideologues used the need for protection that so many Americans felt to promote dubious justifications for war with Iraq and a massive increase in the police and surveillance powers of the government.

Similarly, conservatives have been more successful than liberals in using one other crucial political technique in their attempt to create an experience of community and safety: namely, the evocation of a demeaned "other." While liberals are certainly guilty of this maneuver when they express their disdain for caricatured Evangelical Christians, conservatives are especially skilled at evoking prejudice and erecting devalued caricatures. For example, the satisfying sense of "we-ness" that accompanies being an "American" is deepened and solidified by the creation and demonization of an "enemy." It used to be the Communists; now, it's the terrorists. Membership in a group is enhanced if there are people who are excluded. If these people on the outside are "bad" or "dangerous," then it enables those of us on the inside to feel good, righteous, and safe.

This process of exclusion and demonization is the essential dynamic behind all forms of ethnocentrism, racism, sexism, and homophobia. The feelings of insecurity and disconnectedness that plague us in our personal and social lives can be blamed on the actions of some "other" who is then demeaned and attacked. This process of projection is deliberately used by conservatives to solidify their base. By creating an imaginary "us" and "them," they can then promise satisfaction of deep and legitimate longings for a community safe from both real and illusory threats posed from the outside. On the international front, the currently favored "other" is the swarthy terrorist. On the domestic front, the Religious Right has most recently focused on gay marriage. Both the terrorist and gay newlywed are used as lightning rods to draw out the collective passions of Americans looking to be temporarily relieved of feelings of insecurity and disconnectedness. Ironically, the us/them tactic ultimately serves to undermine a more authentic community that would better meet the psychological needs for connectedness of most individuals. Like a clique of schoolchildren who gain a temporary sense of belonging by demeaning other classmates, the Religious Right promises a temporary and partial remedy for the symptoms of an illness that lies at the heart of the system that they, themselves, promote and defend.

Such solutions—whether promoted by the Left or the Right—are transient and require the constant stimulation and reproduction of paranoid mechanisms. The real reasons that our longings for recognition and safety are continually frustrated are not substantively addressed by the creation of demeaned "others." While the longings are healthy, their frustration is the result of dysfunctional family systems, the ethos of individualism, the greed of the marketplace, the powerlessness people feel at work, and the violence resulting from discrimination and the deterioration of social safety nets.

In this sense, people who lean toward the more progressive end of the political spectrum have a chance, at least, to win hearts and minds, not by erecting an enemy against whom we can all unite, but by appealing in a healthier way to these same unmet needs for security and connection. As Michael Lerner argues in *The Left Hand of God,* progressives need to articulate a politics that is based explicitly on a recognition of the centrality of these desires and that specifically condemns the institutions that frustrate them and fights for social changes that increase the possibility of their real satisfaction.[3]

Schools can play an important role in a political project seeking to identify healthy solutions to the problems of disconnectedness and insecurity. Schools can teach and model empathy; provide recognition;

encourage discussions of values, including those found in the various spiritual traditions; and confront prejudices born of the need to define the self in opposition to a demeaned "other." In other words, schools could try to create an environment in which the legitimate needs of children for connectedness and safety are gratified in ways that inoculate them against the psychological appeal of messages of racism, arrogant nationalism, and moral intolerance.

The psychological needs that drive patriotic fervor are universal. People will always need to be connected and secure. These longings can be gratified in healthy or unhealthy ways. They can be distorted and exploited in the interest of agendas that are immoral, or they can be addressed and gratified in ways that promote the general welfare. Like patriotism itself, the human psyche is intrinsically neither good nor bad. It all depends on the uses to which it's put.

Second Fiddle to Fear

Denise Walsh

Most of us believe that by learning about the past, students can better prepare for the future. As a teacher of U.S. history, I certainly believed it, and for seven years I enthusiastically led my students on an exploration of the American past—until history caught up with me.

I taught at a private secondary school for girls in a town that had lost a disproportionately high number of people in the September 11th attack on the World Trade Center. Perhaps as a consequence, I found that even two years later, student attitudes toward government policy, patriotism, and historical events in general were hampering my ability to create citizens who understood and would protect their rights.

Each year I had been teaching about the Alien and Sedition Acts to show that the Founders were political creatures who struggled to find a balance between individual rights and national security. During the 1790s, the Federalists labeled the Democratic-Republicans as traitors and gleefully passed the Alien and Sedition Acts, which are remembered today for their condemnation of dissent and their draconian immigration policies. These acts aroused intense controversy at the time. But in the end, the Founders earned their laurels: John Adams wisely avoided a full-blown war with France, though historians have argued that doing so cost him a second term. With Thomas Jefferson as President, the Alien and Sedition Acts ignominiously expired.

In 2003, in order to bring the issue of balancing rights against security concerns into sharper focus for my students, I taught the Alien and Sedition Acts in conjunction with the

Patriot Act. My goal was for the students to confront the problem, think critically about it, and take a position. I would not have predicted the outcome.

Given the White, upper-middle-class background of most of my students and our proximity to the Twin Towers, I was not surprised that most of them supported the Patriot Act. But I was astounded that nearly half of them also applauded the Alien and Sedition Acts. They identified strongly with the security concerns of the 1790s, and even though we had just finished studying the American Revolution, they believed that government should be trusted—at the end of the eighteenth century as much as at the beginning of the twenty-first century.

How do I explain my students' response? They had not grown up during the Cold War or during World War II or during the Depression. And the introduction of vulnerability into their lives had been intense and sudden. New York City was still receiving occasional "code orange" warnings, field trips were canceled, and the girls simply craved security. By the following year, the level of fear had ebbed, and the same project yielded little support for the Alien and Sedition Acts.

I still believe that we learn much about the present from our study of the past. I believe that juxtaposing past and present can help students understand that dissent can be patriotic and that the government cannot always be trusted. But these lessons will not be learned when critical thinking plays second fiddle to fear.

Poster encouraging citizens to be mindful of careless talk and to let the military speak for the nation. Artist: Homer Ansley. No. Cal. WPA Art Program, circa 1941–1943. Library of Congress Prints and Photographs Division, Work Projects Administration Poster Collection [LC-USZC2-1169].

President Richard Nixon tossing out a baseball at Senators' opening game, Washington, D.C., 1969. Photographer: Warren K. Leffler. Library of Congress Prints and Photographs Division, U.S. News & World Report Magazine Photograph Collection [LC-USZ62-106488].

Chapter 4

On Patriotism and the Yankees

Lessons Learned From Being a Fan

Deborah Meier

I have a very strong, but perhaps odd, personal connection to the word *patriotism*. I spent my earliest years in what I view, in retrospect, as a very "unpatriotic" family in the period between the two World Wars, when a form of pacifism and internationalism was a common reaction to the horrors of WWI. "No more war" was a view that one did not need left-wing credentials to hold.

My family was not prone to discussing patriotism, yet my parents were loud boosters of what America represented in the larger world, and my grandmother viewed being a Jew and being an American as more or less synonymous with all things noble and great. My mother was determined that neither my brother nor I would go to an Ivy League school because her children had to "know America" by attending school in the Midwest. She was, herself, a first-generation immigrant from St. Louis.

My parents, and even my grandparents, had an instinct for putting people in their place, for avoiding superlatives, and for insisting on seeing the world from the other side of whatever side was getting too popular. For my father, a first-generation New Yorker, deflating other people's pompous beliefs—including those of his children—was a favorite pastime. Flag-waving fell in this category and, until 1941 when America went to war, I watched the annual Memorial

Day parade and all its military pomp from our apartment window with a mix of patriotic fervor and guilt.

Nothing was sacrosanct—not our friends, our schools, the books we read, the movies we watched, or the songs we listened to—not even the liberal politics my parents themselves favored and spent much of their energy defending. My parents may have voted for FDR every chance they got, but they distanced themselves from any form of hero worship. Don't trust famous or powerful people, they would have said, because it's simply unreasonable to assume you can distinguish their ambitions—their PR—from their actual beliefs. Judge them by their record and then keep your fingers crossed. Leave trust to interpersonal relations with people whose eyes you can look into on a daily basis.

Growing up as I did in a lib-lab lefty family—but one that was also rabidly anti-Communist and pro-Democrat—I didn't find it easy to transfer my latent patriotism to other so-called socialist states. Neither real nor imagined utopias were tolerated in my family. We were reminded as children that, by nature, none of us was ever perfect, and that human beings surely could be improved upon as a species and as a society. An open-minded skepticism—even regarding one's own favorite ideals—was always valued in my family. Dreams were necessary, but they were not to be confused with reality.

I was a child of the 1940s—that "magical moment" (especially from the viewpoint of a preteen) when good and evil seemed so clear. Thus, I stirred over the national anthem and was in love with everyone who wore a uniform. I wished only that I, too, could give my life for my country. I loved martial and patriotic music, especially if it also had a socially progressive message tucked into it—as so much of WWII patriotic music did. It would have come as no surprise to me—as it might a generation later—that the Pledge of Allegiance was written by a socialist. In these ways, my patriotism was complicated, hard to pin down, and sometimes contradictory.

Yankee Fandom Versus Love of Nation

But then, I had one other, not-so-secret vice. I was an absolute patriot, loyal to the core, the most rabid of rabid, when it came to the New York Yankees. Toward them I did not experience any edge of skepticism. I owed them total allegiance and loyalty. I was 100% in Mark Twain's camp: A patriot always supports his country, though not always a particular administration. In fact, when it came to the Yankees it was perfectly okay to dislike, and even hate, the management (although I don't recall doing so in the early years of my most devoted fandom). In my youth, to make matters simpler for me, baseball *players* didn't have the opportunity to be traitors. They couldn't jump ship; they could be traded by a benighted management, but they couldn't trade themselves.

I'm grateful for that experience, at the very least because it helps me sort out some of the elements that make up blind patriotism, as well as that other kind of patriotism that I have trouble describing but honor—the kind that kicks in when others unfairly attack, or ignore, or misread my country, state, party, school, or kin. Note the "my." I respect the kind of love of country that made my mother insist that her children see America before they set off on their own, and that led me to show my own children our glorious land before they began to travel abroad. As I recall it, when I was growing up this type of patriotism never seemed to be threatened by the idea that people in other countries might feel similarly about their own country. Nor did it seem to conflict with the idea of dual loyalties—being an Irish-American, for example. It seemed as natural to be loyal to both sides of my cultural heritage, as it was to be loyal to both the maternal and paternal sides of my own family of origin. Why choose? Two is better than one, *ad infinitum*. A multitude of identities could prevent one from feeling too let down if one of those identities seemed vulnerable.

It's the choosing sides that defined my loyalty to the Yankees as different. Their enemies were my enemies, their victories my victories. And both were easy to define. How blessed, but also how painful. My impotence defined my love. I had neither voice nor vote in their future; I was a passive victim of their fate. Their losses were for me more devastating than real losses in my own life for precisely this reason—because the Yankees, like the symbols of misplaced patriotism in general, stood for so much more than a baseball team. They replaced my own self-esteem.

The analogy has its limits, of course. And perhaps I could have learned to be a more temperate fan. But I never learned to be another kind of Yankee fan, as I think I learned to be another kind of American patriot. The other kind of fan is more patient and more open-minded about the virtues of other teams and players. The other kind of fan loves the game, writ large, not just his or her own team's games.

Patriotism Outside of the Ballpark

It's hard, then, to come down on one side or another—for or against patriotism! Of course, I can simply choose to define patriotism in a comfortable way, but that ignores the reality that it's a loaded word. Any effort to discuss it has to start with examining the load. Should we acknowledge defeat, and fight for the idea but not the label, or is this word just too important to turn it over to one's adversaries?

I've spent a lifetime wrestling with this issue. Most of the time I return to literary critic Irving Howe's defense of the term *socialism* on the masthead of *Dissent* magazine, which he launched in the late 1950s. This was at a time when, at least in America, the term was perhaps irreparably associated in the minds of Americans with totalitarianism. Similarly, among educators the term *progressive* is often mistaken as describing classrooms where teachers and students are entitled to "do their own thing," or as "hands-on but minds-off." This has lead some educators to try to invent a new term. But, our labels come with a history and reinventing labels comes with a price that we need to weigh carefully.

So, back to the word *patriotism*. Who has the definition right? Am I close to the truth when I describe my feelings for the Yankees? Or for my grandmother's appreciation of her new homeland? Or for our special history, with all its strengths and warts? What does the etymological history suggest? More important, when all is said and done, how does our concern about patriotism affect our approach to K–12 schooling, especially given the policy climate we currently face?

Some of the facts on the ground (oops, in creeps a military term) are irrefutable. In the name of the War on Terror or the War on Iraq, we have experienced the narrowing of our national understanding of patriotism. Teachers are censored if they discuss complicated or controversial issues, such as the historical and constitutional issues surrounding both the pledge (i.e., the insertion of "under god") and the flag. At a time when vulnerable kids are pressured into joining the ROTC and the army, the view that children of poor families and racial minorities need "more discipline, the Army, boot camps, uniforms, arms crossed, silence in the hall" is gaining prominence. Is this version of education easier to sell at a time when school practices that draw from military models seem particularly relevant and easier to understand? Probably. The glamour of soldiery is creeping back into our culture—especially for young men, increasingly for young women, and above all for those at the bottom of the socioeconomic ladder—and it's bound to impact schooling. The increased popularity of boot camp–style schools for young men of color is not a coincidence. Neither is the popularity of forms of patriotism that are most associated with war, such as an "us-versus-them" style of thought, a style hardly conducive to the nourishing of the intellectual habits of a democracy.

Democracy Is Not "Natural"

Historically, freedom of the mind and intellect has been vulnerable in times of stress, and those who exercise this freedom in such times often face physical coercion and imprisonment. Our democratic habits are hardly well entrenched in the best of times, and are easily shed when under stress. For example, at least half of our fellow citizens believe that in times of crisis homeland security should trump the Bill of Rights. This view is so deeply held as to seem almost commonsensical. If we look closely at our own practices—be it in our families, unions, or schools—we see this tendency played out daily. We become nervous about democratic rights when we feel threatened. We find it difficult to rationalize why we should worry about others' rights if these endanger our own. It is hardly a novel idea that we can't afford the luxury of civil liberties in difficult times. It would take very different training in democracy to expect otherwise.

Democratic habits are fragile, at best. In asking schools to do a better job of instilling them, am I just asking for a more consistent program of brainwashing—even if it is steeped in humanity, poetry, martial music, and history? Is my inability to cross a legitimate union's picket line a form of early brainwashing or the effects of a particular tradition of solidarity—with its own form of martial music? Or are such habits critical, even if often uncomfortable to hold, and worth holding on to, even when what we most cherish seems vulnerable? My central point is that the democratic project is by no means guaranteed to succeed. In fact, it runs counter to much of what we deeply believe. Acknowledging this truth is a first step to developing a sounder definition of patriotism that is consistent with modern democracy. Because, even as democracy is not inborn or natural, it is not unnatural either: It must be learned. So, too, the forms of patriotism that are compatible with it must be learned.

Institutional Versus Personal Loyalties

In raising kids—both in and outside of school—we struggle over loyalty all the time. Love for an abstraction or institution is not, we insist, identical to love for a human being. Thus our loyalty to the one is not the same as our loyalty to the other. Just as nations and even schools are not akin to one's family—even though there are similarities—so, too, what we owe them is different and cannot be easily summed up with slogans. If we treat "my country" as though it were a breathing human being and "my flag" as though it had personal feelings, then we make a foolish mistake. And if we treat these objects as though they are divine, then we commit a profanity. It's amazing how easily we can fall into both traps.

Today, we risk doing all of the above—treating "America" as though it were a conscious human being as well as a symbol of godliness. We're mixing up and confusing all our symbols: the Ten Commandments, the cross, the Bible, the West. Schools are at risk of becoming the recruiting grounds for that other kind of blind, "I'm-the-best" patriotism through the decisions teachers and administrators make about curriculum and pedagogy; disciplinary policy (i.e., the current popularity of "zero tolerance" policies); how to label, categorize, and separate our students; and whether or not to give kids access to multiple views and perspectives—not to mention the ways we use our schools as recruiting grounds for the military.

Telling "Our" Story: The Right to Have More Than One Identity

The most insidious thing about teaching blind patriotism—which would worry me even more if I thought kids were more engaged in schools—is the way it tells our so-called "collective" story. The old story line I grew up with—from Mesopotamia, to Egypt, to Greece, to Rome, to Western Europe, and then to America—has been broken. Even the official global history taught in most American high schools now covers the story of Asia, Africa, and South America, and Native Americans often get as much weight as many a European subculture. It's hard to fix—thank goodness—but it seems we also suffer from the absence of a simple and narrow plot line. We should not be surprised that there is a longing for a unifying story with the happy ending that American democracy is supposed to represent, and that some view increased federal or state control over the local curriculum as a way to bring back a single, heroic *story*. But we need to accept the loss for what it was, a myth that served some far better than others. We need to view the arguments we can have about these varied stories—the picking them apart, the sharing of some stories and the discarding of others as we go—as being both more interesting and better preparation for becoming a good American! Let pop culture take care of the need for common stories, myths, and cherished images. We don't lack these; we lack a place to uncover them, with tender loving care, so that they can't be used to confuse, obscure, or mislead us, at least not without our consent. That's what strong schools are about: uncovering, not covering up.

But it need not be either or. Kids are equally capable of being deeply stirred by an idea of patriotism connected to our shared ownership of the land we currently live in, to its multiple histories, and its yet untold future without insisting on watered-down myths. Our fellow citizens are quite capable of grasping the idea that membership does not require uniformity, but rather suggests mutual demands on behalf of the common good, demands that are always open to appeal. And, as the original contract is challenged, those revisitations, while difficult, can be empowering.

As one's sense of membership expands beyond one's nuclear family, schools can offer alternate visions of a society beyond one ruled by marketplace cohesion. Communities can be suffocating places that demand conformity and isolate dissent. So, even the idea of community has an edge to it that must be attended to. That's why the creation of a school community that crosses the many boundaries of race, culture, ethnicity, and class is both difficult and worthy, if democracy is our goal.

Schools need to fight to hold up open an inviting picture of the marketplace of ideas—all the ways in which we express our different, sometimes very uncommon ideas in music, dance, painting, and so forth. Schools are our first exposure to "the public" as judge and norm-setter. As such, early on they create the kinds of roots that will either flourish for years or, like precious hothouse plants, break under the first adverse conditions. Kids need to experience a public life that is inviting and lively. They have too long associated school with silence, with exercises in answering questions one doesn't care much about, with a bland student government that only gets to decide on whatever is viewed as not sensitive, and with "the rules": keeping the building clean, waiting one's turn, following orders, and being polite. While some of these are virtues, they are equally so in an authoritarian state and a democratic one. In emphasizing these rules, we avoid confronting the truly tough rules—the ones that tell some kids that they belong and tell others that they are outsiders—the habitual practices that often subtly define our place within the community as equally entitled to dignity, voice, and respect, or not. There's a difference between being a novice and an outsider. Kids, like teachers, know when they are one or the other. Democratic schools ensure that no one feels like the latter and that all are, in some respects, the former.

Schools as the Juncture Between the Personal and the Public

In short, my own personal history around patriotism affected the way I saw schooling, and thus influenced the kinds of schools I helped create in New York City and Boston. The Central Park East schools in New York City and the Mission Hill school in Boston were consciously organized to allow participation—first and foremost by the adults, and to a lesser degree by the "novices"—to shape the details that constituted each school's culture. Each school was small enough for a lot of public discourse to take place, for adults and students to know each other well, and for the building of demanding and authentic ways of judging one another's work. Everyone, from the most veteran teacher down to the youngest student, was expected to make sense of what was being asked of them, and to have a voice in the decisions that effected them. Thus the patriotism that we felt towards our school—our stake in its honor—could never be taken for granted, but had to be continuously earned and celebrated.

I came to see each school as the place where ideas could be sorted out without having to settle on the right answer (like the bus schedule and lunchtime). In the Central Park East and Mission Hill schools, the argument was as critical as the vote and changing one's mind was not only honorable, but presumed. Our students may have had less expertise, but, since expertise doesn't always trump good sense, they were no less worthy of being heard. Every experience, no matter how seemingly trivial, had the seeds within it for insight into matters of far wider importance. Thus our schools needed a lean and living constitution if they were to survive over time.

To help guide our day-to-day school interactions and procedures at Central Park East and Mission Hill, we developed the Five Habits of Mind. (For more information on the Five Habits, visit the Mission Hill School's website: www.missionhillschool.org.) The Five Habits of Mind were never actually written down in one final form. There was no agreed upon order for the Five Habits, and different people kept rewording them to fit the circumstance. Since we decided not to add to them, we just fit new "habits" into existing ones, or reworded them to emphasize our favorite part. Similarly, we revisited everything many times—right down to the way we made decisions, the time we took to make them, and the previous year's agreements—and always left room for reconsideration. We agreed that nothing was beyond discussion—by the adults or our students—although there might be agreements about when and where, and even some rules for how to discuss them.

We tried to instill the sense that our differences were sources of strength, not put-downs, and that, when we "attacked" an idea, it was not the person but the idea that was at stake. We were a "nation ruled by law, not men" (or women) in that peculiar sense that so puzzled me as a child. That's why the rules were worth discussing—they were the ground upon which we were equal. Yet in the end we were a community of human beings. No rule or regulation was ever more important than its impact on the living, distinct individuals that made up the whole. And that whole (and here's the rub) required loyalty, perhaps, but not blind allegiance. The honor of the whole had to matter to us—in the way we conducted our classrooms, the aesthetics of the school, how we behaved away from the school, the work we posted on the walls, and the ways in which we talked to and about each other. We were mutually responsible. We didn't have to be the "best" school, or even define what "best" meant. What was important was that in our particular school we had a stake; we were members, with the responsibilities and powers that went with membership. Powers that sometimes differed because of age, role, and so forth, but not in terms of significance to the whole.

Like other loyalties, our loyalty to the school was voluntary. We were not traitors if we moved on or came to the conclusion that this was not the best place to invest our energies. In the end, the definition of what such loyalty required was reconstructed by each of us out of a collective definition we came to together. I suspect that no two of us were entirely sure what our loyalties to the school might require. When one of our teachers said that coming in for professional time on a snow day rubbed her the wrong way, the entire staff spent an hour finding a solution for fear that this issue—although to most a small one—might stretch her loyalty too far. That's the hard balance that we never got entirely right in our little schools, and we surely would not get it right in the bigger city, the nation, or planet Earth.

Some Lessons Learned: Hooks to Schooling

In Central Park East Secondary School (CPESS), which we founded in 1985 (and which died in 2005), we spent a year on a topic that still fascinates me: "Who is an American, anyhow?" America is a particularly interesting nation when it comes to defining patriotism. Many, if not most, nation states have a strong ethnic/blood definition of what constitutes membership— definitions that are only recently coming to terms with the kind of diversity that has for far longer defined being a member of the American clan. But the subclans that make up America draw on their own different roots.

The issue of membership in America has been a struggle to broaden the base of the question of who constitutes "us." Few of those in the original staff of CPESS, we acknowledged, would have been considered a full member of the United States at its inception. The counter claim that we are a nation based on an idea, an aspiration toward some agreed ideal, and not a shared gene pool, was one tack we pursued with out students. Despite the fact that such ideals are often hypocritical, this notion of America as a country working toward an ideal state has a strong tradition in the history of social protest, from Abe Lincoln to Martin Luther King Jr. We explored that tradition of protest. We asked our students to investigate the variety of ideas that constituted American identity, and contrast them with those of our uncommon ancestries. We studied the differences between voluntary and enforced immigration and how the enslavement of African Americans told quite a different story about being an American. Since it is sometimes easier to understand ourselves when confronted with alternatives, we also learned about how other nations defined membership. We never reached a consensus—which might trouble some patriots. If I were doing this today, we might study what the U.S. Immigration Bureau requires immigrants to memorize in order to pass their citizenship tests and discuss who decides these are the right things to know. (Six out of ninety questions on the U.S. immigration exam relate to facts about the American flag, for example.)

We hoped that this yearlong study, along with so much else, would help our students understand that much was hidden between the lines and that all our most cherished books—including the Bible—require constant interpretation, living arguments, and Talmudic reasoning if they are to provide us with more than rhetorical promises. Such ever-shifting interpretation (and reinterpretation) is part of the America I attach myself to and feel patriotic about. And it is my right to be one of a long line of interpreters who defines my membership in America. Our curriculum at CPESS was designed to allow all our students to be interpreters, both of their school and their nation.

What the Central Park East and Mission Hill Schools Might Have in Common with American Patriotism

Building such patriotism in the Central Park East and Mission Hill schools required two features that I think lie beneath the particulars of democracy. These two features were the foundation stones of the schools' Five Habits of Mind, governance agreements, and curriculum and pedagogy: 1) a continual openness to one another's ideas (and not of just those within our school, but the ideas of the living and dead who have influenced the world), and 2) the capacity to imagine ourselves in the shoes of others. In short, patriotic citizens of democratic nations need both skepticism and empathy: two qualities that human infants are at home with as they play with their world—always open to the possibility of being wrong as they do their best to make sense of the world. Such playfulness is central to our humanity, and my hopes for our future rest on the continuing nurturance of this playful spirit not only in the young, but throughout our entire learning lives. These two features were the cement that we at the Central Park East and Mission Hill schools believed would allow for the kind of patriotism we hoped to stir in our students. We hoped they would use these habits of mind in their own lives, in the collective life of the school, in their interactions with the people and families they considered themselves loyal to, and in all the various other frameworks they would come to live within. We hoped they would see skepticism and empathy not as painful chores (which they may occasionally be) but as the habits of a good and joyful life.

The symbols of this brand of patriotism—the logos, flags, songs, poems, rituals—were less important to us at the Central Park East and Mission Hill schools, though we recognized that they were essential in keeping patriotism alive, and thus have deep meaning to us as members of a particular community. At CPESS, we recognized that our "flags" could easily be false idols and dead relics. When some students proposed replacing our logo—a tree under which two young children were reading—with the image of a bulldog, we discussed why some found the new symbol offensive and agreed on the need for a logo we all felt more comfortably identified us. It was an uneasy conversation that raised the kind of issues that any democracy must deal with.

Schools as Places to Explore Versus Places to Instill

Can schools be both places that instill *love of* country and places that explore the *meaning of* country? How do we live with the tensions between these two roles? Schools can be a place to explore the stuff that comes from home and tribe as well as the stuff that cuts across them. I hope so. Not a family, and not a fully blown nation, school is the place to see where our private histories and our shared histories intersect, a place to build the metaphors necessary to make the world manageable while also exposing our metaphors to potential critiques. Yet school is also a place that haunts us forever, the place we learn the habits of public life that are hard to ignore in later years. School plays a role in instilling values, not just exploring them, and there is no way to avoid that.

This fact of school life poses dilemmas and myriad solutions. In such a setting, history is not a *celebration* of our particular tribe's superiority, but an *examination* of our traditions. School is a place where hopefully we are willing to join in the celebration of other people's stories and to give ourselves over to contemplating a view of the world—including ideas in science, literature, and even math—that seems at times odd, incomplete, or even a bit suspect. Surely, if the community seems safe enough, the suspension of one's own favorite views becomes permissible and worth taking a chance on, even if temporarily. It is possible to have both an open mind and firm convictions without being contradictory. Compromise isn't a dirty word but a halfway measure as we explore together what the full-way might be like. Surely then, hearing out the other story is permissible, even if that other story is disturbing. Finding ways to "let live" is not being amoral or immoral; it is an acknowledgment that not all differences are matters of principle, and that we can even survive contradictory principles. These are the dilemmas that patriotism must tackle.

Multiple Patriotisms

Schools can be a place to explore multiple patriotisms and not merely places to impose a single, favorite version. In doing so, schools can foster precisely the brand of patriotism we are so afraid will be lost if it is allowed to be questioned. In such a setting, immigrant students and their families could share the love they have for their country of origin openly and could relish the pleasure of dual and triple loyalties.

We need loyalties, even parochial ones, to be good citizens. We need to love individually if we are to imagine loving on a larger scale. I'm inclined to say that the most important thing we need to fight for in our schools—these days more than most—is the kind of passionate affection for the everyday ways in which we count on each other. We need to caution about writing anyone off as beyond the pale or beyond our capacity for affection. Is that patriotism? Does a flag wave in my heart when I say these things? Does it make me feel like bursting into communal song? Oddly enough, it sort of does.

Patriotism, Nationalism, and Our Job as Americans

James W. Loewen

Let's begin with a distinction between patriotism and nationalism. Frederick Douglass called "a true patriot" one "who rebukes and does not excuse [the] sins" of his or her country. Surely he got that right. A nationalist, in contrast, is one who defends America as right and as having God on its side.

Surely we want our children to grow up to be patriots, not nationalists. That being the case, how shall we educate them? What are we educating them for in the areas of social studies or history? If we are educating them to do their jobs as Americans, what is that? We all do our jobs every day—school bus driver, sociologist (my job), investment banker, carpenter—but what exactly is our job *as Americans*?

Undoubtedly, it is *to bring into being the America of the future.* That job requires our best thinking, our best research, our best actions. What should America do next—regarding our war in Iraq, for example? Or about gay marriage? Or about our still-widening gap between the incomes of the haves and the have-nots? Or about the fact that the planet is running out of oil? Or about the key social issue of next month, whatever that issue may be?

To think about what America should do next requires us to understand what causes what. What should America do next in race relations, for example? Certainly it helps to know that in our past, race relations have sometimes gotten better (1863–76, to name one period) and have sometimes grown worse (1890–1940). Knowing this, we can then investigate the causes of these changes: government policies, cultural trends, and so forth. Then we have some idea about what to do next.

Moreover, learning how *to do* (not just read) history involves researching, interviewing, critical reading, winnowing fact from opinion, and coming to conclusions based on evidence. This is precisely what citizens must do in order to determine what America should do next. History is not just analogous to our job as Americans, it is homologous. The skills are the same.

Studying history also helps students (and adults) to see how the stories we have told ourselves about the past have changed over time. This is historiography—an incredibly empowering concept. In my experience, fourth graders who understand historiography (and fourth grade is not too early to teach the term) learn twice as much from the next historic site they visit. They go around to the back of the monument to see when it went up. They ask questions of the house museum staff to learn why the guides think what they're saying is accurate. They understand that every historic site is a tale of two eras: the one it's about *and the one when it went up.* So is every historic artifact—whether movie, historical novel, or textbook of American history. And sometimes the artifact reveals more about when it was written or constructed than it does about what it allegedly documents.

Textbooks in American history—especially those for middle- and high-school students—have long wrestled with the tension between patriotism and nationalism. Almost always, nationalism has triumphed. That is why their basic underlying storyline is that we started out great and have been getting steadily better ever since. About race relations, as we have seen, this is simply false—as it is about many other topics. So this storyline simply makes us stupider—when it doesn't bore us to tears.

The nationalist storyline is grounded in an unstated distrust of our youth . . . or perhaps of our past. It assumes that if students learned the truth about what we as a nation have done, they could not be counted upon to be good citizens. Indeed, they could not, if by "good citizens" one means "docile nationalists." Since America is always getting better and never did anything wrong—at least not intentionally—all citizens need do is vote.

On the other hand, what a force for improvement our young people can be when they are taught *patriotic* history—a chronicle that includes our failures as well as our accomplishments, uncovers causation, and rebukes and does not excuse our sins. A class of fifth graders rebuked the publisher of their American history textbook for omitting any mention of Washington, Jefferson, Madison, Jackson, et al., as slave-owners. Two sixth-grade girls in Springfield,

Illinois, did the research and planted the seed that led to the astonishing "Race Riot Walking Tour" that teaches visitors to that city about its 1908 attempt to drive out its Black population and become a sundown town. High school students in northern Minnesota convinced the state legislature to eliminate "squaw" as a geographic place name in the state, because they found it to be a racial and sexual slur.[1]

None of them even waited to become of voting age to act as American patriots.

Children stage a patriotic demonstration, Southington, CT. May 1942. Photographer: Fenno Jacobs. Library of Congress Prints and Photographs Division, Farm Security Administration—Office of War Information Collection [LC-DIG-fsac-1a35006].

Chapter 5

Another Way to Teach Politically Without P.C.

Teaching the Debate About Patriotism

Gerald Graff

My daughter, who goes to Stuyvesant High School only blocks from the former World Trade Center, thinks we should fly an American flag out our window. Definitely not, I say: The flag stands for jingoism, vengeance, and war. She tells me I'm wrong—the flag means standing together and honoring the dead and saying no to terrorism. In a way, we're both right.

—*Katha Pollitt, "Put Out No Flags,"*
The Nation, *October 8, 2001*

What should American students learn about patriotism? First and foremost, that the concept is profoundly controversial. How controversial, in the wake of the terrorist attacks of September 11, 2001, is suggested above in the opening of an article by Katha Pollitt that appeared in *The Nation* in October of that year. The passage also suggests a way of teaching contested concepts like patriotism that I have championed for some time: *Teach the debate itself* about such concepts, present students with opposing arguments and ask them to form their own positions.

   This approach offers a democratic alternative to the usual options, in which the teacher supports either the affirmative view of patriotism promoted by the official culture of schooling or the skeptical critique of patriotism favored by many progressive educators. To teach the debate, instead of choosing either option, one stages a classroom controversy over patriotism, with assigned readings that exemplify clashing positions (including essays like Pollitt's, which show that the debate may be not just between us, but inside us). Teaching such debates is not only an excellent way to promote critical thinking, but one that prevents students from feeling politically indoctrinated or browbeaten—a common danger in courses devoted to "teaching for social justice."

To be sure, teaching for social justice usually means not indoctrinating students but provoking them to argue. "Go ahead and disagree with me," we say to our classes. "You'll even get a better grade if you do." Often, however, students do not trust such assurances. By contrast, classes explicitly organized around debates on controversial issues send a more unequivocal message to students that it's not only legitimate to disagree, but a requirement of the course.

A common criticism of teaching the debate is that it assumes a spurious neutrality. According to this criticism, teaching the debate may avoid making students feel indoctrinated, but it does so only by emptying the classroom of real political conflict and turning it into a polite debating society. But this objection misses the point. The proper antidote for the indoctrination and bullying that plague radical advocacy pedagogies is not neutrality but *counter-advocacy.* Indeed, a course organized around a debate between strong views and counterviews allows teachers to become *more* aggressive in taking sides, but with less need to worry about bullying students in the process. For in such a course, the teacher's critical view of patriotism, say, will be resisted by strong defenses of patriotism in the course readings. Students who side with patriotic views against the teacher's critique find their sentiments officially represented and empowered.

Teaching the debate over patriotism can be taken a step further if a second instructor is invited into the class to represent patriotic counterviews, instead of merely representing those views in the syllabus. However much we claim that we want our students to disagree with us, we can hardly expect them to do so if they never see us disagree with each other. If we are serious about the claim, we should put our money where our mouth is and open our classroom to those who are most qualified to challenge our beliefs—our colleagues. Staging periodic debates between instructors (which can be done informally, to avoid the expense and administrative complications of team-teaching) provides students with a vivid model of *how* to conduct intellectual disagreements that students don't get in conventional one-teacher classrooms.

The point is that pedagogical authoritarianism may stem not only from the ideology or personal bias of the teacher, but from the very structure of the one-teacher classroom, in which teachers are sheltered from the disagreements of their colleagues. In this respect, the critical pedagogies of Paulo Freire, Henry Giroux, and other liberatory educators, however transgressive the content of their message may be, are utterly conventional, since they fail to challenge the common assumption that teaching is by nature a solo performance.[1] Though the Freirean classroom may radically question accepted political assumptions, it is thoroughly orthodox in conceiving the classroom itself as a closed space that protects radical instructors from being challenged by their colleagues.

The pedagogical benefits of displacing the one-teacher classroom have been eloquently pointed out by Frank Smith in his book *Joining the Literacy Club*. Smith describes complaining to a colleague that his students "would never argue with me even though I gave them every opportunity. . . . My colleague told me why. They had never heard anyone argue with me. 'Invite me into your next class,' my friend said. 'I'll demonstrate how you can be argued with.'" Smith accepted the offer and

> Within ten minutes my friend and I had a public free-for-all, challenging each other's logic, presuppositions, and evidence. We appealed to students to help us make each other see the light, and soon the entire class was arguing with us and with each other. Everyone was learning, including "the instructors."[2]

To be sure, such classroom set-tos won't always be as smashingly successful as this one. Students can be sullen spectators instead of active participants, and probably will be if the instructors are not clear and incisive or the topic doesn't seem pertinent to the students' lives. But then, such alienated responses occur in one-teacher classrooms too.

For these reasons, teaching the debate, whether over patriotism or any other contested political topic, seems to me fundamentally more democratic than "teaching for social justice" where democratic controversy may be advocated but not enacted and modeled. But teaching the debate is not only more democratic, but more likely to clarify the mysteries of the intellectual world for those many students to whom phrases like "teaching for social justice" are unintelligible academic jargon. There is something misplaced, after all, about attempts to introduce radical intellectual positions to students who have not yet learned the practice of taking "intellectual positions," students who have not learned to enter an intellectual discussion and have a shaky grasp of basic political terminology like "radical," "conservative," "left," "right," and "center."

In order to understand these and other terms in the vocabulary of radical critique, students need to see these terms in comparison and contrast with their conceptual alternatives. That is, such students need to see such terms as they play out in the crucible of actual debates, debates that they can enter and feel they have a stake in, debates in which they gain lots of practice in summarizing (and gaining a sense of what it feels like to live inside) beliefs that challenge their own. The operative principle here is John Stuart Mill's famous observation that we don't understand our own ideas until we understand what can be said against them. As Mill put the point in *On Liberty,* those who "have never thrown themselves into the mental position of those who think differently from them . . . do not, in any proper sense of the word, know the doctrine which they themselves profess."[3]

For example, what is politically at stake in a concept like "social justice" is likely to become intelligible to students only if they have a chance to see that concept in comparison and contrast—that is, in debate—with a term like "social mobility." Though these terms are sometimes seen as synonymous, "social mobility" often presupposes a fair and open economic system in which everyone has an equal chance to succeed, whereas "social justice" implicitly protests against a rigged system in which the already wealthy and privileged start with vastly unfair advantages. Unless students experience discussions in which these opposing assumptions come together and clash, they may never get a clear sense of the key question that underlies most debates about patriotism: Is the American system fair and open or does it stack the social and economic deck unfairly in advance?

In most schools and colleges today, however, students typically go from one classroom in which the openness and fairness of our system is the default assumption to another in which the system is viewed as unfairly rigged. Since such students never encounter a classroom confrontation between these views (except when it may be abstractly summarized by an individual instructor), they are unlikely to grasp the clashing social meanings of "social justice" and "social mobility," and the deeper clash of social philosophies that underlies these different meanings. Indeed, as long as the instructors do not come together to argue out their views with each other and their students, the students may fail to recognize that the instructors fundamentally disagree. But even if the students do recognize the disagreement, the chances are they will respond with the familiar tactic of giving each instructor whatever he or she "wants" in order to meet the obligations of each course with as little trouble as possible. And who can blame students for responding in this cynical way, for the curriculum itself invites such a cynical response by failing to bring clashing perspectives into debate.

In humanities curricula today—to take another example—students may go from one course in which the canonical texts of Western art and literature are seen as an unproblematic heritage to be passed on to another course in which those canonical texts are seen as seriously compromised by racism, sexism, and elitism. Again, the students may not even recognize that the clashing instructors are talking about the same thing—the Western canon—and are disagreeing about it. Again the students will tend to adapt by giving each instructor whatever he or she seems to want even though their demands are contradictory.

The key point is that such a curriculum, in which the dialectical clash of concepts and terms is screened out, or at best is left to individual instructors to reconstruct on their own, is a prescription for political passivity and intellectual illiteracy. When students don't experience terms like "social justice," "multiculturalism," or "patriotism" in comparison and contrast with their conceptual alternatives—that is, when they don't experience such terms in the process of debate—they tend to be deprived of a clear sense of what these terms mean and what is politically at stake in them.

If my argument is correct, then, effective political literacy demands that we not simply air progressive political perspectives in our classrooms, but that we infuse the curriculum throughout with genuine debates between political perspectives.

Pledge of allegiance, 8th Division, 1899. Photographer: Frances Benjamin Johnston. Library of Congress Prints and Photographs Division, Frances Benjamin Johnston Collection [LC-USZ62-14693].

Pledging Allegiance

Walter C. Parker

I pledge allegiance to the flag
of the United States of America,
and to the republic for which it stands,
one nation, under God, indivisible,
with liberty and justice for all.

Reciting the Pledge of Allegiance may be the core civic ritual in the United States and the most common—core because it extracts a personal promise of some sort and most common because it is widely required in schools and concludes the naturalization ceremony for new citizens.

While many people have recited and memorized the pledge, few have interpreted it with others. I've come to this conclusion after leading nearly fifty interpretive discussions or seminars on the pledge. Some have been with high school students, some with elementary students, and many with their teachers and parents. Participants typically say they've not done this before; they have been putting their hands to their hearts and promising something they have not thought much about.

To clarify, a seminar is a discussion of a text for the purpose of plumbing its depths. Discussion accomplishes this better than working alone because one's own understanding is fertilized by the views of others. If the seminar proceeds in a diverse group with a skilled facilitator, so much the better: One's own interpretation is more likely to be challenged in interesting ways.

Leading seminars on the pledge, I'm struck by three arguments that often unfold. First, and most important to many participants, is the phrase "under God" and what it does to the text when it is present or (as before 1954) absent. The mix of nationalism and theism in the pledge can evoke a torrent of opinion.

Second, to what or whom are we pledging allegiance when we recite it? To the flag, say some. To the nation, say others. No, to the republic, say others, pointing to "for which it stands." Does this argument matter? It does, because only one of these is an idea about how to live with one another. Nazis and Romans pledged allegiance to a man (Heil Hitler, Hail Caesar); countless others have pledged allegiance to a plot of land ("land where my fathers died"). But "to the republic" suggests fidelity to the principles of a constitutional democracy.

Then there's the final phrase, "with liberty and justice for all." Here the argument turns on what sort of statement this is. Is it a *description* or an *aspiration*? A *reality* or an *ideal*? Participants can believe one or the other (or both). On this question disagreement runs deep, and for good reason: one side suggests that the citizen's job is to protect democracy (because it has been accomplished); the other, that the citizen's job is to achieve it (because it has not).

There are more arguments I would like to hear, but these are a good start. Listening to them, I've concluded that recitation without interpretation is like fishing in a dry lake. This is not a case for or against reciting the pledge, but for engaging the ideas and issues it raises when you ask it questions, and for doing so with others.

Flag formed by children, girls in white dresses and boys in dark gowns. 1910. Photographer: Redner. Library of Congress Prints and Photographs Division [LC-USZ62-69835].

"Bleeding Flag." Silkscreen, b&w. Artist: Ziva Kronzon. Copyright © 2001 by Ziva Kronzon. Library of Congress Prints and Photographs Division, Exit Art's "Reactions" Exhibition Collection [LC-DIG-ppmsca-01668].

Chapter 6

Patriotism Is a Bad Idea at a Dangerous Time

Robert Jensen

In one of their "Campaign for Freedom" public-service television ads created after 9/11, the non-profit Ad Council captured the mood of a sizable segment of the American population in an ad that begins with a shot of a row of average houses. In somber tones, the voice-over says: "On September 11, terrorists tried to change America forever." The shot fades into a new picture of the same street, this time with U.S. flags flying from every home. "Well, they succeeded," the voice concludes, followed by the slogan of the campaign: "Freedom. Appreciate it. Cherish it. Protect it."

For many, that was the patriotic equation: United States = Freedom = Flag. The conventional image was of a sleeping giant wakened, ready to assert itself in the world, its people brimming with a revitalized sense of patriotism. Such declarations came from virtually every politician and pundit.

And also, to the surprise of some, it came from many in the antiwar movement, who declared, "Peace is patriotic." In the struggle to avoid marginalization—in an attempt to find some rhetorical device that could get traction in mainstream America—many who opposed the U.S. attacks on Afghanistan and Iraq did not argue against patriotism, but instead struggled over the way patriotism should be defined. When faced with the claim that patriotism meant supporting the nation as it went to war, antiwar organizers responded that dissent and critique of an immoral, illegal, and counterproductive war also were expressions of patriotism. These activists tried to distinguish between a reflexive nationalism (my country, right or wrong) and a reflective patriotism (my country, as we try to make it better), framing the former as inappropriate for a democracy and the latter as the best expression of democracy.

A similar debate went on within journalism. There were differences of opinion about whether journalists should publicly proclaim their patriotism and about how aggressive the questioning of officials should be in certain situations. CBS News anchor Dan Rather took flak for various hyperpatriotic comments he made after 9/11, most notably his September 17, 2001, remark on the David Letterman show: "George Bush is the president. He makes the decisions, and, you know, it's just one American, wherever he wants me to line up, just tell me where, and he'll make the call."[1] But Rather was no doubt accurate when he told a newspaper convention in March 2002, "[W]e all want to be patriotic."[2]

Bill Kovach, chairman of the Committee of Concerned Journalists, was one of the strongest mainstream spokespersons for a tough, critical journalism after 9/11. He did not trumpet patriotism, but endorsed the concept in his defense of journalists: "A journalist is never more true to democracy—is never more engaged as a citizen, is never more patriotic—than when aggressively doing the job of independently verifying the news of the day; questioning the actions of those in authority; disclosing information the public needs but others wish secret for self-interested purposes."[3] An editor at one of the top U.S. journalism reviews also implicitly endorsed patriotism in arguing that journalists serve their country best when asking "tough, even unpopular questions when our government wages war." He distinguished "patriotism, love of one's country" from "nationalism—the exalting of one's nation and its culture and interests above all others. If patriotism is a kind of affection, nationalism is its dark side."[4]

I am against nationalism, and I am against patriotism. They are both the dark side. It is time not simply to redefine a kinder-and-gentler patriotism, but to sweep away the notion and acknowledge it as morally, politically, and intellectually bankrupt. It is time to scrap patriotism.

More specifically, it is crucial to scrap patriotism in today's empire, the United States, where patriotism is not only a bad idea but literally a threat to the survival of the planet. We should abandon patriotism and strive to become more fully developed human beings not with shallow allegiances to a nation but rich and deep ties to humanity. At first glance, in a country where patriotism is almost universally taken to be an unquestioned virtue, this may seem outrageous. But there is a simple path to what I consider to be this simple conclusion. After that, there's the difficult task for teachers of figuring out how to walk a fine line in the classroom when teaching about these matters.

What Do You Love?

If we use the common definition of patriotism—love of, and loyalty to, one's country—the first question that arises is, what is meant by country? Nation-states, after all, are not naturally occurring objects. What is the object of our affection and loyalty? In discussions with various community groups and classes since 9/11, I have asked people to explain which aspects of a nation-state—specifically in the context of patriotism in the United States—they believe should spark patriotic feelings. Toward whom or what should one feel love and loyalty? The answers offered include the land, the people of a nation, its culture, the leadership, national policies, the nation's institutions, and the democratic ideals of the nation. To varying degrees, all seem like plausible answers, yet all fail to provide a coherent answer to that basic question.

Land

Many people associate patriotism with a love of the land on which they were born, raised, or currently live. People's sense of place and connection to a landscape is easy to understand. Most of us have felt that, and it's a healthy instinct; it is difficult to care for something that one doesn't know well or have affection for, and we have an obligation to care for the land.

But what has that to do with love or loyalty to a nation-state? Does affection for a certain landscape map onto political boundaries? If I love the desert, should I have a greater affection for the desert on the U.S. side of the border, and a lesser affection when I cross into Mexico? Should I love the prairie in my home state of North Dakota—land where I was born and raised, and where I feel most comfortable and most at home—but abandon that affection when I hit the Canadian border? In discussing connections to the land we can talk sensibly about watersheds and local ecosystems, but not national boundaries. And ties to a specific piece of land (i.e., the farm one grew up on) have nothing to do with a nation-state.

People

It's also common to talk about patriotism in terms of love and affection for one's countrywomen and men. This can proceed on two levels, either as an assertion of differential value of people's lives or as an expression of affection for people. The former—claiming that the lives of people within one's nation-state are more valuable than lives of people outside it—is unacceptable by the standards of virtually all major moral philosophies and religions, which typically are based on the belief that all human life is intrinsically equally valuable. It may be true that, especially in times of war, people act as if they believe the lives of fellow citizens are more valuable, but that cannot be a principle on which patriotism can rest.

This does not ignore the fact that we grieve differently, more intensely, when people close to us die. We feel something different over the death of someone we knew compared with the death of a stranger. But typically when we grieve more deeply for those we knew, it is because we knew them, not because we shared the same citizenship. We all have special affection for specific people in our lives, and it's likely that—by virtue of proximity—for most of us the majority of people for whom we have that affection are citizens of the same nation. But does that mean our sense of connection to them stems from living in the same nation-state and should be understood that way? Given the individual variation in humans, why assume that someone living in our nation-state should automatically spark a feeling of connection greater than someone elsewhere? I was born in the United States near the Canadian border, and I have more in common with Canadians from the prairie provinces than I do with, for example, the people of Texas, where I now live. Am I supposed to, by virtue of my U.S. citizenship, naturally feel something stronger for Texans than Manitobans? If so, why?

Culture

The same argument about land and people applies to cultures. Culture—that complex mix of language, customs, art, stories, faith, traditions—does not map exactly onto the mostly artificial boundaries of nation-states. Indeed, in many nation-states internal differences among cultures can be a source of conflict, not unity. In a society such as the United States, in which battles over these issues are routinely referred to as "the culture wars," it's difficult to imagine how patriotism could be defined as love of, or loyalty to, any particular culture or set of cultural practices.

So, if one were to proclaim that patriotism was about attachment to culture, the obvious question in a nation-state with diverse cultural groups would be, "What culture?" Up until fairly recently in U.S. history, society's answer to that, implicitly, was, "the dominant White, Anglo-American culture." We were a melting pot, but it just always seemed to turn out that the final product of the melting process didn't change much. In an era in which it is widely agreed that people have a right to maintain their particular cultural traditions, few people are going to argue that to be patriotic one must accept that long-dominant culture and abandon other traditions. And to claim that patriotism is about respect for different cultural traditions is nonsensical; respecting different cultures may be a fine principle, but it has nothing to do with love of, or loyalty to, a nation-state.

Leaders

In a democracy it should be clear that patriotism cannot be defined as loyalty to existing political leaders. Such patriotism would be the antithesis of democracy; to be a citizen is to retain the right to make judgments about leaders, not simply accept their authority. Even if one accepts the right of leaders to make decisions within a legal structure and agrees to follow the resulting laws, that does not mean one loves or is loyal to that leadership.

Policies

The same argument about leaders applies to specific policies adopted by leaders. In a democracy, one may agree to follow legally binding rules, but that does not mean one supports them. Of course, no one claims that it is unpatriotic to object to existing policy about taxes or roads or education. War tends to be the only issue about which people make demands that everyone support—or at least mute dissent about—a national policy. But why should war be different? When so much human life is at stake, is it not even more important for all opinions to be fully aired?

Governmental Structures

If patriotism is not about loyalty to a particular leader or policies, many contend, at least it can mean loyalty to our governmental structures. But that is no less an abandonment of democracy, for inherent in a real democracy is the idea that no single set of institutions can be assumed to be, for all times and places, the ultimate vehicle for democracy. In a nation founded on the principle that the people are sovereign and retain the right to reject institutions that do not serve their interests, patriotism defined as loyalty to the existing structures is hard to defend.

Democratic Ideals

When challenged on these other questionable definitions of the object of love or loyalty, most people eventually land on the seemingly safe assertion that patriotism in the United States is an expression of commitment to a set of basic democratic ideals, which typically include liberty, justice, and (sometimes) equality. But problems arise here as well.

First, what makes these values distinctly American? Are not various people around the world committed to these values and to working to make them real in a variety of ways? Given that these values were not invented in the United States and are not distinct to the United States today, how can one claim them as the basis for patriotism? If these values predate the formation of the United States and are present around the world, are they not human ideals rather than American?

An analogy to gender stereotypes is helpful. After 9/11, a number of commentators argued that criticisms of masculinity should be rethought. Though the hegemonic conception of masculinity is typically defined by competition, domination, and violence, they said, cannot we now see—realizing that male firefighters raced into burning buildings and risked their lives to save others—that masculinity can encompass a kind of strength that is rooted in caring and sacrifice? Of course men often exhibit such strength, just as do women. So, the obvious question arises: What makes these distinctly masculine characteristics? Are they not simply *human* characteristics?

We identify masculine tendencies toward competition, domination, and violence because we see patterns of differential behavior; men are more prone to such behavior in our culture. We can go on to observe and analyze the ways in which men are socialized to behave in those ways, toward the goal of changing those destructive behaviors. That analysis is different than saying that admirable human qualities present in both men and women are somehow primarily the domain of one gender. To assign them to a gender is misguided, and demeaning to the gender that is then assumed not to possess them to the same degree. Once we start saying "strength and courage are masculine traits," it leads to the conclusion that woman are not as strong or courageous. To say "strength and courage are masculine traits," then, is to be sexist.

The same holds true for patriotism. If we abandon the crude version of patriotism but try to hold onto an allegedly more sophisticated version, we bump up against this obvious question: Why are human characteristics being labeled American if there is nothing distinctly American about them?

The next move in the attempt to redeem patriotism is to claim that while these values are not the sole property of Americans, it is in the United States that they have been realized to their fullest extent. This is merely the hubris of the powerful. As discussed earlier, on some criteria—such as legal protection for freedom of speech—the United States ranks at or near the top. But the commercial media system, which dominates in the United States, also systematically shuts out radical views and narrows the political spectrum, impoverishing real democratic dialogue. It is folly to think any nation could claim to be the primary repository of any single democratic value, let alone the ideals of democracy.

Claims that the United States is the ultimate fulfillment of the values of justice also must come to terms with history and the American record of brutality, both at home and abroad. One might want to ask people of indigenous and African descent about the commitment to freedom and justice for all, in the past and today. We also would have some explaining to do to the people from nations that have been the victims of U.S. aggression, direct and indirect. Why is it that our political culture, the highest expression of the ideals of freedom and democracy, has routinely gone around the world overthrowing democratically elected governments, supporting brutal dictators, funding and training proxy terrorist armies, and unleashing brutal attacks on civilians when we go to war? If we want to make the claim that we are the fulfillment of history and the ultimate expression of the principles of freedom and justice, our first stop might be Hiroshima. Then Nagasaki.

After working through this argument in class, one student, in exasperation, told me I was missing the point by trying to reduce patriotism to an easily articulated idea or ideas. "It's about all these things together," she said. But it's not clear how individual explanations that fall short can collectively make a reasonable argument. If each attempt to articulate a basis for patriotism fails on empirical, logical, or moral grounds, how do they add up to a coherent position?

Any attempt to articulate an appropriate object of patriotic love and loyalty falls apart quickly. When I make this argument, I am often told that I simply don't understand, that patriotism is as much about feeling as it is about logic or evidence. Certainly love is a feeling that often defies exact description; when we say we love someone, we aren't expected to produce a treatise on the reasons. My point is not to suggest the emotion of love should be rendered bloodless but to point out that patriotism is incoherent because there is no object for the love that can be defended, morally or politically. We can love people, places, and ideas, but it makes no sense to declare one's love or loyalty to a nation-state that claims to be democratic.

Beyond Patriotism

So, there is no way to rescue patriotism or distinguish it from nationalism, which most everyone rejects as crude and jingoistic. Any use of the concept of patriotism is bound to be chauvinistic at some level. At its worst, patriotism can lead easily to support for barbaric policies, especially in war. At its best, it is self-indulgent and arrogant in its assumptions about the uniqueness of U.S. culture and willfully ignorant about the history and contemporary policy of this country. Emma Goldman was correct when she identified the essentials of patriotism as "conceit, arrogance, and egotism" and went on to assert that:

> Patriotism assumes that our globe is divided into little spots, each one surrounded by an iron gate. Those who have had the fortune of being born on some particular spot, consider themselves better, nobler, grander, more intelligent than the living beings inhabiting any other spot. It is, therefore, the duty of everyone living on that chosen spot to fight, kill, and die in the attempt to impose his superiority upon all the others.[5]

We can retain all our affections for land, people, culture, and a sense of place without labeling it as patriotism and artificially attaching it to national boundaries. We can take into account the human need to feel solidarity and connection with others (what Randolph Bourne described as the ability "to enjoy the companionship of others, to be able to cooperate with them, and to feel a slight malaise at solitude"[6]) without attaching those feelings to a nation-state. We can realize that communication and transportation technologies have made possible a new level of mobility around the world, which leaves us with a clear choice: Either the world can continue to be based on domination by powerful nation-states (in complex relationship with multinational corporations) and the elites who dictate policy in them, or we can seek a new interdependence and connection with people around the world through popular movements based on shared values and a common humanity that can cross national boundaries. To achieve the latter, people's moral reasoning must be able to constrain the destructive capacity of elite power. As Goldman suggested, patriotism retards our moral development. These are not abstract arguments about rhetoric; the stakes are painfully real and the people in subordinated nation-states have, and will continue, to pay the price of patriotism in the dominant states with their bodies.

The question of patriotism is particularly important in the United States. The greater the destructive power of a nation, the greater the potential danger of patriotism. Despite many Americans' belief that we are the first benevolent empire, this applies to the United States as clearly as to any country. On this count we would do well to ponder the observations of one of the top Nazis, Hermann Goering. In G.M. Gilbert's book on his experiences as the Nuremberg prison psychologist, he recounts this conversation with Goering:

"Why of course the people don't want war," Goering shrugged. "Why would some poor slob on a farm want to risk his life in a war when the best that he can get out of it is to come back to his farm in one piece. Naturally, the common people don't want war; neither in Russia nor in England nor in America, nor for that matter in Germany. That is understood. But, after all, it is the leaders of the country who determine the policy and it is always a simple matter to drag the people along, whether it is a democracy or a fascist dictatorship or a Parliament or a Communist dictatorship."

"There is one difference," Gilbert pointed out. "In a democracy the people have some say in the matter through their elected representatives, and in the United States only Congress can declare war." Goering responded,

Oh, that is all well and good, but, voice or no voice, the people can always be brought to the bidding of the leaders. That is easy. All you have to do is tell them that they are being attacked and denounce the pacifists for lack of patriotism and exposing the country to danger. It works the same way in any country.[7]

If Not Patriotism?

An argument against patriotism raises the question of whether nation-states are a sensible way to organize our political lives. But if not the nation-state, then what? The simple answer is both the local and the global; politics must, over time, devolve down to levels where ordinary people can have a meaningful role in governing their own lives, while at the same time maintaining a sense of connection to the entire human family and understanding that the scope of high-technology and the legacy of imperialism leave us bound to each other across the globe in new ways. This is a call for an internationalism that understands we live mostly at the local level but can do that ethically only when we take into account how local actions affect others outside our immediate view.

My goal here is not a detailed sketch of how such a system would work. The first step is to envision something beyond what exists, a point from which people could go forward with experiments in new forms of social, political, and economic organization. Successes and failures in those experiments will guide subsequent steps, and any attempt to provide a comprehensive plan at this stage shouldn't be taken seriously. It also is important is to realize that the work of articulating alternative political visions and engaging in political action to advance them has been going on for centuries. There is no reason today to think that national identification is the only force that could hold together societies; for example, political radicals of the nineteenth and early twentieth centuries argued for recognizing other common interests. As Goldman put it:

> Thinking men and women the world over are beginning to realize that patriotism is too narrow and limited a conception to meet the necessities of our time. The centralization of power has brought into being an international feeling of solidarity among the oppressed nations of the world; a solidarity which represents a greater harmony of interests between the workingman of America and his brothers abroad than between the American miner and his exploiting compatriot; a solidarity which fears not foreign invasion, because it is bringing all the workers to the point when they will say to their masters, "Go and do your own killing. We have done it long enough for you." This solidarity is awakening the consciousness of even the soldiers, they, too, being flesh of the flesh of the great human family.[8]

We can, of course, go even further back in human history to find articulations of alternatives. As Leo Tolstoy reminded us in his critique of patriotism published in 1900, a rejection of loyalty to governments is part of the animating spirit of Christianity; "some 2,000 years ago . . . the person of the highest wisdom, began to recognize the higher idea of a brotherhood of man." Tolstoy argued that this "higher idea, the brotherly union of the peoples, which has long since come to life, and from all sides is calling you to itself" could lead people to "understand that they are not the sons of some fatherland or other, nor of Governments, but are sons of God."[9]

In more secular form, this sentiment is summed up in the often-quoted statement of the great American labor leader and Socialist Eugene Debs, who said in 1915: "I have no country to fight for; my country is the earth, and I am a citizen of the world."[10]

Teaching Politics

Teachers, like journalists, are told they should be neutral and objective, and should avoid letting their own political views skew their classroom work. Whatever one's assessment of the intellectual and moral status of patriotism, one thing should be readily evident: A declaration of patriotism—no matter what the definition used—is a declaration of a partisan political position. When teachers are asked to be neutral in political matters yet participate in patriotic events, they are really being asked to endorse the politics of the dominant culture.

Everyone recognizes that individual teachers hold political positions on many subjects; no teacher claims to be politically inert. The conventional argument is not that teachers are devoid of opinions, but that professional practices of fairness, balance, and objectivity help ensure that the classroom is not inordinately influenced by teachers' opinions. As part of that, teachers typically avoid making pronouncements about their political beliefs and affiliations. This is where patriotism is different; teachers typically agree that patriotism is a good thing. On this matter, they are openly political yet see no conflict between this and an obviously contradictory claim to neutrality.

The most plausible explanation is that these teachers take patriotism to be the kind of political judgment that is so universally accepted that to endorse it publicly is uncontroversial. For example, it's likely true that all American teachers believe slavery is wrong, and if asked in public no teacher would hesitate to state that belief. The statement would be a moral and political judgment about the rights and obligations of people, but no one would see it as compromising an accompanying claim to neutrality because to argue for slavery would place one well outside current social norms. It would be seen as an indication of pathology, personal and political.

But unless the argument against patriotism is evidence of such pathology (making me, Debs, Goldman, Tolstoy, and many others—both today and in the past—pathological) patriotism can't be in that category of a moral or political truism. The only way to pretend that declarations of patriotism are not political and open to critique is to erase the many arguments against patriotism. Indeed, a review of contemporary American mainstream commercial education would suggest that is exactly what happens.

Patriotism Makes
Kids Stupid

Bill Bigelow

My stepdaughter works for a firm that gives employees demerits if they fail to use the words "we" and "our" when talking with customers about the company. It's a policy that reminds me of a similar phenomenon in U.S. schools, where the curriculum brands students with a "USA = Us" logo. From their first recitation of the Pledge of Allegiance, students are taught that the most important unit of social analysis is the nation-state and that people on this side of the border constitute "us," whereas those on the other side of the line are "them."

By the time students enter my global studies class as high school juniors, they've had years of nationalistic indoctrination. To be blunt, it's a process that can make youngsters stupid and mean-spirited.

I was reminded of this recently while teaching a unit on the roots of Mexican immigration to the United States. In one of the unit's key lessons, students participated in a role play I wrote on the North American Free Trade Agreement (NAFTA). I wanted students to think about the treaty's effects on both sides of the U.S./Mexican border. NAFTA has flooded Mexico with cheap corn and contributed to throwing over a million and a half farmers off the land. A higher percentage of Mexicans now live in poverty and in extreme poverty than prior to NAFTA. At the same time, the U.S. government has certified that over 800,000 U.S. workers lost their jobs because of NAFTA. And trade unions here were weakened by the greater ease with which companies can flee to Mexico for cheaper labor and lax environmental standards.

But the explosion of U.S. corn exports to Mexico benefited agricultural conglomerates here. And large Mexican farmers who grow cash crops for the U.S. market also benefited, as did many U.S. corporations that set up assembly plants in Mexico, thereby slashing their wage bills. (A $5-a-day minimum wage can do that.)

In the role play, the students represented individuals from different social groups—poor farmers in Chiapas, prosperous farmers in northern Mexico, U.S. executives of frozen food companies, workers in Levi's apparel plants in the United States, cross-border environmentalists, and others. The lesson demonstrates that the question "Did NAFTA benefit the United States?" makes no sense. Who is the United States? Archer Daniels Midland? Factory workers in Ohio? Environmental activists?

In the role play, as poor farmers in Mexico built alliances with U.S. environmentalists and U.S. factory workers, students began to recognize that "us" and "them" do not slice neatly along national lines. U.S. workers, facing lay-offs as their companies outsource production, may have more in common with subsistence farmers in Mexico than they do with corporate executives in the United States.

But even as the students started to grasp the failure of an "us" versus "them" nationalism to explain the world, many still retreated to its reassuring simple-mindedness. Later in the unit, while discussing immigration policy, Beth said, "The United States needs to focus on the United States. We need to make sure that we're all accounted for and okay. We need to worry about us." Marissa echoed Beth, "Maybe it's not nice, but it's true. They're taking our jobs, and it sucks."

"We," "us," "our." My eleventh graders—mostly White and working-class—view their fears about the future through a nationalistic lens. From an academic standpoint, they can't think clearly about global issues when their chief unit of analysis is the nation-state. From a moral and political standpoint, they will consistently misplace blame for their problems as long as they can't think more expansively about who "we" are.

And that's where educators come in. In an era of wagon-circling patriotism, we need to have the courage to challenge our students to question the narrow nationalism that is so deeply embedded in the traditional curriculum.

Children pledging allegiance to the U.S. flag at Weill public school in San Francisco prior to relocation. April 1942. Photographer: Dorothea Lange. Library of Congress Prints and Photographs Division, Farm Security Administration and Office of War Information Collection [LC-USZ62-42810].

New York City, September 11, 2001. Photographer: David Finn. Library of Congress Prints and Photographs Division [LC-DIG-ppmsca-01937].

Chapter 7

Celebrating America

Diane Ravitch

Not long ago, I was among a group of visitors to a public elementary school in New York City. The school had achieved a certain renown for its programs in the arts, and we came to learn more about what the staff was doing. The principal met us at the door and soon began to speak glowingly about the school's accomplishments. He mentioned that the school was attended by children from nearly forty different nations and cultures and that it went to great lengths to encourage the students to have pride in their cultural heritage. There were children in the school from Asia, Latin America, Africa, Europe, and India. All of them were learning to appreciate the foods, dances, customs, and literature of their native countries. Quietly, I asked him whether the school did anything to encourage students to appreciate American culture, and he admitted with embarrassment that it did not.

This seems to me a great paradox in American public education today. Educators believe that children's self-esteem is firmly linked to a positive relationship to their ancestral culture but not to the culture of the country in which they live and are citizens of and in which they will one day raise a family, earn a living, and participate in elections. How strange to teach a student born in this country to be proud of his or her parents' or grandparents' land of birth but not of his or her own. Or to teach a student whose family fled to this country from a tyrannical regime or from dire poverty to identify with that nation rather than with the one that gave the family refuge.

The extent to which we abhor or admire patriotism in the schools depends on how it is taught. If we teach it narrowly as jingoistic, uncritical self-praise of our nation, then such instruction is wrong. It would be indoctrination rather than education. If, however, we teach civic education and define patriotism as a respectful understanding and appreciation of the principles and practices of democratic self-government, then patriotism should be woven through the daily life and teachings of the public schools.

Until the last generation, American public schools took the teaching of patriotism very seriously. The school day began with the Pledge of Allegiance, every classroom displayed an American flag, the flag was raised each day over the school, and students learned the songs of the American civil religion—the national anthem, "God Bless America," "Columbia, the Gem of the Ocean," "America the Beautiful," "My Country, 'Tis of Thee," and so on. Since the earliest days of public education, the schools were expected to teach students about the history, culture, and symbols of America and to encourage them to feel part of the nation. If anything, the public schools in the United States were generally viewed by the public as an institutional expression of national pride, because they were considered the quintessential governmental instrument for building a strong and vibrant national community. It was understood that students and families came from a wide variety of national and ethnic origins, and the public schools were expected to teach everyone about the duties and privileges of citizenship in the United States. The public schools were to instruct students about voting and jury duty, about how the government works, and about national ideals and aspirations.

In many ways, American schools were very much like the state schools of every other nation, which invariably teach students to respect the larger community that supplies and funds their education. No state system teaches its children to despise their own government. But American schools probably went further in their patriotic spirit than the schools of other nations, for two reasons. First, other nations are based on ties of blood or religion, but the United States is a social creation, evolving not from common inherited features but from a shared adherence to the democratic ideology embedded in the Declaration of Independence and the Constitution. The public schools were expected to help forge the American people anew in each generation by teaching children about the nature and workings of democratic self-government. Second, the public school is itself an expression of the nation's democratic ideology, a vehicle created to realize the nation's belief in individualism, self-improvement, and progress. It was in the public schools that students not only would learn what it meant to be an American but would gain the education necessary to make their way in an open society, one in which rank and privilege were less important than talent and merit. If the public schools were ever to abandon their role as an instrument of democratic ideology, they would risk losing their place in the American imagination as well as their claim on the public purse.

Obviously, if teaching patriotism degenerates into vulgar national boasting and a mandate for conformity, then it has failed in teaching the Constitution. For an essential part of the promise of the democratic ideology involves teaching children about the rights of a free people, including the rights of free speech, free expression, and dissent. It is impossible to teach American history without recognizing the important roles played by outsiders, dissenters, and critics, who often turned out to be visionary and prescient in their rejection of the status quo.

The teaching of patriotism in American schools should not be a separate subject. There should not be time set aside for instruction in patriotism. Students who have a solid civic education will study the ideas and institutions of the Founders and learn how democratic institutions work, where they falter, and how they can be strengthened. Students who study American history will learn about the sacrifices of previous generations who sought to safeguard our liberties and improve our society, and they will learn about the men and women of all races and backgrounds who struggled to create a land of freedom, justice, and opportunity. Students must learn too about the failings of our democracy, about the denials of freedom and justice that blight our history.

But to deprive students of an education that allows them to see themselves as part of this land and its history and culture would be a crying shame. Just as students must learn to value themselves as individuals, to value their families, and to value their community, so too should they learn to value the nation of which they are citizens. To love one's country does not require one to ignore its faults. To love one's country does not require one to dismiss the virtues of other countries. Indeed, those who are patriotic about their own country tend to respect those who live elsewhere and also love their respective countries. Love of country may mean love of place, love of the landscape and the people, love of what is familiar. Surely people who have been persecuted may be excused for not having an attachment to their homeland. But for most of us, whatever place we call home and whatever our nationality, Sir Walter Scott's words ring true:

> Breathes there the man with soul so dead
> Who never to himself hath said,
> "This is my own, my native land!"
> Whose heart hath ne'er within him burned,
> As home his footsteps he hath turned
> From wandering on a foreign strand?
> If such there breathe, go, mark him well;
> For him no minstrel raptures swell;
> High though his titles, proud his name,
> Boundless his wealth as wish can claim
> Despite those titles, power, and pelf,
> The wretch, concentred all in self,
> Living, shall forfeit fair renown,
> And, doubly dying, shall go down
> To the vile dust from whence he sprung,
> Unwept, unhonored, and unsung.

Teaching Patriotism— with Conviction

Chester E. Finn Jr.

Americans will debate for many years to come the causes and implications of the September 11 attacks on New York City and Washington, D.C., as well as the foiled attack that led to the crash of United Airlines Flight 93 in a Pennsylvania field. Between the first and second "anniversaries" of 9/11, another development deepened our awareness of the dangerous world we inhabit and of America's role therein—the successful war to liberate Iraq from its dictator and his murderous regime. Of course, the consequences—and contentiousness—of that conflict continue to resonate daily in newspaper headlines and on the evening news. In these challenging times, educators rightly wonder about their proper role. What should they teach young Americans? How should they prepare tomorrow's citizenry? What is most important for students to learn?

These are weighty questions, and there is every reason to expect them to linger. But it is now clearer than ever that, if we wish to prepare our children for unforeseen future threats and conflicts, we must arm them with lessons from history and civics that help them learn from the victories and setbacks of their predecessors, lessons that, in Jefferson's words, "enable every man to judge for himself what will secure or endanger his freedom."

Jefferson was right when he laid upon education the grave assignment of equipping tomorrow's adults with the knowledge, values, judgment, and critical faculties to determine for themselves what "will secure or endanger" their freedom and their country's well-being. The U.S. Supreme Court was right, half a century ago, when, in the epoch-shaping Brown decision, it declared education to be "the very foundation of good citizenship."

Teachers know this better than anyone, and many need no help or advice in fulfilling their responsibility. They're knowledgeable, savvy, creative, caring, and—may I say it?—patriotic, as many fine teachers have always been. They love our country and the ideals for which it stands. Teachers must communicate to their students the crucial lessons from history and civics that our children most need to learn. The events of 9/11 and the war on terrorism that has followed create a powerful opportunity to teach our daughters and sons about heroes and villains, freedom and repression, hatred and compassion, democracy and theocracy, civic virtue and vice.

On April 10, 2003, David McCullough told a Senate committee, "We are raising a generation of people who are historically illiterate. . . . We can't function in a society," he continued, "if we don't know who we are and where we came from." The solemn duty of all educators is to make certain that all our children know who they are. Part of that can be accomplished by teaching them about America's Founders, about their ideals, and about the character, courage, vision, and tenacity with which they acted. From that inspiring history, true patriotism cannot help but grow.

Protesters. New York City, August 30, 2004. Photographer:
Joel Westheimer. Copyright © 2004 Joel Westheimer.

No Child Left Behind. Artist: Christopher C. Kaufman, Livonia, MI.
Used with permission. Copyright by Christopher C. Kaufman.

Chapter 8

Hearts and Minds

Military Recruitment and the High School Battlefield

William Ayers

In her book *Purple Hearts,* the documentary photographer Nina Berman presents forty photographs—two each of twenty U.S. veterans of the American war in Iraq—plus a couple of accompanying paragraphs of commentary from each vet in his or her own words.[1] Their comments cohere around their service, their sacrifice, their suffering. The Purple Heart binds them together—this award is their common experience, this distinction is what they embrace and what embraces them. This is what they live with.

Their views on war, on their time in arms, on where they hope they are headed with their lives, are various; their ways of making sense about the U.S. military mission, wildly divergent.

Josh Olson, twenty-four years old, begins: "We bent over backwards for these people, but they ended up screwing us over, stabbing us in the back. A lot of them, I mean, they're going to have to be killed. . . . As Americans we've taken it upon ourselves to almost cure the world's problems I guess, give everybody else a chance. I guess that's how we're good-hearted. . . ." He's missing his right leg now and was presented with his Purple Heart at Walter Reed Military Hospital by President Bush himself. He feels it all—pride, anger, loss.

Jermaine Lewis, twenty-three, describes growing up in a Chicago neighborhood where "death has always been around." He describes basic training as a place where "they break you down and then they try to build you up." To him, the "reasons for going to war were bogus, but we were right to go in there."

The vets are all young, and several recall deciding to enlist when they were much younger still, more innocent, more vulnerable, but feeling somehow invincible. Jermaine Lewis says: "I've been dealing with the military since I was a sophomore in high school. They came to the school like six times a year, all military branches. They had a recruiting station like a block from our high school. It was just right there."

Tyson Johnson III, twenty-two, wanted to get away from the poverty and death he saw all around him. His life was going nowhere, he thought, and so he signed on: "And here I am, back here. . . . I don't know where it's going to end up."

Joseph Mosner enrolled when he was nineteen. "There was nothing out there," he writes. "There was no good jobs so I figured this would have been a good thing."

Frederick Allen thought going to war would be "jumping out of planes." He joined up when recruiters came to his high school. "I thought it would be fun."

Adam Zaremba, twenty, also enlisted while still in high school: "The recruiter called the house, he was actually looking for my brother and he happened to get me. I think it was because I didn't want to do homework for a while, and then I don't know, you get to wear a cool uniform. It just went on from there. I still don't even understand a lot about the Army." The Purple Heart seemed like a good thing from a distance, "but then when it happens you realize that you have to do something, or something has to happen to you in order to get it."

Recruiting High Schoolers

Military recruiting in high schools has been a mainstay of the so-called all-volunteer armed forces from the start. High school kids are at an age when being a member of an identifiable group with a grand mission and a shared spirit—and never underestimate a distinctive uniform—is of exaggerated importance, something gang recruiters in big cities also note with interest and exploit with skill. Kathy Dobie, quoting a military historian, notes that "basic training has been essentially the same in every army in every age, because it works with the same raw material that's always been there in teenage boys: a fair amount of aggression, a strong tendency to hang around in groups, and an absolute desperate desire to fit in."[2] Being cool and going along with the crowd are big things. Add the need to prove oneself to be a macho, strong, tough, capable person, combined with an unrealistic calculus of vulnerability and a constricted sense of options specifically in poor and working-class communities—all of this creates the toxic mix in a young person's head that can be a military recruiter's dream.

One of the most effective recruitment tools is Junior Reserve Officers' Training Corps (JROTC), the high school version of ROTC that was established by an act of Congress in 1916 "to develop citizenship and responsibility in young people."[3] JROTC is now experiencing the most rapid expansion in its history. Some credit the upsurge to Colin Powell's visit to South Central Los Angeles after the 1992 riots, when he was head of the Joint Chiefs of Staff. Powell stated that the solution to the problems of city youths was the kind of discipline and structure offered by the U.S. military. In the ensuing decade the number of JROTC programs doubled, with over half a million students enrolled at over three thousand schools coast-to-coast, and an annual Pentagon budget allocation in excess of $250 million. Today the evidence is clear: 40% of JROTC graduates eventually join the military, making the program a powerful recruiting device.

Chicago has the largest JROTC program in the country and the "most militarized school system in America,"[4] with more than nine thousand students enrolled in forty-five JROTC programs, including one Navy and five Army JROTC academies that are run as "schools-within-a-school" and two full-time Army military academies, with another slated to open next year. That distinction is only the start: Chicago is also in the vanguard of the Middle School Cadet Corps (MSCC), with twenty-six programs in junior highs and middle schools involving 850 kids, some as young as eleven.[5]

Defenders of the JROTC and MSCC claim that the goal is leadership and citizen development, dropout prevention, or simply the fun of dressing up and parading around. Skeptics point out that the Pentagon money for these programs provides needed resources for starving public schools and question why the military has become such an important route to adequate school funding. Chicago spends $2.8 million on JROTC and another $5 million on two military academies—"more than it spends on any other special or magnet program"[6]—and the Defense Department puts in an additional $600,000 for salaries and supplies.

There is no doubt that JROTC programs target poor, Black, and Latino kids who don't have the widest range of options to begin with. Recruiters know where to go: Whitney Young High School, a large, selective magnet school in Chicago, had fewer military recruiter visits last year than Schurz High School, which is 80% Hispanic.[7] *New York Times* columnist Bob Herbert points out that all high schools are not equal in the eyes of the recruiters: "Schools with kids from wealthier families (and a high percentage of college-bound students) are not viewed as good prospects. . . . The kids in those schools are not the kids who fight America's wars."[8] Absent arts and sports programs or a generous array of clubs and activities, JROTC and its accompanying culture of war—militarism, aggression, violence, repression, the demonization of others, and mindless obedience—becomes the default choice for poor kids attending low-income schools.

The military culture seeps in at all levels and has a more generally corrosive impact on education itself, narrowing curriculum choices and promoting a model of teaching as training and of learning as "just following orders." In reality, good teaching always involves thoughtful and complicated judgments, careful attention to relationships, complex choices about how to challenge and nurture each student. Good teachers are not drill instructors. Authentic learning, too, is multidimensional and requires the constant construction and reconstruction of knowledge built on expanding experiences.

The educational model that employs teachers to simply pour imperial gallons of facts into empty vessels—ridiculed by Charles Dickens 150 years ago and discredited as a path to learning by modern psychologists and educational researchers—is making a roaring comeback. The rise of the military in schools adds energy to that malignant effort.

A vibrant democratic culture requires free people with minds of their own capable of making independent judgments. Education in a democracy resists obedience and conformity in favor of free inquiry and the widest possible exploration. Obedience training may have a place in instructing dogs, but not in educating citizens.

My Recruiter Lied to Me

Today, two years into the invasion of Iraq, recruiters are consistently failing to meet monthly enlistment quotas, despite deep penetration into high schools, sponsorship of NASCAR and other sporting events, and a $3-billion Pentagon recruitment budget. Increasingly, recruiters are offering higher bonuses and shortened tours of duty, and violations of ethical guidelines and the military's own putative standards are becoming commonplace—in one highly publicized case, a recruiter was heard on tape coaching a high school kid about how to fake a mandatory drug test. "One of the most common lies told by recruiters," writes Kathy Dobie, "is that it's easy to get out of the military if you change your mind. But once they arrive at training, the recruits are told there's no exit, period."[9] Although recruiters are known to lie, the number of young people signing up is still plummeting.

The military manpower crisis includes escalating desertions: 4,739 Army deserters in 2001 compared to 1,509 in 1995. According to an Army study, deserters tend to be "younger when they enlist, less educated . . . come from 'broken homes,' and [have] 'engaged in delinquent behavior.'"[10] In times of war, rates of desertion tend to spike upward, and so after 9/11 the Army "issued a new policy regarding deserters, hoping to staunch the flow." The new rules required deserters to be returned to their units in the hope that they could be "integrated back into the ranks." This has not been a happy circumstance for either soldiers or officers: "I can't afford to baby-sit problem children every day," says one commander.

At the end of March 2005, the Pentagon announced that the active-duty Army achieved only about two-thirds of its March goal and was 3,973 recruits short for the year; the Army Reserve was 1,382 short of its year-to-date goal.[11] According to military statistics, 2005 was the toughest recruiting year since 1973, the first year of the all-volunteer Army. Americans don't want to fight this war, and a huge investment in high school recruiting is the military's latest desperate hope.

The high school itself has become a battlefield for hearts and minds. On one side: the power of the federal government; claims (often unsubstantiated) of financial benefits; humvees on school grounds; goody bags filled with donuts, key chains, video games, and T-shirts. Most ominous of all is No Child Left Behind, the controversial omnibus education bill passed in 2001. Section 9528 reverses policies in place in many cities that keep organizations that discriminate on the basis of race, gender, or sexual orientation—including the military—out of schools. It mandates that military recruiters have the same access to students as colleges. The bill also requires schools to turn over students' addresses and home phone numbers to the military unless parents expressly opt out.

On the other side of the recruitment battle: a mounting death toll in Iraq, a growing sense among the citizenry that politicians lied and manipulated us at every turn in order to wage an aggressive war outside any broad popular interest, and organized groups of parents mobilizing to oppose high school recruitment.

A front-page story in the *New York Times* reported a "Growing Problem for Military Recruiters: Parents." The resistance to recruiters, according to the *Times* report, is spreading coast to coast, and "was provoked by the very law that was supposed to make it easier for recruiters to reach students more directly. 'No Child Left Behind' . . . is often the spark that ignites parental resistance."[12]

And parents, it turns out, can be a formidable obstacle to a volunteer Army. Unlike the universal draft, signing up requires an affirmative act, and parents can and often do exercise a strong negative drag on their kids' stepping forward. A Department of Defense survey from November 2004 found that "only 25 percent of parents would recommend military service to their children, down from 42 percent in August 2003."[13]

In a column called "Uncle Sam Really Wants You," Bob Herbert focuses attention on an Army publication called "School Recruiting Program Handbook." The goal of the program is straightforward: "school ownership that can only lead to a greater number of Army enlistments." This means promoting military participation in every feasible dimension, from making classroom presentations to involvement in Hispanic Heritage and Black History months. The handbook recommends that recruiters contact athletic coaches and volunteer to lead calisthenics, get involved with the homecoming committee and organize a presence in the parade, donate coffee and donuts to the faculty on a regular basis, eat in the cafeteria, and target "influential students" who, while they may not enlist, can refer others who might.[14]

The military injunction—hierarchy, obedience, conformity, and aggression—stands in stark opposition to the democratic imperative of respect, cooperation, and equality. The noted New Zealand educator Sylvia Ashton-Warner wrote that war and peace—acknowledged or hidden— "wait and vie" in every classroom. She argued that all human beings are like volcanoes with two vents, one destructive and the other creative. If the creative vent is open, she maintained, then the destructive vent will atrophy and close; on the other hand, if the creative vent is shut down, the destructive will have free rein. "Creativity in this time of life," she wrote, "when character can be influenced forever, is the solution to the problem of war." She quoted Erich Fromm: "The amount of destructiveness in a child is proportionate to the amount to which the expansiveness of his life has been curtailed. Destructiveness is the outcome of the unlived life."[15]

Herbert, himself a Vietnam combat vet, is deeply troubled by the deceptive and manipulative tactics of recruiters: "Let the Army be honest and upfront in its recruitment," he writes. "War is not child's play, and warriors shouldn't be assembled through the use of seductive sales pitches to youngsters too immature to make an informed decision on matters that might well result in them having to kill others, or being killed themselves."[16]

The Reality of War

A little truth-telling, then. War is catastrophic for human beings, and, indeed, for the continuation of life on Earth. With over 120 military bases around the globe and the second largest military force ever assembled, the U.S. government is engaged in a constant state of war, and American society is necessarily distorted and disfigured around the aims of war. Chris Hedges provides an annotated catalogue—unadorned, uninflected—of the catastrophe:

- 108 million people were slaughtered in wars during the twentieth century.
- During the last decade of that spectacular century, 2 million children were killed, 20 million displaced, 6 million disabled.
- From 1900 to 1990, 43 million soldiers died in wars and 62 million civilians were killed. In the wars of the 1990s the ratio was up: between 75% and 90% of all war deaths were civilian deaths.
- Today 21.3 million people are under arms—China has the largest military with 2.4 million people in service (from a population of 1.3 billion citizens), followed by the United States with 1.4 million (from a population of 300 million). About 1.3 million Americans are in Reserve and National Guard units.
- Vets suffer long-term health consequences including greater risk of depression, alcoholism, drug addiction, sleep disorders, and more. About

one-third of Vietnam vets suffered full-blown post-traumatic stress disorder. Another 22% suffered partial post-traumatic stress disorder.[17] This is the nature of the beast. Anyone who's been there knows.

On and on, 119 densely packed pages, fact sheet upon fact sheet, twenty-four pages of evidentiary footnotes, fifteen pages of bibliography, all of it adding up to an inescapable conclusion: War is the greatest organized misfortune human beings have ever constructed and visited on one another. And as Adromache, captive widow of Hector, says at the opening of Seneca's *Trojan Women*: "It is not finished yet. There is always more and worse to fear, beyond imagination."[18] In the course of the play, her young son will be thrown from a tower and murdered, and the daughter of Hecuba and Priam will also be sacrificed. Beyond imagination.

There are now more than 300,000 child soldiers worldwide. Why do children join? Here is Hedges' entire answer to that question:

> They are often forced to. Some are given alcohol or drugs, or exposed to atrocities, to desensitize them to violence. Some join to help feed or protect their families. Some are offered up by their parents in exchange for protection. Children can be fearless because they lack a clear concept of death.[19]

The United States, which consistently refused to ratify the UN Convention on the Rights of the Child, agreed in 2002 to sign on to the "Optional Protocol" to the Convention, covering the involvement of children in armed conflicts. In its "Declarations and Reservations," the United States stipulated that signing the Protocol in no way carries any obligations under the Convention and that "nothing in the Protocol establishes a basis for jurisdiction by any international tribunal, including the International Criminal Court." It lists several other reservations, including an objection to Article 1 of the Protocol, which states, "Parties shall take all feasible measures to ensure that members of their armed forces who have not attained the age of 18 years do not take direct part in hostilities." The United States stipulates that the term "feasible measures" means what is "practical" when taking into account all circumstances, "including humanitarian and military considerations," and that the article does not apply to "indirect participation in hostilities, such as gathering and transmitting military information, transporting weapons, ammunition, or other supplies, or forward deployment."

Because recruiters do lie, because the United States steps back from international law and standards, and because the cost of an education for too many poor and working-class kids is constructed as a trip through a minefield and a pact with the devil, teachers should consider Bill Bigelow's advice to make a critical examination of the "Enlistment/Reenlistment Document—Armed Forces of the United States" that recruits sign when they join up. (Copies can be downloaded as a PDF at www.rethinkingschools.org.) There they will find a host of loopholes and disclaimers, like this one in section 9b:

> Laws and regulations that govern military personnel may change without notice to me. Such changes may affect my status, pay, allowances, benefits, and responsibilities as a member of the armed forces regardless of the provisions of this enlistment/reenlistment document.

When Bigelow's students analyzed the entire contract, they concluded that it would be more honest to simply say something like, "Just sign up. . . . Now you belong to us." They offer sage advice to other students: "Read the contract thoroughly. . . . Don't sign unless you're 100% sure, 100% of the time." One of Bigelow's students, who had suffered through the war in Bosnia, recommended that students inclined to enlist might "shoot a bird, and then think about whether you can kill a human."[20]

Jermaine Lewis, the twenty-three-year-old vet from Chicago who spoke about the war being "bogus" in the book *Purple Hearts,* always wanted to be a teacher but worried about the low pay. Now, with both legs gone, he calculates that a teacher's salary plus disability pay will earn him an adequate income: "So I want to go to college and study education—public school, primarily middle school, sixth to eighth grade." He went through the minefield to get what more privileged kids have access to without asking. It's something.

Rural schoolchildren, San Augustine County, Texas. April, 1943. Photographer: John Vachon. Library of Congress Prints and Photographs Division, Farm Security Administration—Office of War Information Collection [LC-DIG-fsac-1a35427].

Weapons of Fatal Seduction
Latinos and the Military

Héctor Calderón

The opening scene of *Wild Style*, the classic 1982 Hip Hop movie, takes place in a small bedroom in the South Bronx.[1] The walls are covered with graffiti pieces: tags, floaters, top-to-bottoms. The camera focuses on the window as a ninja-like figure sneaks into the bedroom. Dressed completely in black, carrying a bag full of Krylon spray paint, the figure is greeted by his older brother who has just returned from the army. With the subway staccato as background noise, the uniform-clad man screams at his graffiti writing brother:

> You sitting at home and doing this shit, you should be out earning a medal. Stop fucking around and be a man, there ain't nothing out here for you.

The graffiti writer, played by graf pioneer Lee Quinones, responds without missing a beat: "Oh yes there is. This . . . " as he points to his urban masterpieces on the wall.

This scene poignantly illustrates the limited options presented to poor Latinos and other young people of color. They are stuck choosing between the military, community colleges without the prospect of scholarships, working for minimum wage, or prison. While their White counterparts enter the workforce, too many Latinos are left to gain community recognition by tagging local buildings, or worse. Many are eventually lured into military service with promises of job training or money for education. Sadly, very few see the "$30,000 for college" claimed by glitzy army ads, and very few jobs in the armed forces translate to civilian jobs. Outside of careers in law enforcement, gun repair, and truck driving, there are not many civilian job opportunities afforded to military personnel.

The military does deliver on its promise to take Latinos to exotic places like Iraq and Afghanistan. As I write this, there are over 130,000 U.S. troops in Iraq and 10,000 in Afghanistan, according to the Department of Defense.[2] And while Latinos represent approximately 10% of the actively enlisted forces, they constitute over 18% of frontline troops—overrepresented in the most dangerous assignments, including infantry, gun crews, and seamanship.[3]

It is hard to ascertain the present rate of Latino casualties in Iraq. As of August 2003, the DOD put the numbers at 13%. However, based on the number of Latino surnames reported, CNN footage and biographies of the fallen posted on websites, Dr. Jorge Mariscal, Vietnam veteran and Professor at the University of San Diego, estimates that about 20% of casualties are Latino.[4] If these numbers are correct, nearly 1 in 5 casualties is Latino.

Why Latinos Join

According to the 2000 census, Latinos are the largest minority group in the United States: 12.5% of the U.S. population. As the Latino population grows in numbers, Latinos are increasingly targeted by armed forces recruiters.[5] Louis Caldera, Secretary of the Army under Bill Clinton, was one of the architects of the Hispanic Access Initiative, which allows for ROTC recruiters to aggressively target colleges and high schools with large Latino populations. They are well aware that 1 in 7 eighteen-year-olds are of Latino origin, and recruiters gain access to these students' addresses and phone numbers by requesting them from high school records. The No Child Left Behind Act now requires high schools to provide student information for recruitment purposes, unless their parents sign an "opt-out letter," a right made known to very few Latino parents.

Another factor that pressures Latinos to join the military is the unspoken poverty draft. Underlying economic inequalities in communities of color create a fertile ground for military recruitment. Latino and African American households constitute 40% of the lowest fifth of the country's income distribution (those with less than $24,000 in 2001). Although Most Latinos are part of the workforce, over 11% of Latino workers live in poverty.[6] In a recent analysis of government statistics, the Pew Hispanic Center found that the unemployment rate for Latinos was 7.3%, up from 6.6% in 2003, and much higher than the national unemployment rate, which is 5.6%.[7] Given these grim statistics, it is easy to see why military service is an attractive option. The promotional materials of the Armed Forces speak to these inequities with promises of countless job opportunities, "the best education," and social mobility.

The Armed Forces have also bolstered the number of Latino soldiers by targeting non-citizens for recruitment. In July 2002, President Bush signed an executive order that allowed nonnaturalized soldiers who are serving honorably in the "war against terrorism" to apply for a new streamlined citizenship process that would take six months, instead of the usual five years. Department of Defense statistics show that there are about 35,000 non-citizens serving actively in the armed forces,[8] one third of whom are Latino.

Beyond citizenship, many Latinos search for acceptance as Americans by joining the Armed Forces. When Diego Rincón, a Colombian national, was killed in a suicide bombing, his father was quoted as saying, "The only thing that keeps me going now is to make sure that he's buried as an American. That will be my dream come true."[9] Sadly, Latinos are still not fully accepted into the mainstream of the United States, no matter how many soldiers with Latino surnames are listed as war casualties. The fundamental problems of racism are not erased with Latino blood spilled on foreign lands.

Latinos have been manipulated into a war for reasons, as the Senate Intelligence Committee report puts it, that were "overstated" and "not supported by intelligence reports."[10] By now we know that there were no weapons of mass destruction and the people in Iraq did not greet the U.S. Armed Forces as liberators, as former Secretary of Defense Donald Rumsfeld so confidently predicted. Iraq is more unstable today than it was before and has become a magnet for terrorist activity due to the U.S. occupation.

The deadly seduction of Latinos by the military can be described by the historic view of Vietnam veteran Jorge Mariscal:

> What can we say of young Latino men who have sacrificed their lives in Iraq. That they fought without knowing their enemy, played their role as pawns in a geopolitical chess game devised by arrogant bureaucrats, and died simply trying to get an education; trying to have a fair shot at the American Dream that has eluded the vast majority of Latinos for over a century and a half; dying as soldiers who just wanted to be students.[11]

"Our Future Friends." Japanese children parading with U.S. and Japanese flags. September 27, 1905. Photographer unknown. Library of Congress Prints and Photographs Division [LC-USZ62-53239].

A Small Space of Sanity

Studs Terkel

Schoolchildren should learn all they can about the people who stood up for humanity against the war-makers and the powerful. I'm talking about the abolitionists and the suffragettes, the Wobblies and labor organizers, the freedom riders and civil rights marchers, and the antiwar activists. Students should learn about Burr Tillstrom, one of the geniuses of early television, who created the Kuklapolitans and the show "Kukla, Fran, and Ollie." They were puppets, little rags that came to life in Burr's hands: Ollie was the one-toothed dragon; Buelah Witch, the outspoken and independent feminist who always refused to ride her broom sidesaddle; and Kukla, the round-headed enigma. And they became the inspiration for Jim Henson's Muppets. The Kuklapolitans lived in our world, but they created a small space of sanity within it—humane, tender, gentle, filled with humor and good will.

Burr Tillstrom graduated from Senn High School in Chicago, a place the current mayor wants to transform into a military academy, the exact opposite of the world Burr Tillstrom imagined. There's a lot to do to realize Tillstrom's vision, and opposing the militarization of our schools is a part of it. If there's one thing students need to know about patriotism, it's that the only way to love our country is to care about the humanity of the people who live in it.

The Queen of the May, Emily Schwak, at Beecher Street School, whose student body consists of half Americans of Italian descent and half of Americans of Polish descent, Southington, CT. May, 1942. Photographer: Fenno Jacobs. Library of Congress Prints and Photographs Division, Farm Security Administration—Office of War Information Collection [LC-DIG-fsac-1a35007].

Chapter 9

Is Patriotism Good for Democracy?

Joseph Kahne and Ellen Middaugh

Is patriotism good for democracy? Or does a commitment to patriotism threaten democracy? Educators do not agree on this issue.

Chester Finn (former assistant secretary of education in the Reagan Administration) argues that after September 11, "American education has generally made a mess of a teaching opportunity" by focusing on "tolerance and multiculturalism, not civics and patriotism."[1] In an essay titled "Patriotism Revisited," he worries that "it's become a compulsion to pull down America rather than celebrate and defend it."[2] This view aligns with William Damon's perspective that "too many students today learn all about what is wrong with our society without gaining any knowledge of our society's great moral successes. To establish a sound cognitive and affective foundation for citizenship education," Damon writes, "schools need to begin with the positive, to emphasize reasons for caring enough about our democratic society to participate in it and to improve it. Schools need to foster a sympathetic understanding informed by all the facts and energized by a spirit of patriotism."[3]

Other educators see a problem related to patriotism that is very different from the one described by Finn and Damon. Rather than worrying that there is excessive criticism of the United States in schools and a lack of patriotism among youths, they point to pressure, exerted in the name of patriotism, on individual citizens and groups to refrain from criticizing the actions and policies of the U.S. government. In addition, they note a growing set of global problems that require international cooperation.[4] These considerations lead some to flat out reject patriotic sentiments in favor of commitments to global citizenship and principles of international human rights.[5]

Is there a problem or not? And if there is a problem, which problem is it? Are schools turning students into critics of the United States who can't appreciate the country's strengths? Or is the opposite occurring? Is the push for patriotism in response to 9/11 leading students toward patriotic commitments at the expense of critical analysis and an appreciation of the need to protect human rights and democratic principles? Unfortunately, we have little data to draw on when thinking about these issues. Schools systematically monitor the number of eleventh graders who know the difference between equilateral and right triangles, but we often rely on journalists' interviews with three or four students to assess what high school students think about patriotism and democracy.

For this reason, we decided to take a systematic look at high school seniors' views on patriotism and its relationship to democracy. In doing so, we are hoping to reframe the discussion. "Is patriotism good or bad?" The answer is not one or the other but "It depends." The values, priorities, and behaviors associated with patriotism can vary dramatically. Some forms of patriotism are profoundly democratic, and other forms can undermine democratic ideals. It is therefore very important that we clarify the factors responsible for these different outcomes.

In sorting through the ways to make these distinctions, we found it very helpful to consider the two standards provided by John Dewey for a "democratically constituted society": 1) "How numerous and varied are the interests that are consciously shared?" and 2) "How full and free is the interplay with other modes of association?"[6] In other words, a democratic society requires that citizens recognize their common interests and that they fully and openly discuss their differing perspectives on issues related to these common priorities.

The implications for a democratic vision of patriotism are substantial. Patriotic commitments in a democratic society should be motivated by and reinforce recognition of the variety of interests that citizens have in common. In addition, these patriotic commitments should not constrain what Dewey called "free and full interplay" and what we might call informed debate and discussion that considers a wide range of views.

What does this mean for students and for schools? We believe that schools should work to promote a democratic vision of patriotism that is based on Dewey's two standards. In the following sections, drawing on the work of the Harwood Institute and on studies by Robert Schatz, Ervin Staub, and Howard Lavine, we discuss a set of criteria that can help us determine the degree to which students' patriotic commitments align with the needs of a democratic society, as envisioned by Dewey. Specifically, we focus on three dimensions of patriotic belief: commitment to country, attitudes toward critique of country, and active involvement. Then, using this framework as a guide, we share findings from our study of the patriotic commitments of California's high school seniors.

Commitment to Country:
An Uncertain Support for Democracy

It is common to define patriots simply as those who love their country.[7] Why would such a commitment be controversial? Individuals love their families more than they love strangers. They also tend to feel a stronger sense of connection to the town they are from than to a town they have never visited. Shouldn't we expect most individuals to love their country— and to love it more than they love other countries?

Frankly, this isn't the point. The important question is not whether it is common or "natural" to love one's country, but whether such commitments are desirable. After all, jealousy is also a rather common or "natural" emotion, but that doesn't make it a virtue. Indeed, in some cases, one could argue that patriotism is a vice. The term's etymology—loyalty to the fatherland—has nothing to do with a commitment to democracy. Both fascist states and democracies desire loyalty.

To say this is not to deny the potential of patriotic commitments to serve as a support for a democratic society. In line with Dewey's framework, patriotic commitments can support democratic goals by developing a sense of shared interests and a commitment to act. More specifically, patriotic commitments may lead individuals to better balance their own interests with those of the broader society by helping them integrate societal interests into their own sense of what's important.[8] In addition, patriotic commitments (especially when informed by recognition of shared interests) may motivate citizens to actively engage in the civic and political life of the community—a key need in a democracy. Finally, if one's love of country is based in part on recognition of the desirability of life in

a democratic society, such patriotic commitments can help citizens identify with the nation's democratic ideals. "The American trick," Benjamin
Barber writes, "was to use the fierce attachments of patriotic sentiment
to bond a people to high ideals . . . to be an American was also to be
enmeshed in a unique story of freedom."[9] In short, there are democratic
visions of patriotism, ones that focus on loyalty to democratic principles
and practices and that emphasize lateral connections to other citizens
rather than hierarchical commitments to the nation.

Unfortunately, some forms of patriotism that emphasize shared interests fail to meet Dewey's second criterion for a democratic society—
full and free interplay. Indeed, the emphasis on shared interests can become problematic if not balanced by engagement with a broad range of
groups and perspectives. R. Freeman Butts explains it this way: "At its
best, patriotism binds the diverse elements of American society into an
integrated whole, fostering mutual acceptance of citizens as a common
political order. At its worst, patriotism can degenerate into a nationalistic
chauvinism."[10]

Thus patriotic commitments are an uncertain support for democracy.
The key question is not whether one is a patriot. It is the form of one's
patriotic commitments that turns out to be of prime importance. In order
to assess the role schools in a democracy should play with respect to patriotic aims, it is therefore necessary to clarify some other dimensions of
patriotic beliefs. We do so below.

Attitudes Toward Critique:
Blind and Constructive Patriots

Among those who study and theorize about patriotism, the question
of whether patriotic commitments foster democracy often highlights a
crucial distinction—between blind and constructive patriotism.

Blind Patriotism

Blind patriots adopt a stance of unquestioning endorsement of their
country—denying the value of critique and analysis and generally emphasizing allegiance and symbolic behaviors.[11] Studies also indicate that
blind patriots frequently engage in nationalism—asserting their nation's
superiority and supporting their nation's dominance over others.[12] Blind
patriotic commitments are well captured by comments like "My country,

love it or leave it" and by notions that it is "unpatriotic" to criticize one's own country. This form of patriotism is inconsistent with educational and democratic institutions because its intolerance of criticism signifies a lack of "free and full interplay." This perspective obscures the value of reasoned debate and fails to recognize analysis and critique as engines of improvement. Thus, while some forms of patriotism might broaden citizens' concerns to include the whole nation rather than just themselves, their family, and friends, blind or nationalistic patriotic commitments can narrow one's concerns in dangerous and antidemocratic ways.

Constructive Patriotism

Rather than embrace blind or uncritical forms of patriotism, constructive patriots applaud some actions by the state and criticize others in an effort to promote positive change and consistency with the nation's ideals.[13] For example, imperialistic actions, though often advantageous for the imperialist nation's citizens, should be rejected as inconsistent with democratic values. Rather than view critique or debate as unpatriotic (as a blind patriot might), constructive patriots consider a wide range of perspectives and enact what Ervin Staub calls "critical loyalty."[14]

From the standpoint of democracy, this orientation is essential. The point is not to downplay the value of civic knowledge or the promise of America's democratic commitments to equality and justice. Rather, it is to help students use their love of country as a motivation to critically assess what is needed to make it better.

Active Patriotism

If we are interested in determining whether patriotism is good for democracy, there is one more distinction to make—whether a patriotic commitment to one's country requires active participation. While both blind and constructive patriots love their country, neither type is necessarily actively engaged in civic or political life. Both blind and constructive patriots can discuss their perspectives in coffee shops and bars, for example, without acting in any way that substantively supports the nation. Such behavior differs markedly from the kind of active engagement a participatory democracy requires.

Active patriots, whether blind or constructive in their orientation, are those who take it upon themselves to engage in democratic and civic life in an effort to support and sustain what they feel is best about the country and to change features they believe need improvement. Their actions may begin with, but will move beyond, voting. Their forms of engagement may include PTA meetings or political protests. Active patriots may volunteer with the elderly or work on a campaign. Their love of country and their desire for it to thrive are demonstrated by their deeds.[15]

Patriotism Among High School Seniors

Drawing on these criteria for a democratic vision of patriotism, we now attend to students' perspectives. Specifically, we describe findings from the California Survey of Civic Education—a survey of high school seniors we developed to inventory students' civic commitments and capacities as well as the opportunities schools have provided to foster them. The survey is part of a broader school change initiative called "Educating for Democracy: California Campaign for the Civic Mission of Schools."[16]

In the spring of 2005, we gave the survey to 2,366 high school seniors from a very diverse set of twelve California high schools. We assessed students' commitments and capacities in the spring of their senior year because at that time they were completing their state-funded public schooling and they had reached or were reaching voting age—becoming eligible to assume the full responsibilities of citizenship. One component of the survey measured the different kinds of patriotic commitments we discuss in this chapter.[17] In an effort to probe more deeply, we also conducted 10 focus groups with fifty students from five of these high schools. Though the survey is clearly an early step in the effort to understand patriotic outcomes, our hope is that it will help move the conversation forward by providing useful indicators of student commitments and their relationship to a democratic vision of patriotism.[18]

Commitment to Country

In our focus groups, students frequently expressed strong patriotic commitments. As one student told us, "I definitely love America. I don't think we're a bad country. We try to help people—of course we have our flaws, and sometimes our reasons for doing that are sketchy, but I think overall we try to do our best and help. We have so many rights, and I can't imagine living anywhere else."

Seventy-three percent of the seniors we surveyed agreed, for example, that "the United States is a great country," while only 10% disagreed (the remaining 17% were neutral). And their level of agreement declined only slightly—to 68%—when the statement became "I have a great love for the United States" (with only 12% disagreeing).[19] Thus, while we will argue that high school students' vision of patriotism should be developed to better align with the responsibilities of democratic citizenship, it seems clear that there is little reason to worry that students are being turned into critics who focus on the country's shortcomings and fail to appreciate its strengths. For the most part, California's adolescents endorse patriotic sentiments.[20]

Constructive Patriotism

In focus groups, many students also expressed a clear sense that patriots sometimes offer critiques in an effort to improve the country. One said, for example, "I think a lot of people get confused and say being patriotic means that you think America is perfect. I think being patriotic is trying to make a difference in your country because you care so much about it. Whether you're Republican or Democrat doesn't matter, it's just that you want to make it a better country."

Some students also distinguished between supporting the country's principles and supporting its particular practices and policies. As one young woman explained, "I like the moral ideas that America has. I don't like how they are going about it."

Our survey results were consistent with these sentiments. For example, 68% agreed with the statement (with only 11% disagreeing) "I oppose some U.S. policies because I care about my country and want to improve it." Similarly, 69% agreed that "if you love America, you should notice its problems and work to correct them." (Only 12% disagreed.)

Active Patriotism

As discussed above, patriotic citizens in a democracy must do more than express their love for the country or talk about ways it could improve. For democracy to work, citizens must also be willing to act. Less than half of the students we surveyed, however, shared this belief. Indeed, in response to the statement "To be truly patriotic, one has to be involved in the civic and political life of the community," only 41% agreed. This response is similar to what the Harwood Institute found when it first asked this question of adults in 2002. These findings also mirror findings of numerous other studies of both youths and adults. Participation in many forms of civic and political engagement has declined markedly over the course of the past several decades. To a significant degree, we seem to be a nation of spectators. The risk this tendency poses to democracy is substantial.[21]

Blind Patriotism

Our survey indicates that, for many students, commitments to patriotism are associated with antidemocratic orientations that emphasize blind or uncritical support for the country. For example, more high school seniors agreed (43%) than disagreed (29%) with the statement "I support U.S. policies because they are the policies of my country." In fact, even when we asked students more pointedly whether they thought "it is un-American to criticize this country," 22% agreed and 21% were neutral. Thus 43% of the high school seniors in our sample, having completed required courses in U.S. history and in U.S. government, failed to reject this patently antidemocratic stance.

These findings do not demonstrate that California's high school seniors are blind patriots, but they do indicate that patriotic sentiments rather than analysis may often guide assessments of the nation's policies and practices—as well as responses to critiques by others.

A Democratic Vision of Patriotism

Unfortunately, while the majority of students in our sample endorsed statements associated with love of country, few of these high school seniors endorsed all three of our other indicators of democratic patriotism. Indeed, only 16% expressed that they were committed patriots, endorsed active and constructive patriotism, and rejected blind patriotism.[22] We would not expect every student to consistently support these four criteria for a democratic vision of patriotism, but 16% is hardly impressive. If patriotic education consistent with the demands of democracy is a goal for our schools, it appears that we are coming up quite short.

Two Problems in Need of Attention

While there are clearly limits to what this survey can tell us, it does provide some guidance. First, it appears that some of the most impassioned remarks related to schools and patriotism overstate the case. Schools are neither turning students into critics of the United States who cannot appreciate its virtues, nor are they failing to help students recognize the role critique can play as a means to make society better. At the same time, the fact that only 16% of the diverse group of students we surveyed in California expressed consistent support for a democratic vision of patriotism is cause for concern. We have identified two problems, in particular, that deserve our attention.

Problem 1: Passive Patriots

Many students fail to appreciate the importance of civic participation. Only 41% of students surveyed believed that loving one's country requires being civically or politically active. This finding parallels other studies that highlight young people's increasingly passive conceptions of "good citizenship."[23]

Fortunately, recent research is beginning to provide a clearer sense of curricular approaches that promote commitment to active engagement. These include instruction in history and government that emphasizes the importance of informed civic engagement, as well as such strategies as service learning, discussing social problems, and the use of simulations. Creating a school climate that allows students to participate in meaningful aspects of school governance, to be active in afterschool clubs, and to openly discuss controversial issues in the classroom also appears efficacious.[24] Of course, given the current emphasis on No Child Left Behind and related standards, whether schools will choose to focus on such priorities and will do so effectively is far from clear.

Interestingly, one argument for patriotism is that a commitment to one's country will lead to active engagement. Indeed, we see evidence from our survey that supports this claim. Fifty-four percent of those who say they love their country endorse the value of civic and political engagement, while only 34% who do not agree that they love their country endorse the value of civic and political engagement. This finding would seem to back up the proposition that a sense of patriotic commitment motivates citizens to be more active.

Problem 2: Patriotic Commitments Sometimes Lead to Blind Patriotism

While committed patriots may be more civically and politically active, patriotic commitments do not appear to help with the problem of blind patriotism—indeed, at times they appear to contribute to it. Our survey indicates that those who say they love their country are three times more likely than those who do not (28% vs. 9%) to endorse the idea that it is "un-American to criticize the country." In short, love of one's country seems to be distracting some students from recognizing the need for critique in a democracy.

Reflecting a similar pattern, the value of critique is endorsed by high school seniors when it is framed as a way to make the country better. For example, 68% agreed with the statement "I oppose some U.S. policies because I care about my country and want to improve it" (only 11% disagreed). But when a conflict is implied between patriotism and critique of the country, comfort with critique drops markedly. In fact, more students agreed (42%) than disagreed (38%) with the statement "There is too much criticism of the U.S. in the world. We, its citizens, should not criticize it."

Thus, for a significant number of students, invoking notions of patriotism appears to lead them to want to stifle critique. This finding makes the need for educators to strengthen students' understandings of both patriotism and democracy quite clear. To do so they must ground commitments to patriotism in appreciation of our country's democratic ideals and practices rather than in a sense of blind loyalty.

Unfortunately, there is little evidence that policy makers are considering such issues. Margaret Nash, who recently examined how state education policies attend to patriotism, found that many states include patriotism among their list of goals, but often without specifying how to promote patriotism or what exactly this goal entails. To the extent that they do specify a means of fostering patriotism, however, Nash found that reciting the Pledge of Allegiance is the most common strategy.[25] Indeed, following 9/11, when the interest in patriotism surged, 17 states either enacted new pledge laws for schools or amended current policies.[26] As former Senator S. I. Hayakawa (R-Calif.) once commented, "Patriotic societies seem to think that the way to educate children in a democracy is to stage bigger and better flag saluting."[27]

This tendency isn't surprising. The pledge is our nation's most explicit patriotic exercise, and the practice has long been integrated into the school day. Unfortunately, reciting the pledge is inadequate. The problem is not that saying the pledge is a symbolic act. Symbols have a place in society. The problem is that symbols can complement, but not substitute for, substance.[28]

What Educators Can Do

Educators can do a great deal to foster understandings of patriotism that support democratic values and practices. Rather than "teaching" students to love their country, teachers need to help students build an explicit connection between their "love of country" and democratic ideals—ideals that include the role of informed analysis and, at times, critique; the importance of action; and the danger of blind loyalty to the state.

Clearly, countless opportunities exist, especially in literature, history, and government courses. Teachers can deepen students' love of country by explaining the value of democratic ideals. We should teach about key instances in which the implications of patriotic commitments were debated and about the actions of critics who, in support of our ideals, worked to change the country. We should teach about the sacrifices patriotic citizens have made and consider our debt to them. We also need students to learn about those who may have used the rhetoric of patriotism to constrain liberty and stifle dissent. True to the demands of democracy, this curriculum will engage controversial issues and will require debate, discussion, and analysis. Even when broad democratic principles are agreed upon, not all will agree about the implications of such principles in particular instances. This curriculum should examine the past and should also rely on current events. To support students' recognition of the need for participation in a democracy, opportunities for action may also be included. Our goal here is not to lay out a particular curriculum—though we do believe that such a curriculum should be developed. Our point is that attention to patriotism and democracy should become sustained and coherent components of the broader school curriculum—just like other important learning objectives. Right now, with only 16% of students consistently endorsing commitments associated with a democratic vision of patriotism, it appears that we have much work to do.

This effort deserves the attention of teachers and principals and of those in district, state, and federal offices that shape curricular priorities. Students' patriotic commitments can develop in ways that meaningfully support and enhance our democratic society. Alternatively, some kinds of patriotic commitments can undermine our most precious values. Citizens do not instinctively or organically develop understandings of patriotism that align with democratic ideals. Educators have a role to play—helping students to think carefully about forms of patriotism that support our democracy and forms that do not.

California Student Peace Strike, UC Berkeley, April 19, 1940. About half of the university's students assembled at the Peace Strike. Most of them have books. They have "cut" their 11:00 A.M. classes. Copyright © 1940 by Rondal Partridge (photographer). Used by permission. For information, visit: www.rondalpartridge.com

I Solemnly Swear

Joan Kent Kvitka

In 1972, Michigan stipulated that I sign a loyalty oath before it granted me my first teaching license. It was a politically charged era, especially on the campus of the University of Michigan, and this requirement threw me into a quandary. Would endorsing this prerequisite to teaching in the state be consistent with my embrace of our true democracy, a government "of, by, and for the people," or would it be an act that would compromise necessary and protected freedoms? Unbeknownst to me, the U.S. Supreme Court was deliberating on the same issue at the same time. In April 1972, the majority decision upheld the constitutionality of loyalty oaths that require an "affirmation" to "uphold and defend the Constitution [and to] oppose the overthrow of the government . . . by force, violence or by any illegal or unconstitutional method. [This would] assure that those in positions of public trust were willing to commit themselves to live by the constitutional processes." Six years previously, the Court had struck down "disclaimer" oaths that required public servants to avow that they were not and never had been members of the Communist Party.

I signed Michigan's oath. To uphold the spirit of our democratic ideals has become the cornerstone of my social science teaching practices spanning twenty-eight years in public school classrooms from Michigan to Oregon. Although I am no longer required to swear my allegiance, investigating the concepts cherished by the framers of our Constitution has been central to the curriculum I teach, whether my students and I are excavating prehistory, mapping ancient civilizations, or debating contemporary global issues. Nothing in the examination of societies within authentic historical contexts precludes asking questions relevant to democratic ideals: How does this society view justice? Whence does power come, and how is it distributed? What protections are in place to safeguard against the abuse of power? What happens when empires or nations compete for power and resources? How are natural resources exploited or protected, and who determines this? Do tensions exist between social classes? What social institutions are in place for resolving conflicts? How is human labor valued? How do traditions forge identities? How does change occur?

My students are lively and eager to explore diverse political, economic, and cultural systems from multiple points of view. They come to understand that living in the United States in the nascence of the twenty-first century is both a privilege and a responsibility. They feel that, in order to navigate the road from the innocence of childhood to the responsibilities of adulthood, they must ask such questions as "What is more just for more people more often?" They are becoming adept at viewing the world in its complexities, rather than accepting people and ideas and decisions at face value.

Over three decades of teaching, I have come to a deep understanding of the commitment I made in swearing my loyalty to a governing system dedicated to the virtues of democracy and equality for all—both those within our diverse society and those across a global mosaic of cultures. Every day in my classroom, teacher and students alike put into practice the patience and courage of citizenship. Being patriotic, my students and I are constantly learning, is not simply embracing "America right or wrong." Being patriotic requires the audacity to explore equally what is right and wrong about our nation and the courage to accept responsibility for both.

Public school students in art class sketching a live model wearing a stars-and-stripes dress and holding a U.S. flag. 3rd division, Washington, D.C. Photographer: Frances Benjamin Johnston. Library of Congress Prints and Photographs Division, Frances Benjamin Johnston Collection [LC-USZ62-68425].

Children bringing in salvaged scrap at a headquarters civilian defense office. Chicago, Illinois, December 1942. Photographer: Jack Delano. Library of Congress Prints and Photographs Division, Farm Security Administration—Office of War Information Photograph Collection [LC-USW33-014786-D].

Chapter 10

Patriotism and Ideological Diversity in the Classroom

Diana Hess and Louis Ganzler

Given the current debate about patriotism in United States politics—what patriotism is and what patriots do—it is helpful to recognize the diversity of perspectives and passionate disagreement that the subject provokes. Indeed, one person's patriot is another's traitor. Debates about the meaning of patriotism can be contentious, and we wade into this dispute knowing that others will disagree with what we have to say. But, in many ways, the fact that people will disagree is part of the point that we hope to make. Our definition of patriotism is based on the ideal of popular sovereignty and the reality that too much agreement is a bad thing for democracy. To be patriotic, then, is to engage with others in the noble and challenging process of *deliberating* the nature of the public good and how it should be achieved.

By deliberation, we do not mean dogmatic ranting that involves more speaking than listening, nor do we mean the insipid acceptance of all ideas in an attempt to create a conflict-free community. Instead, we endorse Walter Parker's conception of inclusive deliberation as a process "where marginalized voices are encouraged to speak, listening is generous, students have studied the alternatives they are weighing, claims are supported with evidence and reasoning, and a rich inventory of historical, scientific, and literary knowledge is brought to bear."[1] Therefore, teachers who are preparing student-patriots need to aim for opening (and not simply filling) minds. They should also encourage students to learn that a diversity of views is to be sought after, not repressed.

From 2004 to 2006, we have traveled to high schools in three states trying to understand how teachers cultivate this kind of student-patriot in their classrooms. In this extensive, ongoing study, we are looking at various approaches to democratic education in high school social studies classes and are assessing how they influence the development of students' civic knowledge, skills, and actual political participation. In particular, we have been investigating what students learn from classroom-based discussions of highly controversial political issues. Over 950 students in twenty schools have participated in our study, in which we observed classes, interviewed teachers, and analyzed questionnaires. Because our interest is in what students actually take away from civic education, we have talked with hundreds of students about their experiences and learning in their social studies classes. We will conduct final interviews with the students after the national election in November 2008, when they will have been out of high school for a few years. While the study will not be finished until then, what we have learned to date has sparked our interest in the role that ideological diversity within classes plays in democratic education.

When we use the term "ideology" we are referring to the set of beliefs related to one's political perspective. We are particularly interested in the degree to which there is open disagreement in the classroom over salient political issues. We have measured students' political ideology by asking them in our pre- and post-course questionnaire where they stand on a host of key political issues such as taxes, the death penalty, abortion, and immigration. We have also asked who they would have voted for in the last presidential election.

To illustrate how ideological diversity affects democratic education in the classes we have observed, we would like you to imagine you are a high school student in each of the following three classes in our study. In the first class, an ideologically diverse group of students frequently discusses controversial political issues. The second class also has an ideologically diverse group of students, but rarely holds discussions on controversial issues. The third class has very little ideological diversity but holds some discussions on controversial issues. If you were a high school student, in which class would you feel most challenged? Which class would best prepare you to participate as a citizen in a deliberative democracy?

Hazel Brown's Class: Diversity and Deliberation

Our first visit is to a twelfth-grade government course in a large, suburban public school. The teacher, Hazel Brown, has been teaching for thirty years and will retire in June. Brown wants her students to actively engage in politics and directs her curriculum toward that end. Her students meet politicians, work as election judges, learn how to vote, participate in legislative simulations and moot courts, and frequently engage in discussions of highly controversial political issues that affect the world outside of their school.

Brown's class is a microcosm of the political diversity that exists in the United States: Half the class reports that they would have voted for Bush in the 2004 presidential election and the other half says they would have voted for Kerry. Because their views on many political issues are similarly divided, genuine conflict surfaces often in the controversial discussions in Brown's class. Despite acknowledging that discussions "sometimes . . . get a little tense," as one student put it, the students view conflict as a regular and welcome component of the class. "There were a lot of disagreements, but I don't think it would stop anybody" from expressing their views, says one student. Indeed, the presence of conflict often spurs students into joining a discussion they might otherwise avoid. As one frequently quiet student says, "when something really rubbed me the wrong way I would definitely participate." Students report that they talk more about politics as a direct result of the class, and some are even inspired to become more active politically. According to one student, "This class actually made me want to get into politics a little more than before. . . . It made me feel like you have to almost be in politics to be able to change things."

The debates about politics in Brown's class increase students' sophistication in considering differing views. One student believes that the frequent discussions "make me think deeper on every issue, not just government issues." Another student, who says her family doesn't "listen to what anyone else has to say," thinks that these classroom discussions on controversial issues have helped her appreciate the diverse political perspectives of others: "If you have an opinion, but then you get to hear what someone else has to say about the other side of it, [it makes you] think about it a little more." In sum, the presence of and emphasis on ideological diversity in Brown's class allows students to be aware not only of the diversity of ideas in their class, but also in the world around them.

Matt Lincoln's Class: Dormant Differences

Now imagine that you are in another twelfth-grade class, this one an Advanced Placement course on U.S. and comparative government and politics. This course is designed to replicate a college-level course and prepare students for the Advanced Placement examinations that occur in May. Your teacher is Matt Lincoln, an experienced, mid-career teacher who typically lectures for most of each class period, although he often asks his students questions and is frequently asked questions by them. He is an articulate and lively lecturer, and students pay careful attention and take course notes. Some of his lectures touch on controversial political issues, but there are few sustained and planned issues discussions. One student describes the class's relationship with controversy this way: "If it happened to come up and someone had a question about it, then we talked about it. But it wasn't like 'today we are going to talk about the death penalty' or something."

As in Brown's class, there is a fairly equal division among Lincoln's students between Bush and Kerry supporters, and our surveys show that among the students there is a wide range of ideological difference about political issues. Because controversial issues discussions are infrequent, however, conflict and debate about political issues is rare in the classroom. As a result, the students in Lincoln's class are unaware of the ideological diversity among their peers. In fact, a number of students say it seems that their classmates are "pretty much in the middle" of the political spectrum.

Although the students are not learning about the wide range of political views held by their classmates, they told us they are gaining a much better understanding of how governments function. This increased knowledge causes students to pay more attention to current events and politics. One student said she was "more aware of how things happen and why they happen," and another said the class "fosters my awareness of political news or current events." Unfortunately, because there are so few opportunities to discuss their political views, Lincoln's students are unaware of the diversity of ideas in their midst.

Tom Walter's Class: Debate Without Conflict

The third class we want you to imagine is an eleventh-grade course on civics. It is held in a small, Christian high school that requires students and their parents to sign a statement testifying that they hold fundamentalist

Christian beliefs. Most, but not all, of the school's teachers also subscribe to these beliefs. Tom Walter is one such teacher. Energetic and thoughtful, he often lectures during class, frequently asks his students open-ended questions, and occasionally facilitates discussions in small groups.

Walter allows opportunities for students to state their views on politically controversial issues, even though the class is almost entirely ideologically homogenous. One student told us that because they all come from a similar background, they tend to have the same political views—especially about whether Bush or Kerry should have won the 2004 presidential election. In fact, all but one of the students from this class who participated in our study indicated that, had they been old enough to vote in the last election, they would have voted for Bush. Students report hearing some competing perspectives, however. One student explains that the all-Christian make-up of the school means students share personal beliefs, but politics can be debated. In terms of gay marriage, he says, "Christians can disagree about the government's rules over the issue, but not over the personal choice of being homosexual." The teacher echoes the distinction raised by this student when explaining what he wants them to decide on their own compared to what he hopes they all will believe. He says,

> Certainly we are trying to train our students to have a Christian worldview. I am going to say, "This is how I think one would think Christianly about this issue." [But] while I would never balk at sharing with a student how I felt about these political and social issues and why I felt it, I wouldn't say, "This is how you should feel."

While the students' ideological diversity is limited by the school's policy of allowing only "saved" Christians to attend, Walter looks outside the school and involves his civics students in a multi-school deliberation program to ensure that his students hear other political views. Although these events allow the students to be exposed for brief interludes to fellow students with varied political opinions, the day-to-day homogeneity of their own classroom seems to limit the impact of such exposure. Because of the ideological homogeneity in the class, the students are not *regularly* exposed to opinions that sharply depart from their own. As a result, they seem unable to seriously grapple with differing viewpoints, relying instead on oversimplification and ideological clichés to defend their positions. One student, for example, dismissed all the opposing views that he heard as left-wing ideology, unworthy of respectful consideration and deliberation. He surmised that the interschool deliberation event was predicated on the notion that, "America has made terrible mistakes. We are terrible people, the Right is wrong. Now go from here."

Walter's students are exposed to controversial issues, but compared to Hazel Brown's and Matt Lincoln's classes, they are much more ideologically homogenous. As a consequence, there is little authentic political conflict in the class.

What Difference Do Differences Make?

If patriotism in a democratic society means being able to engage with others in genuine deliberation about important political issues, then the preparation of open-minded citizens requires specific types of teaching and learning. Our study shows us that teaching students how to engage with those who hold different views can be either fostered or inhibited by the range of political difference that exists among the students and the teacher's willingness to provide the students with opportunities to discuss those differences. While we are impressed by the skill and commitment of Hazel Brown, Matt Lincoln, and Tom Walter and believe there is value in what all of their students are learning, we think that Brown's students are getting the most practice in what it takes to productively contribute to a democratic community.

Brown's students stand out from the students in the other two classes in several important ways. We found that Brown's students were motivated to become involved in politics in order to change the status quo. They also consistently recognized and valued the different perspectives they encountered from their peers. Finally, political conflict was normalized in Brown's classroom, and, as a result, students both respected and engaged their peers in political discourse even when they disagreed with them.

It is clear to us that classes in which there are a range of political views are more interesting spaces for discussions of issues than classes where most of the students are ideologically aligned. But ideological diversity among students must be engaged by the teacher if it is to be a useful tool in preparing students to participate democratically in efforts to improve society. Teachers can expose ideological differences and facilitate this kind of engagement through issues discussions, which allow students to recognize not only that there is conflict, but also that the airing of conflicting political views is normal, interesting, and productive. Where there is little discussion of issues in a politically diverse class, as in Lincoln's class, students may believe that everyone is in the political middle. While this may seem like an innocuous misperception, we believe the political consequences are potentially harmful. Similarly, when all the students' views are politically homogeneous, as in Walter's class, the discussions that do take place appear to elicit only facile dismissal of viewpoints that differ from the ones the students in the class share.

Political scientists Hibbing and Theiss-Morse claim that people in the United States consistently underestimate the level of disagreement that exists among the electorate. They suggest that most voters believe themselves to be moderate and that the majority of other voters are too.[2] This phenomenon describes why the students in Lincoln's class erroneously believed they were "all in the middle." The condition that allows this misperception to flourish is a lack of exposure to political conflict. Because people in the United States—as compared to other democracies worldwide—tend to avoid political conflict, they are unaware of how many different political opinions their fellow citizens hold. Lincoln's class, in this context, can be viewed as a miniature model of U.S. politics. Due to the absence of discussion about controversial issues in the classroom, students' awareness of their own political diversity lays dormant. This is potentially harmful to the health of a democracy because when these students do encounter political opinions that run counter to their own, they are likely to mislabel such views as being out of the mainstream. Worse, they are unprepared to engage in deliberation. Some of Walter's students at the inter-school deliberation recoiled when they encountered political views different than their own, perceiving dissenting views as assaults on their own beliefs and unworthy of proper consideration. In schools, after all, students have the opportunity to learn norms of debate that make healthy interchanges possible. Such learning opportunities, however, can be too easily squandered.

Hibbing and Theiss-Morse also believe there is a connection between how citizens view conflict and whether they actually engage politically.[3] If this link exists (and we are persuaded by their research that it does), then our study shows that two factors are crucial in order to activate ideological awareness among students: 1) ideological diversity within a class, and 2) teacher practices that capitalize on differences of opinion. Moreover, in classes with wide political difference that is unawakened, there is a high opportunity cost, since most young people are unlikely to engage in such discussions in politically diverse climates elsewhere. Consequently, policies and pedagogies that create ideologically homogeneous educational settings or cause existing ideological heterogeneity to be hidden will most likely fail to live up to their potential as democracy builders.

A Proposal

We think there are concrete steps that people interested in democratic education can take to ensure that all students are taught how to deliberate thorny and authentic political issues in a diverse political environment. The most obvious, and perhaps most challenging, step is to create schools and classes that are as politically heterogeneous as possible. While especially skillful teachers taking advantage of curricular and democratic education programs can add diversity to an otherwise homogenous classroom environment, it is much easier to awaken diversity than create it. Themed schools that are developed to attract like-minded students may seem like nurturing communities, but, in fact, may lack the very diversity that is necessary to make it possible for their students to thrive in more politically heterogeneous, real democratic communities that exist outside the school. In a similar fashion, we should be wary of courses that are designed to attract students with similar political views and should promote the purposeful creation of politically diverse classes and curriculum.

Where classes are ideologically diverse, we should encourage teachers to put this diversity to good use by ensuring that students have many opportunities to engage in vigorous discussions of political issues. It is important to remove the barriers to this kind of teaching that exist in many schools, districts, and states. For example, rigid district and state tests that define social studies by content only make it extremely difficult for teachers to take the time to engage their students in meaningful discussions. Most importantly, teachers who engage students in discussions of contentious political issues need to be supported by administrators and the community, especially when there is criticism about whether schools are the proper place to engage young people in such discussions.

Talking seriously with others about the nature of the public good and how it can be achieved is not an easy form of patriotism. Teaching students to discuss hot issues is hard work, but if we want to help young people become patriots of the *deliberative* sort, then it is work worth supporting.

Toeing the Line and the Law
First Amendment Rights in Schools

karen emily suurtamm
with Edwin C. Darden, Esq.

The constitutional right to free speech is guaranteed to all American citizens, and what better place to practice this right to investigate, debate, and express one's opinions than the classroom. But recent events have demonstrated that there are limits to the first amendment rights of teachers and students. In the wake of 9/11 and the continued occupation of Iraq, educators and students have been suspended, punished, and fired for expressing their diverse views about the current political scene. These cases demonstrate that the protection of first amendment rights is often in precarious tension with the interests of the school at large, as perceived by school administrators and policymakers. Moreover, they reveal the ambiguous and subjective nature of distinguishing between controversial speech (acceptable) and offensive speech (unacceptable). For example, the administrators at Occoquan Elementary School in Virginia demonstrated a clear political position when they punished two students (aged five and eight) for wearing t-shirts with a slogan they believed would disrupt and cause injury to other students: The shirts read "Latinos Forever."[1]

While some teachers aim to make classrooms fertile ground for discussing controversial social and political issues, a number of precedent-setting cases limit the ability of teachers and students to express those opinions. The law can limit first amendment rights in the schools for the following reasons:

1. Students are usually minors and schools have a custodial responsibility to maintain a safe and orderly environment.
2. Students are a captive audience (due to mandatory attendance laws).
3. Teachers act as role models for students.
4. When operating in their official capacity, teachers are "state actors" who act as an extension of the government power represented by the school administration. According to the U.S. Supreme Court, "The state has interests as an employer in regulating the speech of its employees that differ significantly from those it possesses in connection with regulation of the speech of the citizenry in general."[2]

Teaching with Care: Limitations on the Speech of Educators

Elementary, middle, and high school teachers do not have the same right to academic freedom as post-secondary educators do. Control of the curriculum—both what is taught and how it is taught—is vested with the board of education and the administration. When performing their professional duties, teachers are bound to the mission of the school. Outside the school, teachers are also limited, and court rulings have traditionally balanced the interests of the teacher (and his/her individual right to free speech) against the interests of the school district. In order to be protected by first amendment rights, the speech of government employees is governed by two tests. First, the courts ask whether the speech is of a public or private concern. If private, the speech is protected. If public, the courts then ask whether the interest of the teacher in speaking as a private citizen is outweighed by the state's interest in promoting efficiency in the delivery of educational services. Of course, legal decisions are largely contextual. Here are a few important cases:

*   1968: The U.S. Supreme Court ruled that a public school teacher could not be discharged for making comments on school expenditures in letters published in the local newspaper. However, she did not have the right to publicly criticize supervisors, because this would undermine the workplace.[3]
*   1972: The U.S. Supreme Court decided that a teacher could refuse to participate in the flag salute if the teacher stood silently with her hands by her side.[4]

- 1972: A federal circuit court decided a teacher could not be dismissed for wearing a black armband to class to protest the Vietnam War.[5]
- 1987: The Supreme Court heard the case of a clerical employee in a Texas constable's office who was discharged when she allegedly told a co-worker—after John Hinckley Jr. shot president Reagan—"If they go for him [Reagan], I hope they get him." The courts ruled that the speech was of public concern, but since it was not heard by the public and did not affect the functioning of the office, her first amendment rights should be protected.[6]
- 2003: The 2nd Circuit Court upheld the dismissal of a New York City teacher for his active membership and leadership in the North American Man/Boy Love Association (NAMBLA), even though there was no evidence of its influence on his conduct with his students. In this case, they decided that, given the highly controversial moral position of NAMBLA and the teacher's position as someone working with minors, his return to school would disrupt the school's functioning, and "his active involvement with the group disrupted the board's educational mission."[7]

Limitations on the Speech of Students

Court decisions on students' first amendment rights are governed by two influential Supreme Court cases. First, in *Tinker v. Des Moines* (1969), the court ruled that students' speech can be limited if schools demonstrate that it substantially disrupts school activities, or that such disruption is likely to occur.[8] Second, in the case of *Bethel v. Fraser* (1986) the courts ruled that first amendment rights do not protect student speech that is lewd, vulgar, obscene, and plainly offensive.[9] School boards, however, cannot limit freedom of expression because of "a mere desire to avoid [the] discomfort and unpleasantness that always accompany an unpopular view point,"[10] or because speech merely "contains a potentially offensive political viewpoint."[11] Here are a few important cases:

- 1970: A federal circuit court upheld the decision of Shaw High School in Cleveland to forbid students from wearing buttons in an anti-war protest because the history of school disturbance and the wearing of insignias suggested to officials that disruption would ensue.[12]
- In August of 2005, the Ohio federal district court ruled against a school board that supported a principal's demand that a student

remove a t-shirt that read, "Homosexuality is a sin! Islam is a lie! Abortion is murder!" because the school board could not prove that the speech "interfered with the work" of the school nor "collided with the rights of other students to be let alone."[13]

Schools can have speech-limiting policies that guide internal decisions, but they cannot be discriminatory, vague, or overbroad. Instead, such policies must be specific, apply to all people equally, and must not place unnecessary limits on Constitutional free speech rights. Of course, teachers and students should not shy away from discussing controversial political and social topics. Instead, they should do so armed with the passion of their convictions and the prudence to express that conviction in appropriate ways.

The safest guardians of Liberty's Flag—the public schools—welcoming President McKinely, El Paso, Texas. June 20, 1901. Library of Congress Prints and Photographs Division [LC-USZ62-55731].

Poster created circa 1915 by Howell Lith. Co., Ltd., Hamilton, Canada. Library of Congress Prints and Photographs Division, WWI Posters [LC-USZC4-12709].

Chapter 11

"Patriotism, Eh?"
The Canadian Version

Sharon Anne Cook

It's 8:15 A.M. on a typical day at Anyschool in Canada. Adolescents are charging down hallways, slamming locker doors, and tripping over one another and any unwary supervising teacher, trying to make it through the classroom door before the playing of the Canadian national anthem. Most will manage it; some are stranded in mid-flight. A teacher might have to remind them to "stand at attention." Instead, they remain still-ish (just like their swifter friends in the classroom), looking unhappy, staring vacantly until their purgatory ends after this single demonstration of national respect demanded of students. There is no Pledge of Allegiance, no hand on the heart, not even a working knowledge of the words to the anthem.

Many students, however, could quote verbatim the Molson Canadian beer commercial from April 2000:

> I have a Prime Minister, not a President; I speak English and French, not American; and I pronounce it "about," not "a boot."
> . . . I can proudly sew my country's flag on my backpack. I believe in peacekeeping, not policing; diversity, not assimilation; and that the beaver is a truly proud and noble animal. . . . My name is Joe! And I am Canadian! Thank you.[1]

Here we have it: patriotism, Canadian style, apparently composed of vague anti-American pride in our presumed peacefulness, our diversity, and the lowly beaver. And courtesy, too, represents a proud Canadian value: The "oath" ends by thanking the listeners. This bland self-identification with qualities perceived to be less abrasive or aggressive than those defining the American character, voiced more politely than pronouncements of American patriotism—available for mass comparison on television or in film—is what most Canadians would define as Canadian "nationalism," the closest thing we have to "patriotism."

What are the roots of this seemingly pale thing we might call Canadian Patriotism, and how has the formal school curriculum intersected with popular notions of what it is to be a patriotic citizen? One of Canada's best-known philosophers, John Ralston Saul,[2] argues that Canada's contribution to the world has been to build a new type of quiet nationalism, characterized most fundamentally by the tradition of compromise between our three founding peoples: French, English, and First Nations.[3] And it is no coincidence that Saul is the husband of the woman who has just retired from the office of governor general, a quintessentially Canadian political institution. Adding to its heterogeneous mixture, Canada has welcomed a larger percentage of immigrants compared with its population base than has any Western nation over the past century, Saul asserts, including the United States. The concepts and proclivities underpinning this tradition of compromise—self-effacement, careful and endless debate on a shifting agenda of priorities, the notion of "limited identities" to describe the range of competing factors (regional, linguistic, racial, and ethnocultural among others) in every Canadian's sense of self—all of these are incompatible with strident patriotic fervor. In fact, patriotism is actively feared as having the potential to undo this frail consensus.

Through the school curriculum, particularly in the prescriptions for history and social studies, objectives for citizenship training in this country have privileged understanding through debate rather than patriotism. Both curricular and school authorities have consistently taken the position that, while loyalty is good, patriotism is to be approached with caution. In recounting the Canadian government's efforts to whip the nation into unified support for the First World War, the authors of one leading textbook for eighth graders note that, although English Canadian supporters of the draft eventually triumphed, "the price of victory was steep. . . . It was Quebec against the rest of Canada. The bitterness lasted for years to come."[4]

Patriotism and Canada's Three Cultures

Canada is a tricultural and, since 1971, an officially bilingual nation. The often-uneasy relationship between French and English Canadians has been a feature of our national life from the 1840s, when the infamous Durham Report suggested that the greatest kindness to French Canadians would be to gradually eliminate their language and culture. No matter what Lord Durham thought was best for the colony, one can only marvel at the resilience and vigor of French Canadian life, whether in the "home province" of Quebec or in one of the many minority francophone communities across Canada. French Canadians are here to stay, but their interests have been pitted against the English majority views on many occasions. The two rebellions in western Canada (in 1869 and 1885) both had a strong subtext of French Canadian dissatisfaction, as did the major eastern Canadian rebellion in Lower Canada (Quebec) in 1837; the threat of the draft almost split the nation in two during both World Wars, as noted above; and the rise of modern Quebec separatism remains a persistent worry for most Canadians. The "French Canadian fact," as it is delicately termed in many school curricula, has forced Canadians to emphasize the need to protect unity rather than patriotism while respecting customs and traditions that arise from this linguistic community. For a province like Alberta, this takes the form of requiring students to respect the franco-Albertan community, along with Ukrainian Canadians and First Nations groups, and to accept that "some people prefer to live in or belong to a special community so they can keep their customs and traditions."[5] Few Canadians feel that the luxury of patriotic fervor is possible or wise in the face of French Canadians' needs and aspirations to protect their language and culture.

One essential element of the Canadian style of patriotism derives from our British forebears. From the earliest Canadian-produced history readers dating from the 1860s, Canadian children learned about their political, economic, and moral indebtedness to Mother Britain. Canadians waited until 1982 to produce a formal constitution under the Canada Act, and our ties to Britain have been cemented through a political system closely modeled on the British, a judicial and education system with strong echoes of British values, and large-scale British immigration. Public values rooted in respect for reserve, fair play, and hard work remain closely linked in popular perceptions to our heritage in the British Empire.

In the early twentieth century, Canadian schoolchildren were challenged, as one textbook of 1910 put it, to civilize "a vast solitude of uncultivated plains, unbroken forests, and lonely mountains" by using these same British values.[6] Today, curricular guidelines phrase objectives in environmental terms: Responsible citizens must "promote diversity and . . . not compromise the natural world for any species in the future."[7] As the challenge has been framed in school materials, then, the demands of taming Canada's vast geography while acting respectfully toward the environment and remaining mindful of British values of fair play have remained in the forefront of educators' concerns. And yet, even here, one does not find a patriotic impulse to that duty. Issues associated with the immensity of the land, the husbanding of resources, and the protection of border and region have traditionally portrayed Canada as the junior partner, first to Britain, then to the United States—a willing partner, to be sure, but in deference to those with access to more resources, larger populations, and greater appetites. National patriotism seems unnecessary if one already finds inclusion in the family of a respected imperial power, whether British or American.

The influence of the third major component of Canadian culture, Canada's First Nations, in producing a muted sense of patriotism most likely derives from the early and sustained economic partnerships that the English and the French each developed separately with the aboriginal peoples through the fur trade. There is no doubt that occasional flashes of violence erupted in this relationship. Instances such as the Battle of Long Sault in 1660, in which Dollard Des Ormeaux and his sixteen companions were overcome by Iroquois, continue to live in French Canadian annals and in history textbooks read by generations of Canadian children. Aboriginal and Métis peoples' resistance to the fledging Canadian government's "manifest destiny" over western Canada, in addition to starvation and disease, resulted in the North-West Rebellion in 1885 in what is now Saskatchewan. Nevertheless, examples of violent resistance are relatively rare beyond the eighteenth century, as the fur trade provided the underpinning for western development through the patronage of the Hudson Bay Company for the British and the North-West Company for the Scots and French. The First Nations and Métis peoples were *commercial* allies, providing a practical reason to resolve any disputes peacefully. This tradition was further reinforced by the establishment in the late nineteenth century of the North-West Mounted Police (now the Royal Canadian Mounted Police), a force that

Canadian children are taught continues to work closely in dispute resolution all through Western and Northern Canada.

The evocation of partnership with First Nations peoples is, of course, belied by the appalling poverty and distress of many native communities in Canada. Yet the official curriculum—however that might be subverted in practice—underscores the unity of purpose. The Northwest Territories curriculum, for example, asserts that "whatever one might desire for the future of the territories, it is a fact that we—easterners and westerners; Dene, Métis, Inuit, and non-Natives—live together now, sharing our lives in a single, vast political jurisdiction."[8]

Patriotism and Peacekeeping

The Canadian tradition of peacekeeping probably developed naturally from such initiatives in the 1870s as the creation of the North-West Mounted Police to remove rum-runners from the West and to make the area compatible to settlement. Clearly, it was also reinforced during the Cold War by the establishment of the United Nations, an institution to which Canadians and especially the Canadian education establishment gave strong support. Doubtless, the widespread enthusiasm for the United Nations—characterized by student UN assemblies held from the 1950s across Canada and overt support through curriculum documents—was partly due to the UN Charter's provision for maintaining international peace through the use of collective security forces. This approach was developed as a reasonable way to ensure that the horrors associated with World War II would never again occur. It was a Canadian, Lester Pearson, who successfully organized a UN peacekeeping force during the Suez Crisis, an accomplishment duly recognized by the international community through the Nobel Peace Prize in 1956 and celebrated in virtually every Canadian history textbook since. Whatever the cause, Canadian schools and institutions have seen Canadians as peacekeepers since that time at least and have immortalized this image through texts, popular films, and commemorative statues.

Patriotic Aberrations

This is not to say that Canada has never experimented with patriotic values or excess. It has done so fairly often and, predictably, in xenophobic ways that have excluded many and privileged the usual few. As elsewhere, Canadian patriotism has been most evident during periods of national crisis when Canadians' safety or that of the nation-state has been thought to be endangered. The Chinese during the building of the transcontinental railway in the 1880s, German and Italian Canadians during World War I, Ukrainian and Japanese Canadians during World War II, French Canadian nationalists during the FLQ terrorism of the late 1960s, and the invocation of the War Measures Act in 1970—all suffered the loss of civil liberties, of the presumption of innocence, or of the right to earn a fair living wage. Clearly, Canadians can make no claims to treat minority interests more fairly than is done elsewhere.

Patriotism, Canadian Style

Counterpoised to the occasional political aim of invoking patriotism has been the official position of the education establishment (which, however, has not been immune to the xenophobic assumptions of any given era): suspicion toward the extremes of propaganda. One persistent dispute in eastern Canada involved cadet training in the schools from the 1890s to the end of World War I. By 1923, the National Council of Education worried that high school history could become a means to promote patriotism. It argued that "history should not be prostituted to the service of propaganda."[9] The concern was that combining historical and civics education in the same curriculum would increase the propagandistic potential of history and social studies courses to an unacceptable level.

Rather than promoting explicit patriotism, Canadian curricula have typically celebrated our pride in democratic institutions; the 1952 curriculum guidelines for history in Canada's largest province, Ontario, called on students to develop such vague qualities as "tolerance, respect and good will;"[10] the current civics guidelines call on young people to become "informed," "purposeful," and "active" citizens, by, for example, demonstrating "an understanding of the various ways in which decisions are made and conflicts resolved in matters of civic importance."[11] One cannot be certain about the meaning of such statements; they are surely a long way from overt patriotism, however.

It is an open question as to how persuasive this educational discourse of "peace and good government" rather than spirited patriotism is to the general public. However, there is some evidence that it reflects general Canadian norms. During the winter of 2004, the Canadian Broadcasting Corporation—which provides a national radio and television service to all parts of Canada—ran one of the "Greatest Canadian" contests, modeled on the British contest that had resulted in Churchill's being proclaimed as the "Greatest Briton." Whom did Canadians choose as their "Greatest," casting 1.2 million votes for the winner? A Churchillian political master, perhaps, like Pierre Elliott Trudeau or Lester Pearson, holding the country together during times of strife? A famous hockey player, or even a hockey commentator? A scientist? All of these, and others as well, were nominated and promoted with an embarrassing level of hype. But no, we chose a mousy, slight man with wispy hair and a sharp, reedy voice, a former Baptist minister, premier of Saskatchewan, leader of Canada's left-wing New Democratic Party. Best known these days as Kiefer Sutherland's grandpa, Tommy Douglas was hailed as the best this country has ever produced because he introduced the first universal medicare program in the West, setting the stage for this unique Canadian national health plan. This is the type of person who most captures the Canadian imagination and symbolizes our pride: the little guy from Saskatchewan who ensured that everyone would have the right to health care. If contests to discover the greatest Canadian reveal something of the national psyche, then perhaps we can also find here the national aspirations of Canadians: a tradition of populism that encompasses environmentalism and peaceful dispute resolution; health care for everyone; public life grounded in an ethic of fairness, honesty, and plain hard work rather than glitz and glitter. Maybe that is the true definition of patriotism, Canadian style.

Students listen to the speaker at the California Student Peace Strike, University of California, April 19, 1940. Copyright © 1940 by Rondal Partridge (photographer). Used by permission. For information, visit: www.rondalpartridge.com

Chapter 12

Patriot Acts
This Isn't the First Time

Cecilia O'Leary

In the 1990s, during the flush years of an exuberant dot-com economy, being an American meant little more than enjoying the freedom to consume. However, in the aftermath of the terrorist attack on September 11th, 2001, rituals and symbols of patriotism seemed omnipresent, particularly in schools. In the days after 9/11, the flag represented a sense of loss and grief, and was flown by a broad spectrum of people for a variety of reasons. It wasn't long, however, before the range of what it meant to be patriotic and loyal was limited to unquestioning loyalty and obedience to the government. This attitude was all but legislated with the passing of the Patriot Act in 2001, which gave the domestic intelligence apparatus unprecedented power, justified racially motivated arrests, and curtailed civil liberties in the name of national security. The preemptive invasion of Iraq in 2003 and the on-going war there make it highly unlikely that there will be an easing of these neo-conservative foreign and domestic policies, which both encourage and thrive off of this singular vision of patriotism.

In an atmosphere of fear and distrust, some Americans are once again lobbying for an unquestioning patriotism in schools. The battle cry has sounded for reinstituting a daily pledge of allegiance, threatening to reverse a trend begun after the Vietnam War when educators were disinclined to place form over substance and rote memorization over democratic participation. In the United States, where being an American is considered a choice rather than a birthright, those who claim cultural authority to shape and define patriotic attitudes and symbols hold great influence. Patriotism is a powerful cultural phenomenon that generates not only solidarity, unity, and remembrance, but also mistrust, divisiveness, and amnesia. For patriots, loyalty to family, friends, religion, and place are subsumed under allegiance to one's country.[1] A historical overview of the twentieth century suggests, however, that this militarist form of patriotism—shaped by the demands of war, infused by racism, narrowed by anti-immigrant positions and political intolerance of dissent—has more often than not undermined the very ideals it purports to protect.

In order to bring a historical perspective to contemporary divides over the meanings of patriotism, I will explore how five overlapping themes converged between the Civil War and World War I when voluntary organizations imagined, constructed, and institutionalized a national culture. During this time, public schools became the locus of culture wars, impacted by the emergence of mass organizations of self-proclaimed "patriots" who developed and defined patriotic culture. Specifically, these organizations sought to rally the patriotic fervor of the nation's youth around the flag and the institutionalization of the Pledge of Allegiance.

First, patriotic rituals and symbols emerged in the nineteenth century, not from harmonious, national consensus, but out of fiercely contested debates over whose memories would be enshrined in national holidays, what exactly constituted disrespect for the flag, whose heroes would be memorialized in monuments, and what narratives would become the nation's founding myths. Similar discussions continue today, as people debate how history and civics should be taught in the classroom, if military recruiting should be allowed on school grounds, and whether a daily swearing of allegiance to the flag should be mandatory. The struggle over what kind of patriotism should be taught in the schools is not new.

Second, concern for youth and education have always been at the heart of these debates—children represent the future of the nation and the kind of patriotism they practice symbolizes national aspirations. During the 1890s, despite differences over goals and constituencies, nationalists cooperated in their effort to raise the flag over every school, institutionalize the pledge of allegiance, introduce patriotic rituals aimed at galvanizing children's hearts, and create civic curriculums aimed at securing children's minds.

Third, regardless of individual motivations, the Civil War became more than a test of whether there would be two nations; also at stake was whether patriotism would be grounded in the ideal of freedom and equality for all Americans. For many anti-slavery reformers, the Emancipation Declaration of 1863 played a critical role in expanding the meaning of patriotism from a willingness to die for the United States to the reciprocal obligation of the nation to make the idea of liberty a reality. After Abraham Lincoln established the doctrinal basis for an activist liberal state (with a government that might, for example, initiate programs to attack discrimination and inequality or buttress civil liberties), Frederick Douglass, the leading Black Abolitionist, predicted that Emancipation Day would become the "most memorable day in American Annals." July 4th marked the political birth of the nation, but Douglass believed that the Emancipation Proclamation promised to "put peace forever between the conscience and the patriotism of the people."[2] But after the Civil War, divisions deepened along racial lines, even though the language of patriotism continued to speak in universal terms of democracy. By 1877, the racialization of patriotism was already underway and the defeat of Reconstruction officially opened the door to the reassertion of a "Whites only" brand of patriotism. Nonetheless, as detailed in Gloria Ladson-Billings's essay in this book, African Americans did continue to keep the most progressive traditions of patriotism alive.

Fourth, the patriotic rituals and symbols that many now take for granted and consider inviolable traditions are, in fact, relatively recent inventions whose sacred status was far from inevitable. For example, the first national observation of Memorial Day took place in 1868, but it was not uniformly observed on the last Monday of May until 1971; the schoolhouse flag movement did not get underway until the 1880s; Francis Bellamy's Pledge of Allegiance was not written until 1891; and Congress did not enact a national law against "flag desecration" until 1968. The flag, which stands as the preeminent symbol of the nation, lacked any standardized design until the invasion and subsequent conquest of Mexico in 1848 when, for the first time, mass-produced flags replaced the kaleidoscope of homemade flags that creatively placed stars in different arrangements, added other icons, and freely combined a patchwork of colors. Reverence for the flag as a sacred symbol only became a popular sentiment during the Civil War. Similarly, "The Star-Spangled Banner," written by Francis Scott Key in 1812, was not initially sung as a sacred hymn. While the words express a nationalist pride in surviving a British assault, the melody was inspired by an eighteenth century English drinking song. "The Star-Spangled Banner" would not be finally approved as the official national anthem until 1931.

Fifth, unlike many other countries, the creation of patriotic culture in the United States did not originate with government-sponsored initiatives but from the efforts of voluntary organizations and community mobilizations. Leaders in the patriotic movement included the Grand Army of the Republic (GAR), made up of Civil War veterans; The Woman's Relief Corps (WRC), made up of women who had proven their loyalty to the United States during the Civil War; Daughters of the American Revolution (DAR), who claimed hereditary links to the American Revolution; civic-minded business associations; progressive reformers; and the National Education Association (NEA). What distinguished this movement from earlier efforts to forge a mass sense of patriotism was that each of the aforementioned organizations emphasized youth as the standard-bearers of the nation and the public school as the primary location for instilling patriotic values.

Mobilizing the Nation's Youth

After the Civil War, there were a variety of competing images of patriotism, including the idealization of heroic male warriors, antebellum associations with virtuous men, and Emancipation's promise that America would live up to its civic ideals. A broad range of nationalists sought cultural authority to reinterpret the meaning of loyal Americanism, especially as it pertained to educating the nation's children and young adults. One of the most influential voices was the Grand Army of the Republic (GAR), the first mass organization of veterans that made loyalty to the Union the only criterion for membership. As its membership swelled, the GAR staged spectacular encampments where tens of thousands of veterans pitched their tents in the middle of all the major cities and paraded through streets lined with thousands of men, women, and children in awe of those who marched as embodiments of patriotism. The veterans saw themselves as the nation's custodians of memory and as a living link between the Civil War and future generations. The GAR expected every local post to become a "school of patriotism, a school of intelligent Americanism, a school of high obedience to law and order." Activist veterans held monthly campfires with local children to tell "thrilling stories of heroic deeds, brave encounters, desperate battles . . . and wondrous suffering."[3] Members regularly visited schools in their old uniforms, and brought a war-tattered flag as emotional reminders that patriots must be willing to fight and die to preserve the union.

The GAR was also one of the only integrated organizations in the nineteenth century. Black veterans joined out of the belief that the organization's formal commitment "to equality, sealed in the blood of soldiers, was a patriotism worth embracing."[4] However, the GAR forged an uneasy alliance of Black and White veterans and, thus, while Black veterans could join the GAR as equals, they faced an informally enforced segregation. Moreover, the Grand Army projected a singularly male-warrior image and refused to admit women, despite their heroic service during the Civil War. Overcoming these rebuffs, women formed their own mass organization, the Woman's Relief Corps (WRC) and opened membership to any woman who had proven her loyalty to the Union. Finally, in 1883, the Grand Army relented and allied with the WRC. The WRC, whose membership numbered more than 100,000 from 1892 to 1919, not only joined the patriotic movement, but also played a pivotal role in crafting the rituals of Memorial Day and making the day the most important new national holiday of the nineteenth century—not to mention a significant educational force for the nation's youth.

The WRC understood that the only way to preserve the memory of patriotism after the Civil War veterans died was to turn the day into a "kindergarten of Union sentiment" when imparting lessons of loyalty to the living were as essential as remembering the dead.[5] The WRC shifted the locus of citizenship instruction from the home to civic spaces and made Memorial Day into an important new site for public civic education. On the day, women ensured that wagonloads of flowers were brought to cemeteries and school children were organized to decorate each Union grave with a flower. For example in 1909, the WRC brought out 324,000 schoolchildren waving 240,000 flags in Detroit. The WRC envisioned the next generation as the "greatest standing army in the world," ready to spread the "gospel of patriotism."[6] The WRC succeeded in transforming children from sentimental symbols of the nation into active participants.

"The Great Fusing Furnace": Americanization in the Public Schools

Thirty years after the Civil War, nationalists believed that the new threat to the nation came from the arrival of immigrants from Europe. They demanded that the only way to deal with this "alien element" was to Americanize their children "in the common schools of the nation."[7] In the late 1880s, the GAR marched forward under the motto, "The schoolhouse stands by the flag, let the people stand by the school." But as the GAR veterans aged and died in larger numbers, a new breed of professional nationalists, including progressive reformers, civic-minded businessmen, advertisers, magazine publishers, and newspaper editors, succeeded them, drawing upon modern technology and new means of communication to organize the first national propaganda campaign on behalf of the nation. Despite the effectiveness of these new nationalists within the growing system of public education, the movement continued to include a variety of ideological perspectives and encouraged a degree of debate about who and what stood for the nation.

Within the public schools, organized patriots urged teachers to experiment with teaching flag ceremonies to foster an emotional patriotism among the students. Throughout the 1880s, teachers created pageants and schoolyard rituals; this, in turn, developed into children's daily recitation of the Pledge of Allegiance. Even though the Constitution does not prescribe a daily oath, the notion of pledging loyalty had become more commonplace during the Civil War and Reconstruction, when teachers from Southern border states were required to swear their allegiance to the Constitution of the United States.

George T. Balch, an educator, veteran, and GAR spokesman, wrote the first pledge to gain widespread recognition: "We give our heads and hearts to God and our country, one nation, one language, one flag."[8] In 1890, he wrote *Methods for Teaching Patriotism in the Public Schools,* which became an immediate success as teachers adopted his series of flag rituals that combined religious fervor and military discipline. Balch was principally interested in form and argued that even though children did not understand the word "nation," patriotic teachers could predispose children to feelings of love and duty for their country, just as religious teachers taught love of God before students could grasp its full significance. Balch's plan, with its stress on regulated and uniform behavior, appealed to teachers charged with Americanizing immigrants in the new urban schools and to government schools charged with assimilating more than 250 Native American tribes by removing "Indian" children from their homes and placing them into state boarding schools.

Although organized groups of patriots such as the GAR veterans; activists in the WRC and DAR; and educators had laid the groundwork for patriotic education by lobbying for flags to be flown over every schoolhouse, it was not until a national paper, the *Youth's Companion,* added its expertise in modern advertising techniques that the schoolhouse flag movement became a truly national phenomenon. By 1900, some national magazines claimed a circulation of more than 100,000 subscribers and, as national markets grew, advertising ceased to be just a long list of products and was transformed into a dynamic social force capable of attracting consumers and shaping public opinion. For example, the *Youth's Companion,* a family paper read by parents with children and teachers with students, used its advertising know-how and access to teachers to mobilize students as patriotic activists in the schoolhouse flag campaign. The paper's editors decided that having the nation's children simultaneously pledge their allegiance to the flag on Columbus Day would make a fitting prelude to the 1892 Columbian Exposition, scheduled to take place in Chicago. The *Youth's Companion* proposed to place the public schools at the center of this celebration, which marked the four hundredth anniversary of Columbus's "discovery" of America. Francis Bellamy, a nationalist and Christian Socialist, took charge of the national campaign. Bellamy believed in the social gospel and agitated for the broadening of governmental powers to correct social injustice. Unlike George Balch, Bellamy denounced the privileging of individual liberty over social equality and fraternity.

Competing Political Goals for Patriotic Education

In a time of major class formation and social dislocation, most national presses stood behind the rights of property, condemned calls for economic justice, and denounced militant labor demonstrations for an eight-hour workday as un-American. Bellamy countered these views by calling for a new nationalist spirit in which equality would mean equal rights to employment and education. He used the flag campaign of the *Youth's Companion* to popularize this civic-minded version of patriotism. When the *Youth's Companion* asked him to write a pledge for the Columbian Public School Celebration, Bellamy decided to move beyond Balch's simplistic formula in favor of a pledge that delivered a sense of U.S. history. In August 1891, Bellamy undertook the writing of the pledge, asking himself, "What of our purpose as a Nation?" Bellamy was tempted to use the "historic slogan of the French Revolution which meant so much to Jefferson and his friends, 'Liberty. Equality, Fraternity.'" He grappled with whether or not the nation was prepared to move beyond a philosophy of individualism, and in the end settled for the final line, "with liberty and justice for all." This way, Bellamy reasoned, the pledge would be ideologically "acceptable to either an individualist or a socialistic state," leaving the option open for future generations to decide. Only two hours after beginning his task, the Christian socialist and muckraker emerged from his office with the text for what would become the nation's official Pledge of Allegiance.[9]

With only eight months left to organize the Columbian Public School Celebration, Bellamy put his advertising skills to work. First, the promotional department for the Celebration devised slogans that used simple words, what we would call "sound-bites." Celebration organizers also launched a full-scale letter-writing campaign, aimed at every type of press, in hopes of generating coverage for the campaign. But more needed to be done to move beyond the mainstream press. In order to create news stories, meetings with elected officials seeking the Celebration's endorsement were turned into interviews about the officials' opinions on patriotism. The promotional department then took the content of these discussions and crafted them into news releases and news items that the American Press Association distributed to small town presses for a modest fee.

The organizing paid off when the National Education Association (NEA) gave the Columbian Public School Celebration its unanimous endorsement. After weeks of lobbying, President Harrison gave his endorsement, and leaders from both houses of Congress passed a joint resolution on June 29, 1892 authorizing the president to proclaim Columbus Day a national public holiday. In less than a month, President Harrison made October 21st a day that would link the "discovery" of America with the schoolhouse flag movement. The Columbian Exposition, not scheduled to officially open until May 1893, moved its dedication ceremonies up to October 1892 to coincide with the four hundredth anniversary of Columbus's "discovery of the New World." Tens of thousands of visitors came to Chicago for the dedication ceremonies and millions more read about it in the news.

During the first day of the exposition, people's attention shifted from the dizzying array of products and industrial wonders to masses of patriotic youth. Chicago took the lead in carrying out the flag exercises that would be repeated across the country. By the end of Columbus Day in

1892, millions of schoolchildren had participated in the first nationally orchestrated day devoted to raising and saluting the flag. Whereas only four years earlier the flag had seldom been flown over schoolhouses, more than 100,000 schools now raised the flag. The public school proved to be one of the most important institutions for political socialization in the last half of the nineteenth century.

However, what it meant to pledge allegiance to the flag remained an open question. The pledge was flexible enough to be seen by some as a way to stress the principles of justice and liberty, while others emphasized its capacity to promote military discipline and obedience to authority. In the wake of the Spanish-American War, state-sanctioned rituals of patriotism became even more common. In New York, soon after the war was declared in April 1898, the legislature instructed the state superintendent of public instruction to institute the pledging of allegiance at the beginning of each school day. Daily rituals aimed at reaching children's hearts were reinforced with new civic curricula to secure their minds with heroic images of virile soldiers and the notion of dying honorably for one's country.

Debates about which textbooks to use in the schools turned into a full-scale cultural battle between organized Confederate veterans and northern publishers. The first area of contention centered on each side's insistence that its interpretation of the Civil War be taught to succeeding generations. Through the 1890s, GAR veterans vigorously demanded that it be made clear that the South's withdrawal from the Union represented treason. Southern authors, in turn, insisted on depicting the war as a heroic struggle for constitutional freedom in which Confederate soldiers fought for what they believed to be right. The growth of public education lent added urgency to the textbook debates. Before 1860 only six states had required the study of history, but after the Civil War numerous states passed legislation aimed at regulating textbooks, and by 1900 twenty-three states required the study of history. Negotiation of a mutually acceptable interpretation of the Civil War did not begin to emerge until professional historians at the turn of the century sought a consensus around a "usable past." Most southern historians grudgingly accepted the GAR's demand that the unconstitutionality of secession be recognized. Northern historians, while maintaining a pro-Union view, were increasingly influence by Social Darwinism and found common ground with their White southern colleagues in a shared racism.

Within the emerging historical profession, Woodrow Wilson led the revision of Civil War history. In *A History of the American People,* Wilson eliminated the role of Black Union soldiers and their proven patriotism altogether, and instead wrote about the "extraordinary devotion and heroism" of men from both armies who shared the "same race and breeding." Taking the view that Reconstruction was a tragic aberration, Wilson describes the early Ku Klux Klan as "frolicking comrades" and titled his chapter on the end of Reconstruction "Return to Normal Conditions."[10] It would not be until the 1930s that these kinds of patently racist reinterpretations of the Civil War and Reconstruction would be significantly challenged. W.E. B. Du Bois condemned the degeneration of history into "lies agreed upon" and argued that, rather than Black failure, White fear of Black success had fueled reaction and led to Reconstruction's defeat.[11]

During World War I, anti-immigrant prejudices led to increasingly virulent attacks on so-called "hyphenated" Americans believed to be harboring dual-allegiances. As the war continued in Europe, nationalists upped their demands for national conformity and made the daily recitation of the Pledge of Allegiance by every public school student the normative expectation. In Chicago in 1916, a young African American student was arrested because he refused to respect what he saw as a symbol of Jim Crow and lynching. "I am willing to salute the flag," Hubert Eaves explained, "as the flag salutes me." The *Chicago Defender* broadcasted the story in bold headlines: "Youngster, Eleven Years Old, Starts New Philosophy of American Patriotism."[12]

At the other end of the political spectrum, militant nationalists who had failed to institutionalize military drilling in the public schools at the turn of the century, succeeded during World War I in the creation of a masculine culture of order and discipline within the Boy Scouts. Trained to express an unquestioning and jingoistic allegiance, Boy Scout troops from across the country joined the Americanization campaign and helped to spread the slogan "One country, one language, one flag" in their words and actions.

Determined to demonstrate their loyalty, immigrant groups held massive rallies. In 1918, nearly 100,000 foreign-born men, women, and children staged one of the most spectacular celebrations of Independence Day in Philadelphia's history. Representing more than thirty nationalities, participants assembled at Independence Hall and pledged an oath of "allegiance to the country of their adoption."[13] But despite such patriotic displays, demand for cultural conformity grew more strident and charges of un-Americanism were used against anyone who deviated from mainstream wartime politics. German Americans came under intense attacks for not sufficiently changing their cultural traditions. In an atmosphere of wartime xenophobia, towns banned German books from libraries, stopped the teaching of German in the public schools, and destroyed the German-language presses. By the end of World War I, Americanizers had effectively eradicated German-American culture. In the war's aftermath, the American Legion and the DAR succeeded in changing the Pledge's words "my Flag" to "the Flag of the United States of America" in order to ensure that immigrants could not use the pledge to swear a secret loyalty to another country.

Between the world wars, intolerant patriots persecuted thousands of Jehovah's Witnesses and insured that their children were expelled from schools for refusing to salute the flag. What had begun in 1892 as an attempt to encourage loyalty to the nation "with liberty and justice for all" devolved into the suppression of dissent and unquestioning homage to the flag. In 1943, the Supreme Court ruled that an obligatory loyalty oath was unconstitutional; the law sided with any student who refused to participate in patriotic or religious rituals. But throughout the Pledge's history it has taken courageous students of resolute convictions to cross the blurred line between voluntary and compulsory participation. The Pledge remained the same until Flag Day 1954, when President Eisenhower approved the addition of the constitutionally questionable phrase "under God" to differentiate the United States from the Soviet Union, its godless Cold War antagonist. At the time, President Eisenhower said, "From this day forward, the millions of our schoolchildren will daily proclaim in every city and town, every village and rural schoolhouse, the dedication of our nation and our people to the Almighty."[14]

After the Vietnam War and before September 11, some schools had begun to slowly redefine patriotism more inclusively to address the needs of a multiethnic, polyglot population living in an increasingly global world. Today, as misplaced concerns for national security advance a "my country right or wrong" version of patriotism, government officials and policy makers are pressuring schools to return to standardized curriculums that emphasize rote memorization over critical thinking and democratic participation. The historical struggle over whether or not patriotism can coexist with more democratic forms of citizenship continues. Wouldn't our students make a better use of their time debating these questions rather than marching in lock-step loyalty?

Protesters with sign. New York City, August 30, 2004. Photographer: Joel Westheimer. Copyright © 2004 Joel Westheimer.

Patriotism's Secret History

Peter Dreier
and Dick Flacks

Since 9/11, patriotic fervor has revitalized the conventional wisdom that love of country is synonymous with conservatism. Conservatives, we are told, wave the flag. Or wear it on their lapels. Or paste it on their cars. Leftists, by contrast, only scorn it. Or burn it.

But conservatives have never had a monopoly on Old Glory. For example, during the weeks before Bush's invasion of Iraq, the anti-war movement countered with bumper stickers illustrated with an American flag that proclaimed, "Peace Is Patriotic." Indeed, throughout the nation's history, many American radicals and progressive reformers proudly asserted their patriotism. To them, America stood for basic democratic values: economic and social equality, mass participation in politics, free speech and civil liberties, elimination of the second-class citizenship of women and racial minorities, and a welcome mat for the world's oppressed people. The reality of corporate power, right-wing xenophobia, and social injustice has only fueled progressives' allegiance to these principles and their struggle to achieve them. As a symbol of the nation, the flag is not owned by the administration in power, but by the people. We battle over what it means, but *all* Americans—across the political spectrum—have an equal right to claim the flag as their own.

Most Americans—and most educators—are unaware that much of our patriotic culture has been created by writers of decidedly progressive sympathies. Students rarely learn about the origins of many of the songs, poems, and inscriptions that are now considered synonymous with American patriotism.

For example, the Pledge of Allegiance was originally authored and promoted by a leading Christian socialist, Francis Bellamy (cousin of best-selling radical writer Edward Bellamy), who was fired from his Boston ministry for his sermons depicting Jesus as a socialist. Bellamy penned the Pledge of Allegiance in 1892 to celebrate the 400th anniversary of Christopher Columbus's discovery of America. He hoped the pledge and the use of the flag in public schools would promote a moral vision to counter the climate of the Gilded Age, with its robber barons and exploitation of workers. Bellamy intended the line "One nation, indivisible, with liberty and justice for all" to express a more collective and egalitarian vision of America.

Or consider the lines inscribed on the Statue of Liberty: "Give me your tired, your poor/Your huddled masses yearning to breathe free." The author, Emma Lazarus, was a poet of considerable reputation in her day and was a strong supporter of Henry George and his "socialistic" single-tax program. She was also a friend of William Morris, a leading British socialist. Her welcome to the "wretched refuse" of the earth, written in 1883, was an effort to project an inclusive and egalitarian definition of the American Dream.

And there was Katharine Lee Bates, a professor of English at Wellesley College. Bates was an accomplished and published poet whose book *America the Beautiful and Other Poems* includes a sequence of poems expressing outrage at U.S. imperialism in the Philippines. Bates, a member of progressive-reform circles in the Boston area, was concerned about labor rights, urban slums, and women's suffrage. An ardent feminist, for decades she lived with and loved her Wellesley colleague Katharine Coman, an economist and social activist. "America the Beautiful," written in 1893, not only speaks to the beauty of the American continent but also reflects her view that U.S. imperialism undermines the nation's core values of freedom and liberty. The poem's final words—"and crown thy good with brotherhood, from sea to shining sea"—are an appeal for social justice rather than the pursuit of wealth.

During both the Depression and World War II, the fusion of populist, egalitarian, and anti-racist values with patriotic expression reached full flower. Aaron Copland, whose *Fanfare for the Common Man* and *A Lincoln Portrait* are now patriotic musical standards that are regularly performed at major civic events, was a member of a radical composers' collective. In 1939, composer Earl Robinson teamed with lyricist John La Touche to write *Ballad for Americans*, which was performed on the CBS radio network by Paul Robeson, accompanied by chorus and orchestra. This 11-minute cantata provided a musical review of American history, depicted as a struggle between the "nobody who's everybody" and an elite that fails to understand the real, democratic essence of America.

Robeson, at the time one of the best-known performers on the world stage, became, through this work, a voice of America. Broadcasts and recordings of *Ballad for Americans* (by Bing Crosby as well as Robeson) were immensely popular. In the summer of 1940, it was performed at the national conventions of both the Republican and Communist parties. The work soon became a staple in school choral performances, but it was literally ripped out of many public school songbooks after Robinson and Robeson were identified with the radical left and blacklisted during the McCarthy era. Since then, however, *Ballad for Americans* has been periodically revived, notably during the bicentennial celebration in 1976 when a number of pop and country singers performed it in concerts and on TV.

Many Americans consider Woody Guthrie's song "This Land Is Your Land," penned in 1940, to be our unofficial national anthem. Guthrie, a radical, was inspired to write the song as an answer to Irving Berlin's popular "God Bless America," which he thought failed to recognize that it was the "people" to whom America belonged. The words to "This Land Is Your Land" reflect Guthrie's assumption that patriotism, support for the underdog, and class struggle were all of a piece. In this song, Guthrie celebrates America's natural beauty and bounty, but criticizes the country for its failure to share its riches, reflected in the song's last, and least-known, verse:

One bright sunny morning in the shadow of the steeple
By the relief office I saw my people.
As they stood hungry I stood there wondering
If this land was made for you and me.

In the 1940s, left-wing performers like Guthrie, Pete Seeger, the Almanac Singers, Josh White, Burl Ives, Leadbelly, and Robeson created songs to promote the war effort, expressing the passionate fervor of left-wing resistance to fascism. Their songs also expressed the conviction that the fight against fascism had to encompass a struggle to end Jim Crow and achieve economic democracy at home. Indeed, President Franklin Roosevelt's speeches during that period reflect many of the same themes and images. If you add to these songs the scripts of numerous Hollywood war movies and radio plays by some of America's leading writers—some of whom were later blacklisted in the McCarthy era—it becomes clear that popular culture in support of that war was largely the creation of American leftists.

During the 1960s, American progressives continued to seek ways to fuse their love of country with their opposition to the government's policies. The

March on Washington in 1963 gathered at the Lincoln Memorial, where Martin Luther King, Jr. famously quoted the words to "My Country 'Tis of Thee," repeating the phrase "Let freedom ring" eleven times.

Phil Ochs, then part of a new generation of politically conscious singer-songwriters that emerged during the 1960s, wrote an anthem in the Guthrie vein, "The Power and the Glory," that coupled love of country with a strong plea for justice and equality. The words to the chorus echo the sentiments of the anti-Vietnam War movement:

> Here is a land full of power and glory;
> Beauty that words cannot recall;
> Oh her power shall rest on the strength of her freedom
> Her glory shall rest on us all.

One of its stanzas updated Guthrie's combination of outrage and patriotism:

> Yet she's only as rich as the poorest of her poor;
> Only as free as the padlocked prison door;
> Only as strong as our love for this land;
> Only as tall as we stand.

Interestingly, this song later became part of the repertoire of the U.S. Army band.

In 1968, in a famous anti-war speech on the steps of the Capitol, Norman Thomas, the aging leader of the Socialist Party, proclaimed, "I come to cleanse the American flag, not burn it."

In recent decades, Bruce Springsteen has most closely followed in the Guthrie tradition. From "Born in the USA," to his songs about Tom Joad (the militant protagonist in John Steinbeck's *The Grapes of Wrath*), to his anthem about the September 11 tragedy ("Empty Sky"), Springsteen has championed the downtrodden while challenging America to live up to its ideals. Children and adults alike may best know Steve ("Little Stevie") Van Zandt as the guitarist for Bruce Springsteen's E Street Band and, most recently, for his role as Silvio Dante, Tony Soprano's sidekick on *The Sopranos*. But his most enduring legacy should be his love song about America, "I Am a Patriot," including these lyrics:

> I am a patriot,
> and I love my country,
> because my country is all I know.

Wanna be with my family,
people who understand me.
I got no place else to go.
And I ain't no communist,
and I ain't no socialist,
and I ain't no capitalist,
and I ain't no imperialist,
and I ain't no Democrat,
sure ain't no Republican either.
I only know one party,
and that is freedom.

When right-wing critics challenge the patriotism of progressives and liberals, there is no better way to celebrate America than to listen to Bates's, Robinson and Robeson's, Guthrie's, Ochs's, Springsteen's, or Van Zandt's patriotic anthems. And while doing so, maybe wave a flag and remember these songs are also yours.

"Patriotism Starts at Home." Artist: Steven Dana. Copyright
© 2001 by Steven Dana Collage on paper. Library of Congress Prints and Photographs Division, Exit Art's "Reactions"
Exhibition Collection [LC-DIG-ppmsca-01692].

Chapter 13

Politics and Patriotism in Education

Joel Westheimer

Living now here but for fortune
Placed by fate's mysterious schemes
Who'd believe that we're the ones asked
To try to rekindle the patriot's dream

—Arlo Guthrie, "Patriot's Dream," 1976

In November of 2001, less than two months after the terrorist attacks on the World Trade Center, Nebraska's state board of education approved a patriotism bill specifying content for the high school social studies curriculum in accordance with the state's 1949 statute—the Nebraska Americanism law. Social studies, the bill read, should include "instruction in . . . the superiority of the U.S. form of government, the dangers of communism and similar ideologies, the duties of citizenship, and appropriate patriotic exercises." The board further specified that middle school instruction "should instill a love of country" and that the social studies curriculum should include "exploits and deeds of American heroes, singing patriotic songs, memorizing the 'Star Spangled Banner' and 'America,' and reverence for the flag."[1]

Nebraska was not alone. Within a few months, more than two dozen state legislatures introduced new bills or resurrected old ones aimed at either encouraging or mandating patriotic exercises for all students in schools. Seventeen states enacted new pledge laws or amended policies in the 2002–03 legislative sessions alone.[2] Since then more than a dozen additional states have signed on as well. Twenty-five states now require the pledge to be recited daily during the school day, and thirty-five require time to be set aside in school for the pledge.

The federal role in encouraging patriotic passion has been significant as well. On October 12, 2001, the White House, in collaboration with the politically conservative private group Celebration U.S.A., called on the nation's 52 million schoolchildren to take part in a mass recitation of the Pledge of Allegiance. Four days later, the U.S. House of Representatives passed a resolution (404–0) urging schools to display the words "God Bless America" in an effort to reinforce national pride. In 2002, six months before the Iraq War, the federal government announced a new set of history and civic education initiatives aimed squarely at cementing national identity and pride. These initiatives, President George W. Bush declared, would "improve students' knowledge of American history, increase their civic involvement, and deepen their love for our great country." To engender a sense of patriotism in young Americans, we must, Bush emphasized, teach them that "America is a force for good in the world, bringing hope and freedom to other people."[3] The 2005 federal budget allocates $120 million to grants that support the teaching of "traditional American History." In addition, a campaign by the National Endowment for the Humanities seeks to fund the celebration of traditional "American heroes."

The drive to engage students in patriotic instruction shows no sign of abating and, in fact, may be taking on new fervor. These efforts share at least two characteristics. First, as I detail below, the form of patriotism being pursued by many school boards, city and state legislatures, and the federal government is often monolithic, reflecting an "America-right-or-wrong" stance—what philosopher Martha Nussbaum warns is "perilously close to jingoism."[4] Many educators have condemned these developments as a legislative assault on democratic values in the school curriculum. Second, few of these initiatives have included teachers or local school administrators in their conception or development. The direction has come from on high—from the U.S. Department of Education, from local and state boards of education, and from politicians.

But the grassroots response has been far more complex. At the level of the classroom and the school, the efforts of individual teachers, students, principals, and community organizations paint a broad array of curricular responses to the calls for patriotic education. Many teachers and administrators have implemented mandatory policies, shunned controversy, and reinforced the America-is-righteous-in-her-cause message, just as the Bush Administration and politically conservative commentators want them to. However, terrorism, war, and the threat of fundamentalist intolerance have sparked other educators' commitments to teaching for democratic citizenship, the kind of citizenship that recognizes ambiguity and conflict, that sees human conditions and aspirations as complex and contested, and that embraces debate and deliberation as a cornerstone of patriotism and civic education. In the nation's classrooms, patriotism is politically contested terrain.

What Is Patriotism?

It has often been said that the Inuit have many words to describe snow because one would be wholly inadequate to capture accurately the variety of frozen precipitation. Like snow, patriotism is a more nuanced idea than is immediately apparent. Political scientists, sociologists, and educators would do well to expand the roster of words used to describe the many attitudes, beliefs, and actions that are now called "patriotism." So before we can talk about the politics of patriotism in schools, it makes sense to get clear on at least a few definitions.

Although it is beyond the scope of this essay to delve deeply into the many forms of patriotic attitudes and actions, two umbrella categories of patriotism are worth brief exploration. Each is relevant to debates over curriculum and school policy, and each represents a political position that has implications for what students learn about patriotism, civic engagement, and democracy. I will be calling these two manifestations of patriotism *authoritarian patriotism* and *democratic patriotism,* and their distinctive characteristics are displayed in the table on the next page.

Authoritarian Patriotism

In a democracy, political scientist Douglas Lummis argues, patriotism reflects the love that brings a people together rather than the misguided love of institutions that dominate them. "Authoritarian patriotism," he notes, "is a resigning of one's will, right of choice, and need to understand to the authority; its emotional base is gratitude for having been liberated from the burden of democratic responsibility."[5] Authoritarian patriotism asks for unquestioning loyalty to a cause determined by a centralized leader or leading group. In his 1966 book, *Freedom and Order,* historian Henry Steele Commager observed, "Men in authority will always think that criticism of their policies is dangerous. They will always equate their policies with patriotism, and find criticism subversive."[6] Authoritarian patriotism demands allegiance to the government's cause and therefore opposes dissent.[7]

Schools have a long history of implication in projects of authoritarian forms of patriotism. In Chapter 12 of this book, Cecilia O'Leary pointed out that schools are often enlisted to encourage students' support of national and foreign policies as well as to promote the Americanization of immigrants. During wartime, in particular, schools tend to adopt an unquestioning stance towards citizenship. As Stephan Brumberg details in his portrayal of New York City Schools' participation in fostering patriotism during World War I, when the United States went to war, so too did its public schools.[8]

The Politics of Patriotism

	Authoritarian Patriotism	**Democratic Patriotism**
Ideology	Belief that one's country is inherently superior to others.	Belief that a nation's ideals are worthy of admiration and respect.
	Primary allegiance to land, birthright, legal citizenship, and government's cause.	Primary allegiance to the set of principles that underlie democracy.
	Non-questioning loyalty.	Questioning, critical, deliberative.
	Follow leaders reflexively, support them unconditionally.	Care for the people of society based on principles such as liberty, justice.
	Blind to shortcomings and social discord within nation.	Outspoken in condemnation of shortcomings, especially within nation.
	Conformist; dissent seen as dangerous and destabilizing.	Respectful, even encouraging, of dissent.
Slogans	My country, right or wrong.	Dissent is patriotic.
	America: Love it or leave it.	You have the right to *not* remain silent.
Historical Example	McCarthy Era House Un-American Activities Committee (HUAC) proceedings, which reinforced the idea that dissenting views are anti-American and unpatriotic.	The fiercely patriotic testimony of Paul Robeson, Pete Seeger, and others before HUAC admonishing the committee for straying from American principles of democracy and justice.
Contemporary Example	Equating opposition to the war in Iraq with hatred of America or support for terrorism.	Reinforcing American principles of equality, justice, tolerance, and civil liberties, especially during national times of crisis.

For example, immediately following the declaration of war, the New York City Board of Education moved to ensure that all teachers demonstrated "unqualified allegiance" to administration policies by signing the following statement:

> We, the undersigned teachers in the public schools of the City of New York, declare our unqualified allegiance to the government of the United States of America, and pledge ourselves by word and example to teach and impress upon our pupils the duty of loyal obedience and patriotic service as the highest ideal of American citizenship.[9]

Loyal obedience, to be sure, left little room for dissent or debate about foreign policy. More significantly for schools, however, the educational implications were clear: A patriotic citizen is one who does not question or critically explore government policy.

To say that authoritarian patriotism comes only from the ruling authority would be too simplistic. The social psychology of authoritarian patriotism (especially in a democracy) depends on a deliberate and complicit populace. Following September 11, an abundance of American flags and bumper stickers suddenly sprouted in virtually every city, suburb, town, and rural district in the country. While the flags signaled understandable solidarity in a time of crisis, other public expressions of national pride carried more worrisome messages. Fiercely nationalistic and jingoistic sentiments could be seen and heard on bumper stickers, news broadcasts, and television, as well as in politics. Schools were no exception, and students soon witnessed adults showcasing authoritarian responses to issues of enormous democratic importance.[10]

For example, in 2004 more than 10,000 high schools, community colleges, and public libraries were mailed a free video called "Patriotism and You" by the Washington, D.C.–based group Committee for Citizen Awareness. The group boasts that the video has now been seen by 30 million children and adults nationwide. Teacher Bill Priest of Rock Bridge, Maryland, showed the video to his class as "an example of propaganda of a sort."[11] Statements such as "Patriotism is respecting authority" and "We should manifest a unity of philosophy, especially in times of war" pervade the video. Priest wondered why nobody in the film talks about the right to express patriotic dissent. As this video and dozens of other recent initiatives that aim to teach patriotism illustrate, the primary characteristic of authoritarian patriotism is disdain for views that deviate from an official "patriotic" stance. And proponents of an authoritarian kind of patriotism have once again looked to the schools to help deliver a unified message and have sought to punish educators who allow or offer dissenting perspectives.

Democratic Patriotism

In a National Public Radio show titled "Teaching Patriotism in Time of War," social historian Howard Zinn eloquently described a possible counterstance to authoritarian patriotism. "Patriotism," he said, "means being true and loyal—not to the government, but to the principles which underlie democracy."[12] Democratic patriotism aims to remain true to these principles. A few historical examples illustrate this position.

In 1950, Senator Margaret Chase Smith (R-Me.) was the first member of Congress to publicly confront Senator Joseph McCarthy (R-Wis.). She prepared a Declaration of Conscience urging her fellow senators to protect individual liberties and the ideals of freedom and democracy on which the United States was founded. As she presented the declaration, Senator Smith said the following:

> Those of us who shout the loudest about Americanism are all too frequently those who . . . ignore some of the basic principles of Americanism—the right to criticize, the right to hold unpopular beliefs, the right to protest, the right of independent thought.[13]

Many educators, policy makers, and ordinary citizens have embraced a vision of patriotism that reflects these ideals about democracy and the duties of democratic citizens. When he sang Woodie Guthrie's "This Land Is Your Land," Pete Seeger expressed many patriotic sentiments about the United States, but when he appeared before McCarthy's House Un-American Activities Committee (HUAC), he noted:

> I have never done anything of any conspiratorial nature, and I resent very much and very deeply the implication . . . that in some way because my opinions may be different from yours . . . I am any less of an American than anybody else. I love my country very deeply.[14]

African American actor, performer, and All-American football player Paul Robeson addressed HUAC in even starker terms: "You gentlemen . . . are the non-patriots, and you are the un-Americans, and you ought to be ashamed of yourselves."[15]

Protest sign. New York City, August 30, 2004. Photographer: Joel Westheimer. Copyright ©
2004 Joel Westheimer.

More recently, some citizens agree with former Attorney General John
Ashcroft's admonition that anyone who criticizes the government is giving "ammunition to America's enemies" (a notably authoritarian-patriotic
position). Others see things differently: Dissent is important and, as a popular march placard indicates, in a democratic nation "Protest Is Patriotic."
William Sloane Coffin captures the sentiments of many who wonder about
Ashcroft's thinking and the threat to a democratic form of patriotism that
it represents: "Today, our danger may lie in becoming more concerned
with defense than with having things worth defending."[16] Another look
into history reveals a democratic vision of patriotism as well. Although millions of schoolchildren recite the Pledge of Allegiance every day, far fewer
know much about its author. Francis Bellamy, author of the original 1892
pledge (which did not contain any reference to "God"), was highly critical of many trends of late-nineteenth-century American life, most notably
unrestrained capitalism and growing individualism. He wanted America
to reflect basic democratic values, such as equality of opportunity, and he
worked openly to have his country live up to its democratic ideals.

Was Bellamy patriotic? Of course, but his was not patriotism of the authoritarian kind. Indeed, many of America's national icons shared a democratic vision of patriotism. For instance, Emma Lazarus wrote the poem that became the inscription on the base of the Statue of Liberty: "Give me your tired, your poor / Your huddled masses yearning to breathe free." Katharine Lee Bates, an English professor and poet at Wellesley College, wrote the lyrics to "America the Beautiful," including the words "America! America! God mend thine every flaw!" Bellamy, Lazarus, Bates, and many like-minded reformers throughout America's history asserted their patriotism by strongly proclaiming their beliefs in democratic values such as free speech, civil liberties, greater participation in politics, and social and economic equality.[17] In particular, all echo the quintessentially American belief in critique. A recent *Boston Globe* editorial in honor of the Fourth of July noted that we are a nation "born in a challenge to authority."[18] Indeed, many of the founding fathers foresaw the importance of such challenges and the courage required of citizens to live up to this awesome expectation. Abraham Lincoln, for example, observed that "To sin by silence when they should protest, makes cowards of human beings."Caring about the substantive values that underlie American democracy is the hallmark of democratic patriotism.

This does not mean that democratic patriots leave no room for symbolic displays of support and solidarity. Few would argue with the power of symbols. The authors and composers mentioned above created the very symbols of American patriotism on which proponents of authoritarian patriotism rely. But democratic patriotism seeks to ensure that "liberty and justice for all" serves not only as a slogan for America but also as a guiding principle for policies, programs, and laws that affect Americans. To be a democratic patriot, then, one must be committed not only to the nation, its symbols, and its political leaders, but also to each of its citizens and their welfare. "This land is your land, this land is my land," "Life, liberty, and the pursuit of happiness," "Crown thy good with brotherhood"—for democratic patriots, these visions represent the ideal America, one worth working toward openly, reflectively, and passionately.

Increasing Authoritarian Patriotism in Schools

I have already detailed several district, state, and federal campaigns to promote one particular view of American history, one narrow view of

U.S. involvement in the wars in Iraq and Afghanistan, and so on. There are others. Hundreds of schools, for example, now use the Library of Congress's new "Courage, Patriotism, Community" website. Advertised widely among educators, this website was founded "in celebration of the American spirit" and includes "patriotic melodies" and "stories from the Veterans History Project."[19] Despite a few prominently posted questions—such as "Does patriotism mean displaying the flag or practicing dissent or both?"—there is little material on the site that lends anything but a pro-war, America-can-do-no-wrong vision of patriotism. Similarly, the Fordham Foundation produced a set of resources for teaching patriotism called *Terrorists, Despots, and Democracy: What Our Children Need to Know*, which, under the guise of teaching "indisputable facts," presents storybook tales of "good" and "evil" in the world. But the smaller stories—those taking place in the nation's classrooms and individual schools—might portray more tangible causes for concern.

In New Mexico, five teachers were recently suspended or disciplined for promoting discussion among students about the Iraq War and for expressing, among a range of views, antiwar sentiments. One teacher refused to remove art posters created by students that reflected their views on the war and was suspended without pay. Alan Cooper, a teacher from Albuquerque, was suspended for refusing to remove student-designed posters that his principal labeled "not sufficiently pro-war." Two other teachers, Rio Grande High School's Carmelita Roybal and Albuquerque High School's Ken Tabish, posted signs about the war, at least one of which opposed military action. And a teacher at Highland Hills School was placed on administrative leave because she refused to remove a flier from her wall advertising a peace rally. Roybal and Tabish were suspended, and all of the teachers in these cases were docked two to four days' pay by the Albuquerque Public Schools. Yet, each of these schools posts military recruitment posters and photographs of soldiers in Iraq.[20]

In West Virginia, high school student Katie Sierra was suspended for wearing a t-shirt with a rewritten version of the pledge on it: "I pledge the grievance to the flag," it began, and it ended with, "With liberty and justice for some, not all." Some of her classmates at Sissonville High School told reporters that they intended to give Katie a taste of "West Virginia justice." The school's principal, Forrest Mann, suspended Katie for three days and forbade her to wear the controversial shirt, saying that her behavior was "disrupting school activity." Indeed, at least one of Katie's classmates felt that the shirt disrupted her studies, writing that Katie's actions "greatly saddened me and brought tears to my eyes. I watched as a young lady was permitted to walk down the hallways of Sissonville High School wearing a t-shirt that spoke against American patriotism." No students were disciplined for wearing shirts emblazoned with the American flag.[21]

In Broomfield, Colorado, 17-year-old David Dial was suspended for posting fliers advertising an "International Student Anti-War Day of Action." He noted that it was "just a peaceful protest against the war in Iraq," adding that his suspension was hypocritical given the fanfare at the school surrounding new curricula promoting student civic and political involvement.[22]

But perhaps two of the most interesting cases involve the Patriot Act. In the first case, a Florida teacher handed out to his students copies of a quotation: "They that can give up essential liberty to obtain a little temporary safety deserve neither liberty nor safety." He asked students to interpret this statement in light of current events. (The class had previously studied the circumstances surrounding the internment of Japanese Americans during World War II.) After discussing the implications of the quotation, the teacher asked the class whether anyone knew who wrote it. When none guessed correctly, he showed them an overhead slide that included the name and a drawing of its author: Benjamin Franklin. They then discussed the intentions of the nation's Founders, constitutional protections, and so on. This teacher was supported by parents but was disciplined by the principal for straying from the mandated civics curriculum standards. A letter of reprimand remains in his personnel file.

The second case might be apocryphal, but this story (and many others like it) has been circulating among teachers, professors of education, and concerned parents. I have been unable to find solid documentation, but I include it here to demonstrate the degree to which these stories invoke teachers' and the public's sense that, in the current climate of intimidation, dissent in the context of civic education is subject to repression and regulation. The story goes roughly thus: A New York State high school teacher was reprimanded for having his students examine historical comparisons of crisis times in U.S. history. He introduced students to the Alien and Sedition Acts of 1798 and the Sedition Act of 1918. The earlier acts allowed President John Adams to arrest, imprison, and deport "dangerous" immigrants on suspicion of "treasonable or secret machinations against the government" and to suppress freedom of the press. The more recent act restricted criticism of the government, the Constitution, and the military. Pairing these acts with the text of today's Patriot Act, the teacher asked students to assess the three time periods and argue for the justice or injustice of each law. Several parents complained that he was not encouraging patriotism, and the principal instructed the teacher to discontinue the lesson.

Patriotism as a Substitute for Politics

Much of the rationale behind the cases of teachers being reprimanded in schools rests on the idea that patriotism, especially where public schools are concerned, should remain above partisan politics. Dissent, rather than being viewed as an essential component of democratic deliberation, is seen as a threat to patriotism. Indeed, in this view, politics is something unseemly and best left to mudslinging candidates for public office: Being political is tantamount to devaluing the public good for personal or party gain. Education, in this way of thinking, should not advance politics but rather should reinforce some unified notion of truth that supports—without dissent—officially accepted positions.

For example, Senator Lamar Alexander (R-Tenn.), a former U.S. secretary of education under President Reagan, introduced the American History and Civics Education Act in March 2003 to teach "the key persons, the key events, the key ideas, and the key documents that shape [our] democratic heritage."[23] According to Senator Alexander, this legislation would put civics back in its "rightful place in our schools, so our children can grow up learning what it means to be an American."[24]

These efforts by the Congress and by conservative members of the Bush Administration have been applauded by those who view education primarily as a means of conveying to American youths and young adults a monolithic set of important historical facts combined with a sense of civic unity, duty, and national pride. Reaching back to a 1950s-style understanding of the American past and the workings of American society, Senator Alexander and like-minded politicians suggest that Americans, despite diverse backgrounds and cultures, all share a unified American creed or a common set of beliefs and that these beliefs are easily identifiable. Explicitly borrowing from consensus historian Richard Hofstadter, Senator Alexander believes that "it has been our fate as a nation not to have ideologies but to be one."[25]

Telling students that history has one interpretation (e.g., that the United States is pretty much always right and moral and just in its actions) reflects an approach to teaching love of country that too easily succumbs to authoritarianism. Yet teaching this one unified creed—especially in the wake of the September 11 attacks—is rarely viewed as being political. "Being political" is an accusation most often reserved for exploring views that are unpopular—the kind of views, not surprisingly, that come from critical, reflective, and democratic forms of patriotic teaching.

In many schools throughout the United States, this tendency to cast patriotism and politics as opposites runs especially deep. So strong are the anti-politics politics of schooling that even mundane efforts at teaching for democratic understandings, efforts that aim to encourage discussion around controversial topics, for example, are often deemed indoctrination. After a teacher allowed students at a school assembly to recite an antiwar poem they had written, one parent argued in a parents' forum, "We live in the USA, so singing a patriotic song isn't inappropriate. But politics has no place in the school."[26]

Similarly, after the National Education Association developed lesson plans about the events of September 11, politicians, policy makers, and some parents worried that the curriculum—titled "Tolerance in Times of Trial"—did not paint a positive enough picture of U.S. involvement in world affairs. Conservative political commentator and talk show host Laura Ingraham attacked the curriculum as indoctrination, warning that the lessons encouraged students to "discuss instances of American intolerance." Curricular materials developed by the Los Angeles-based Center for Civic Education that included discussion of controversial issues in multiculturalism, diversity, and protection of the environment drew similar criticism. And we are already seeing evidence of attacks on curriculum that examines the social, economic, and political implications of Hurricane Katrina.[27]

Politics Is Not a Dirty Word

But politics is not a four-letter word. Patriotism, if it is to reflect democratic ideals, needs politics. In a lecture on citizenship in the twenty-first century, Harry Boyte, co-director of the University of Minnesota's Center for Democracy and Citizenship, argued that politics is the way people with different values and from different backgrounds can "work together to solve problems and create common things of value."[28] In this view, politics is the process by which citizens with varied interests and opinions negotiate differences and clarify places where values conflict. Boyte cited *In Defense of Politics* by Bernard Crick in calling politics "a great and civilizing activity." For Boyte, accepting the importance of politics is to strive for deliberation and a plurality of views rather than a unified perspective on history, foreign policy, or domestic affairs. For those seeking to instill democratic patriotism, being political means embracing the kind of controversy and ideological sparring that is the engine of progress in a democracy and that gives education social meaning. The idea that "bringing politics into it" (now said disdainfully) is a pedagogically questionable act is, perhaps, the biggest threat to engaging students in discussions about what it means to be patriotic in a democratic nation.

It is precisely this aspect of politics with which educators wrestle. While many, like Boyte, see education as an opportunity to teach the critical and deliberative skills that are consistent with democratic patriotism and enable students to participate effectively in contentious public debates, others are uncomfortable with approaches to teaching that encourage dissent and critique of current policies. For example, the events of the Iraq War and the ongoing "reconstruction" have led policy makers and educators who favor authoritarian patriotism to prefer celebrating what President Bush has repeatedly called "the rightness of our cause."

The classroom dramas described above illustrate the intensity with which battles over controversial issues in the classroom can be waged. Yet there are dozens, perhaps hundreds, of curricular efforts that deliberately engage politics as a healthy embodiment of the diversity of opinions, motivations, and goals that make up democratic patriotism.

Teaching Democratic Patriotism

Many valuable debates about patriotism do not take as their starting point the question "Should patriotic instruction be apolitical or political, obedient or critical?" Rather, they begin with questions such as "Whose politics do these education programs reflect and why?" or "Which citizens benefit from particular policies and programs and which do not?" Such approaches aim toward democratic patriotism.

Initiatives that emphasize a vision of democratic patriotism tend to come from nongovernmental education organizations, small groups of curriculum writers, and individual teachers rather than from textbook companies or district, state, and federal education departments. As Operation Iraqi Freedom began in March 2003, Oregon teacher Sandra Childs asked students to consider the relationship between patriotism and the First Amendment, using the words of Senator John McCain (R-Ariz.) as a starting point: "The time for debate is over." A school in Chicago reorganized its interdisciplinary curriculum around the theme of competing national concerns for civil liberties and safety. Some efforts encompass an entire school as the vision is infused into nearly every aspect of the curriculum, extracurricular activities, and even the physical space. I briefly describe two such programs here, but I encourage readers to search out others.[29]

El Puente Academy for Peace and Justice

The El Puente Academy for Peace and Justice is located in the Williamsburg neighborhood of Brooklyn, New York.[30] It was established in 1993 by El Puente ("The Bridge"), a community organization, in partnership with the New York City Board of Education. The school is academically successful. It has a 90% graduation rate in an area where schools usually see 50% of their students graduate in four years. But what makes the school especially compelling is its firm commitment to reverse the cycles of poverty and violence for all community residents. It teaches love of country by teaching caring for the country's inhabitants. The curriculum, organization, and staff embody a living vision of democratic patriotism at work.

One of the concerns of both El Puente, the organization, and El Puente, the academy, is the health of the community. Williamsburg and nearby Bushwick are called the "lead belt" and the "asthma belt" by public health researchers. As Héctor Calderón, El Puente's principal, declares, "Williamsburg reads like a 'Who's Who of Environmental Hazards.'"[31] Students at El Puente study these toxic presences not only because they are concerned about the health of the natural environment, but also because these hazards directly affect the health of the community. Science and math classes survey the community in order to chart levels of asthma and provide extra services to those families affected by the disease. One year, students and staff became intrigued when they found that Puerto Ricans had a higher incidence of asthma than Dominicans. They wondered if Dominicans had natural remedies not used by Puerto Ricans. Their report became the first by a community organization to be published in a medical journal. Another group of students successfully battled against a proposed 55-story incinerator that was to be built in the neighborhood (which is already burdened with a low-level nuclear waste disposal plant, a nuclear power plant, and an underground oil spill). While math and science classes measured and graphed levels of toxicity, a humanities class produced a documentary on their findings.

That all men (and women) are created equal is indeed a truth that is self-evident to these urban students. That all members of their community are entitled to a healthy life—as well as liberty and the pursuit of happiness—is also self-evident in the academy curriculum. For El Puente students, patriotism means love of American ideals, whether that entails supporting current social and economic policies or critiquing them. El Puente principal Calderón asserts that "Patriotism should be based on deep reflection and profound understanding of the values that tie us as a community."[32]

La Escuela Fratney Two-Way Bilingual Elementary School

A spiral notebook labeled "Questions That We Have" is always accessible in Bob Peterson's elementary class. Peterson is one of many teachers at La Escuela Fratney, which opened in Milwaukee in 1988 and is Wisconsin's only two-way bilingual elementary school. All of its 380 students begin their schooling in their dominant language (English or Spanish), and by grade 3, they have begun reading in a second language. Rita Tenorio, teacher and co-founder of Fratney, explains that the school's mission includes preparing students "to play a conscious and active role in society," thereby enabling them to be active citizens who can participate in democratic forums for change and social betterment.

Peterson, who is founding editor of *Rethinking Schools* and the 1995 Wisconsin Elementary Teacher of the Year, placed the notebook prominently at the front of the classroom on September 12, 2001, after a fifth grader pointed out the window and asked, "What would you do if terrorists were outside our school and tried to bomb us?" Peterson's notebook, relatively ordinary in ordinary times, appeared extraordinary at a time when unreflective patriotic gestures commonly associated with authoritarian patriotism abounded. Recall President Bush's admonition to both the world and to U.S. citizens that "you are either with us or you are with the terrorists" or White House Press Secretary Ari Fleischer's dire warning to Americans to "watch what they say and watch what they do."[32] It was in these times that Escuela Fratney teachers felt especially compelled to teach the kind of patriotic commitments that reflected such American ideals as freedom of speech, social justice, equality, and the importance of tolerating dissenting opinions.

Using a curriculum Peterson developed for *Rethinking Schools* that is focused on 9/11, terrorism, and democracy, teachers at Escuela Fratney encouraged students to ask tough questions, to explore many varied news sources, and to share their fears, hopes, and dreams about America. For example, after reading a poem by Lucille Clifton titled "We and They," students responded through stories, poems, and discussion. One student wrote her own poem, "We Are from America," about what ordinary citizens of the United States think about ordinary citizens of Afghanistan and vice versa: "We are from America / they are from Afghanistan / We are rich to them / they are poor to us," and so on. Another class discussed the history and meaning of the Pledge of Allegiance. Through exercises like these, students learn a kind of patriotism that gives space to thoughtful reflection and that honors the ideals of democracy on which the United States was founded. Ironically, Peterson's curriculum may do more to teach students "traditional" history and the Founding Fathers' ideals than those lessons suggested by Lamar Alexander and his colleagues. Peterson's curriculum won the Clarke Center's national competition for innovative ways to teach 9/11 in the classroom (elementary division). Classroom activities and assignments at La Escuela demonstrate that teaching a commitment to democratic ideals is not facile. La Escuela Fratney puts its mission into practice by encouraging teaching that makes clear the connections between students' lives and the outside world, between their communities and the larger national community, and between the concerns of our nation and the global concerns of all nations.

Many other educators pursue similar aims. Nel Noddings, for example, would like to see school teachers help students explore and discuss the psychology of war, varying motivations for battle, the conflicting meanings of patriotism, an understanding of propaganda, and compassion for "the enemy."[34] Stephen Thornton argues that students should gain an understanding of internationalism and the ways that a focus on the peoples of other nations can help us to strengthen connections to our own.[35] Herbert Kohl calls for students to re-examine some of our favorite historical "stories" in an effort at democratic renewal of the importance of dissent and social movements. As the resources section at the end of this book reveals, there are a rich array of resources available to those educators who aim to teach a democratic vision of patriotism to their students.[36]

Conclusion

In June 2006, the Florida Education Omnibus Bill (H.B. 7087e3) enacted legislation specifying that "American history shall be viewed as factual, not constructed, shall be viewed as knowable, teachable, and testable. . . . The history of the United States shall be taught as general history" (see www.flsenate.gov). This most recent addition to the growing body of politics aimed at legislating mindless adherence to an "official story" has been widely derided by historians and educators alike. But the impact of these laws should not be underestimated.

There is evidence that many students are learning the lessons of authoritarian patriotism well. A poll of California high school students found that 43% of seniors, having completed courses in U.S. history and U.S. government, either agreed with or were neutral toward the statement "It is un-American to criticize this country" (see Chapter 9 of this book, "Is Patriotism Good for Democracy?"). Another poll shows that a majority of students nationwide have some ideals consistent with democratic patriotism (and this is probably due in no small part to the efforts of individual teachers and administrators), but a sizable minority (28%) believe that those who attend a protest against U.S. military involvement in Iraq are "unpatriotic."[37]

In a climate of increasingly authoritarian patriotism, dissent grows ever more scarce. But a democratic public is best served by a democratic form of patriotism. To ensure the strength of our democratic institutions and to foster a democratic patriotism that is loyal to the American ideals of equality, compassion, and justice, adults must struggle with difficult policy debates in all available democratic arenas. Trying to forge a national consensus in any other way or on any other grounds (especially through attempts at authoritarian patriotism) is what leads to troubled waters. And students need to learn about these contentious debates with which adults struggle and prepare to take up their parts in them. To serve the public interest in democracy and to reinforce a democratic kind of patriotism, educators will need to embrace, rather than deny, controversy.

Langston Hughes, in his 1936 poem "Let America Be America Again," speaks of the gap between a rhetorical patriotism rooted only in symbolic gestures and love of the American ideals of liberty and equality:

> O, let my land be a land where Liberty
> Is crowned with no false patriotic wreath,
> But opportunity is real, and life is free,
> Equality is in the air we breathe.

That's the best kind of patriotism we can hope for.

Poetry and Patriotism

Maxine Greene

A month or so ago, I was invited to speak at a poetry slam conducted by Urban Poets, a group of teenage poets who perform their own works with the most passionate intensity. Some poems are profoundly personal; some, expressions of outrage at injustices and discrimination; others, protests against "school" and its unfairness or irrelevance to their lives; still others, outcries against the war in Iraq and the lies that sustain it.

Should schools be teaching these students to recite the Pledge of Allegiance? Liberty and justice for all? Patriotism? Enforcers of the Patriot Act lurk around libraries; recruiters for the armed services try to seduce high school boys and girls into enlisting. False promises, adult untruths, tests, achievement gaps, the sense of being human resources rather than singular persons and participants in a community. And allegiance to what? To the United States of America? To the President and his cronies?

I had trouble deciding what to say to that young generation whose world differed so much from my own. So I turned to Walt Whitman and a poem he wrote, "Poets to Come," telling them it was up to them to change the world. Like many artists, Whitman spoke of imagination and unrealized possibility. He knew about oppression and poverty and corruption, the rot beginning to erode democracy. But in his poetry and in his Democratic Vistas, he was asking for the kind of unease that would ward off complacency and compliance, that would awaken people enough to move them to act, to see democracy as an open possibility, always in the future, not as an achievement in the past.

This view may be the stuff of an emancipatory curriculum, something worth our teenagers' allegiance. Patriotism—forever uncertain, forever in the making—may become a dimension of learning, directed toward what might be, what should be, rather than toward the fixed, the unshakable "is." I apologized to the young people for the shape of the world we were leaving to them and urged them to continue imagining and making their voices audible, to continue creating occasions for hope.

Patriotism by the Numbers

Cindy Sheehan

I receive a lot of e-mail. Just the other day, I received this message:

> Dear Ms. Sheehan,
> My cousin, "brave soldier," 30, originally of Indiana, was one of the five U.S. soldiers killed on Saturday, October 15th—Iraq's "peaceful day." He is survived by his wife, his two children, his parents, his sister, our grandma, his aunt, his two uncles, and his two cousins. We are currently awaiting confirmation per DNA identification.
> I thank you for taking notice. The loss of his life and that of his comrades does not make for a peaceful day—may their souls rest in peace.

And this one came from a "Gold Star" mother:

> How?
> I have so many questions. . . . How do I stop the vulgar pain in my chest? How do I do this? How do I continue to breathe but cannot live? How do I do this? How do I keep my soul in my body? How do I do this? How do I close my eyes wondering if sleep should come but yet knowing if I sleep I will awaken to know this is not a nightmare but my life? How do I do this? How do I love someone with my very being but cannot ever hold him again? How do I do this? How do I go on without that sweet face that brought more joy to my life than I ever deserve—never to be seen by my eyes again? How do I do this? How do I stop the scream that no one hears but me? How do I do this? PLEASE TELL ME . . . how do I live

without my child, my son, my heart, my soul, my joy, my validation to
my life. . . . Please tell me . . . how do I do this? How does the world go
on without Steven . . . how do I do this?

This letter came from a mom whose son was aggressively recruited until
he finally agreed to enlist—then discovered he had a made a big mistake:

> I find that I can't get Jeffrey out of my mind. I can see him at 11
> or 12 years old, jumping in the car when I'd pick him up at a friend's.
> It's so real . . . it's almost like you can reach out and touch him. What
> a world of hell this administration has put us in. One we will live in all
> the rest of our days. . . .

As you read these painful testaments, thousands of American families are
going about their normal lives wondering if a terrible shoe is about to drop.
Will it be their lives that are destroyed today? Or will it be another family
randomly picked by the universe to suffer this violent assault on their homes?
But while these families wait, there is not one member of this Administration, not one member of Congress, not one hate-spewing, right-wing radio
talk-show host who will worry that their darling child may be the next one
killed in a meaningless war. Not one of these supporters of the war has any
idea of the horror of lying awake at night or walking around all day with an
icy-cold stomach because of hearing that soldiers were killed in Iraq today.
Why? Because not one of these supporters of the war has any loved ones in
harm's way—a harm they created or support, either actively or tacitly. And they
support this war in the name of democracy and patriotic duty. The day of the
fraud-ridden constitutional referendum in Iraq, George Bush said: "Democracies are peaceful countries."

If every student in every school learns only one thing about patriotism,
it should be this: Life is precious. We honor our country by holding precious
the life of its youth. Every teacher in every school should convey this message.
If students were to take signs to their congressional offices near them and
demand that each and every member of Congress do everything in his or
her power to bring our precious lifeblood home, these would be profoundly
patriotic acts.

My son Casey had such a bright future ahead of him. Someone asked me
the other day what I miss most about him. I just miss him. I miss everything
about him. I miss his presence on this planet. I miss his naive joy and heart-

breaking hope for the future. I miss his future, and I remember his past with love and pain. We recently passed the sorrowful day when the 2,000th U.S. soldier was killed in Iraq, and by the time you are reading this, there will have been countless more unnecessary deaths. On the day of the 2,000th, I went to D.C. I went to the White House. Our house. I sat on the sidewalk outside of our house and demanded that the war criminals who live and work there bring our troops home.

Our young people are not just numbers. Our young people are confined to early graves because of criminals who should be confined to prison, who are profiting handsomely from the undeclared mess in Iraq. The Iraqi people are even less than numbers. If they are counted or thought of at all, they are very often wrongly counted as "insurgents," when they are so often children and women. More than sixteen young American men and women have lost their lives in Iraq *each week* since the Bush Administration's March 2003 invasion. Some 30 Iraqi civilians are killed each day that the war continues.

If mere numbers will awaken America's true patriotic spirit, then think of the predictions of Donald Rumsfeld and Condoleeza Rice: That this occupation could last a dozen years or more. What number are you comfortable with? One was too much for me.

Fox News coverage of the Republican National Convention. Photo taken in the midst of thousands of people marching up the Avenue of the Americas in New York City to protest the Republican National Convention, August 30, 2004. Photographer: Joel Westheimer. Copyright © 2004 Joel Westheimer.

Resources for Educators

Agenda for Education in a Democracy

Seeks to support young people's participation in a social and political democracy through research and programs that promote democratic citizenship. Includes the Institute for Educational Inquiry and the Center for Educational Renewal: depts.washington.edu/cedren/AED.htm

American Political Science Association—Civic Education Organizations

Extensive online list of civic education organizations: apsanet.org/content_7501.cfm

Campaign for the Civic Mission of Schools

Works with forty coalition partners to bring about changes in state, local, and national policy that promote civic learning and implement the recommendations in the Civic Mission of Schools report: www.civicmissionofschools.org

Campus Compact

Organization representing nine hundred college and university presidents who are committed to the civic purposes of higher education: www.compact.org

Center for Civic Education

Specializes in civic/citizenship education, law-related education, and international educational exchange programs for developing democracies: www.civiced.org

Center for Democracy and Citizenship

Develops citizenship initiatives around the concept of public work: www.publicwork.org

Center for Information and Research on Civic Learning and Engagement (CIRCLE)

Funds and disseminates research on the civic and political engagement of Americans between the ages of fifteen and twenty-five: www.civicyouth.org

Citizenship Education Research Network

Researchers, policy makers, and practitioners interested in citizenship education and research in Canada: www.canada.metropolis.net/research-policy/cern-pub/overview.html

Civic Practices Network

A collaborative and nonpartisan project designed to bring schooling for active citizenship into the information age: www.cpn.org

Civnet

Online resource that promotes civic education all over the world: www.civnet.org

Close-Up Foundation

Works to promote responsible and informed participation in the democratic process through a variety of educational programs for middle and high school students, teachers, and adults. The website describes programs and provides a range of links to resources and organizations: www.closeup.org

Constitutional Rights Foundation (CRF) and the Constitutional Rights Foundation Chicago (CRFC)

Both offer civic education curricula, activities for students, and professional development for teachers: www.crf-usa.org and www.crfc.org

Corporation for National and Community Service

Provides opportunities for community service through Senior Corps, AmeriCorps, and Learn and Serve America. Part of USA Freedom Corps, a White House initiative to foster a culture of citizenship, service, and responsibility: www.nationalservice.org

Democracy.org

Resources for promoting democratic citizenship, character education, and service learning: www.democracy.org

Democratic Dialogue

Promotes international collaborative inquiry into democracy, education, and society. For educators, political scientists, sociologists, philosophers, teachers, policymakers, artists, critics, and the broader public concerned with the ideals, tensions, policies, and practices of education for democracy: www.democraticdialogue.com

Educators for Social Responsibility

Helps educators create safe, caring, respectful, and productive learning environments that foster democratic participation and change. Their New York City chapter's website, www.esrmetro.org/resources.html, includes resources for teachers on a variety of issues, including a number of excellent curriculum examples under the umbrella title "Reflecting on 9/11": www.esrnational.org

El Puente Academy for Peace and Justice

A small learning community high school that emphasizes curricular and extra-curricular activities in the community to strengthen civic engagement and democratic citizenship: http://elpuente.us/

e.thePeople

Digital town hall that "promotes intelligent and diverse discussion and political action": www.e-thepeople.org

Facing History and Ourselves

Offers professional development services, teacher resources, and publications that encourage educators to use history to teach students about "civic responsibility, tolerance, and social action": www.facinghistory.org

Highlander Research and Education Center

Highlander sponsors educational programs and research into community problems, as well as a residential Workshop Center for social change organizations and workers active in the South and internationally. Over the course of its history, Highlander has played important roles in many major political movements, including the Southern labor movements of the 1930s, the Civil Rights Movement of the 1940s–60s, and the Appalachian people's movements of the 1970s–80s: www.highlandercenter.org

Institute for Democracy and Education at Ohio University

Provides teachers, administrators, parents, and students committed to democratic education with a forum for sharing ideas, a support network of people holding similar values, and opportunities for professional development: www.ohiou.edu/ide

Kids Can Make a Difference

School program and detailed curriculum to inspire young people to realize that it is within their power to help eliminate hunger and poverty in their communities, their country, and their world: www.kidscanmakeadifference.org

National Alliance for Civic Education

Selected resources and guidelines for civic education: www.cived.net

National Association of School Psychologists: One Year Later—A 9/11 Memorial
www.nasponline.org/NEAT/911memorial.html

North Carolina Civic Education Consortium
Works with schools, governments, and community organizations to prepare North Carolina's young people to be active, responsible citizens: www.civics.unc.edu

The Political Engagement Project—Carnegie Foundation for the Advancement of Teaching
A collaborative study of twenty-one college and university based programs that strengthen students' political understanding and engagement. The website includes curriculum resources: www.carnegiefoundation.org/PEP

Project 540
Gives students the opportunity to talk about issues that matter to them and to turn these conversations into real change in their schools and communities: www.project540.org

Project Vote Smart
Project Vote Smart is dedicated to providing all Americans with accurate and unbiased information for electoral decision-making: www.vote-smart.org/index.htm

Public Achievement
People of all ages work with others, meet challenges, solve problems, and learn from one another the meaning of citizenship and democracy: publicachievement.org

Public Broadcasting System: America Responds
www.pbs.org/americaresponds/educators.html

Rethinking Schools
Writing, resources, and advocacy for public education reform in the pursuit of equity and social justice. See, especially, lesson plans by Bill Bigelow: www.rethinkingschools.org

Rouge Forum
Meetings and resources for educators, students, and parents interested in teaching and learning for a democratic society: www.pipeline.com/~rgibson/rouge_forum

Social Science Research Council
Provides teaching guides covering a range of issues: globalization, terrorism and democratic values, war, building peace, and fundamentalism: www.ssrc.org/sept11/essays/teaching_resource/tr_guides.htm

Street Law Inc.
Practical, participatory education about law, democracy, and human rights. Street Law features the curriculum Street Law and many other curricular resources for teachers and students: www.streetlaw.org

Teachers First
See their lesson on terrorism and tolerance: www.teachersfirst.com/lessons/terrorism.cfm

Teaching for Change
Provides professional development workshops, publications, parent-empowerment programs, and catalog of K–12 resources for teachers and parents. Focus is on diversity and global citizenship: www.teachingforchange.org

Teaching Tolerance
Founded by the Southern Poverty Law Center, Teaching Tolerance supports the efforts of K–12 teachers and other educators to promote respect for differences and appreciation of diversity: www.tolerance.org

Notes

Dedication page

1. Adapted from the text included in an exhibit at the Canadian War Museum, Ottawa, Ontario.

Introduction

1. See Edward S. Herman, *The Myth of the Liberal Media: An Edward Herman Reader* (New York: Peter Lang, 1999).

2. See, respectively, Martha Nussbaum's notion of cosmopolitan patriotism (drawing on Kant's ideas about patriotism and cosmopolitanism) in M. Nussbaum and J. Cohen, *For Love of Country: Debating the Limits of Patriotism* (Cambridge, MA: Beacon, 1996); Mark Green (Ed.), *What We Stand For: A Program for Progressive Patriotism* (New York: New Market, 2004); and Chapter 13 of this volume.

3. Pew Research Center survey, "The 2004 Political Landscape: Evenly Divided and Increasingly Polarized," November 2003. Available at: people-press.org/dataarchive

4. George Balch, *Methods of Teaching Patriotism in Public Schools* (1890), cited in Cecilia O'Leary, *To Die For: The Paradox of American Patriotism* (Princeton, NJ: Princeton University Press, 1999), p. 175.

5. Katherine D. Blake, "Peace in the Schools," National Education Association Proceedings (Chicago: University of Chicago Press, 1911), pp. 140-46, cited in Susan Zeiger, "The Schoolhouse vs. the Armory: U.S. Teachers and the Campaign Against Militarism in the Schools, 1914–1918," *Journal of Women's History*, Summer 2003, p. 150.

6. Michael Walzer, *Spheres of Justice: A Defense of Pluralism and Equality* (New York: Basic Books, 1984), p. 310.

Chapter 1

1. Cornel West, *Democracy Matters: Winning the Fight Against Imperialism* (New York: Penguin, 2004), p. 171.

2. George Lakoff, *Don't Think of an Elephant: Know Your Values and Frame the Debate* (White River, VT: Chelsea Green, 2004).

3. Ann Coulter, *Treason: Liberal Treachery from the Cold War to the War on Terrorism* (New York: Crown Forum, 2003).

4. See Adrienne D. Dixson, "'Let's Do This!' Black Women Teachers' Politics and Pedagogy," *Urban Education*, 38, 2003, pp. 217-35; and Daniel G. Solorzano, "Critical Race Theory, Race and Gender Micro-aggressions and the Experience of Chicano and Chicana Scholars," *Qualitative Studies in Education*, 11, 1998, pp. 121–136.

5. Michael W. Apple, *Educating the "Right" Way* (London: Falmer, 2001).

Charles Payne Point of View

1. Cited works include: Wallace Terry, *Bloods: An Oral History of the Vietnam War by Black Veterans* (New York: Ballantine, 1985); Charles Moskos, *The American Enlisted Man: The Rank and File in Today's Military* (New York: Russell Sage Foundation, 1970); and Ron Harris, "African-American Youths Are Rejecting Army, Military Says," *St. Louis Post-Dispatch*, 15 March 2005. Downloaded April 2, 2006 from www.commondreams.org/headlines05/0315-08.htm

Chapter 2

1. John Gehring, "Recruiting in Schools, a Priority for Military, Is Targeted By Critics," *Education Week*, 22 June 2005, p. 6.
2. See David Jackson, "Bush Continues to Stump for War Support," *USA Today*, 13 January 2006.
3. See Mahmood Mamdani, *Good Muslim, Bad Muslim: America, the Cold War, and the Roots of Terror* (New York: Doubleday, 2004).
4. James W. Loewen, *Lies My Teacher Told Me: Everything Your American History Textbook Got Wrong* (New York: New Press, 1995), pp. 67–129; and Walker LaFeber, *The American Age: U.S. Foreign Policy at Home and Abroad, 1750 to the Present* (New York: Norton, 1994), pp. 1–125.
5. Mark E. Brandon, "War and the American Constitutional Order," in Mark Tushnet, ed., *The Constitution in Wartime: Beyond Alarmism and Complacency* (Durham, NC: Duke University Press, 2005), p. 11.
6. Andrew J. Bacevich, *The New American Militarism: How Americans Are Seduced by War* (New York: Oxford University Press, 2005), passim.
7. Ariel Dorfman, *Other Septembers, Many Americas: Selected Provocations, 1980–2004* (New York: Seven Stories, 2004), p. 41.
8. Quoted in William B. Whitman, *The Quotable Politician* (Guilford, CT: Lyons, 2003), p. 242.

Delaine Eastin Point of View

1. Quote taken from the electronic edition of John Adams's diaries, published by the Massachusetts Historical Society: www.masshist.org/digitaladams
2. Neil Postman, *The Disappearance of Childhood* (New York: Delacorte, 1982), p. xi.

Chapter 3

1. For a good review of the relevant psychological literature, see Peter Fonagy, *Attachment Theory and Psychoanalysis* (New York: Other Press, 2001).
2. Malcolm Gladwell, "The Cellular Church," *New Yorker*, 12 September 2005, pp. 60–67.
3. Michael Lerner, *The Left Hand of God: Taking Back Our Country from the Religious Right* (San Francisco: Harper, 2006).

James W. Loewen Point of View

1. The first two examples are from the author's research, no published source. The Minnesota reference is commonly available on the web; see, Tom Robertson, "Squaw Lake Resists Name Change," Minnesota Public Radio, April 30, 2001, at: news.minnesota.publicradio.org/features/200104/30_robertsont_squawlake-m

Chapter 5

1. For a more fully developed version of this argument for teaching the debate over Frierean critical pedagogy, see my "Teaching Politically Without Political Correctness," *Radical Teacher*, 58, 2000, 26–30; and my *Beyond the Culture Wars: How Teaching the Conflicts Can Revitalize American Education* (New York: Norton, 1992).
2. Frank Smith, *Joining the Literacy Club: Further Essays into Education* (Portsmouth, NH: Heinemann, 1988), p. 76.

3. John Stuart Mill, "On Liberty," in *Utilitarianism, Liberty, Representative Government* (London: Dent & Sons, 1951), p. 129. For a recent writing textbook based on Mill's dialectical principle, see Gerald Graff and Cathy Birkenstein, *"They Say/I Say": The Moves That Matter in Academic Writing* (New York: Norton, 2006).

Chapter 6

1. L. Brent Bozell, "Media Coverage at Its Best," *Washington Times*, 25 September 2001, p. A-18.

2. Mike Tolson, "Remain Objective Despite War, Rather Tells Texas Journalists," *Houston Chronicle*, 19 March 2002, p. 19.

3. Bill Kovach, "Journalism and Patriotism," talk given to the annual meeting of the Organization of News Ombudsmen, 30 April 2002. Available online at: www.newsombudsmen.org/kovach.html.

4. Russ Baker, "Want to Be a Patriot? Do Your Job," *Columbia Journalism Review*, May 2002, pp. 78–79.

5. Emma Goldman, "Patriotism: A Menace to Liberty," in *Anarchism and Other Essays* (New York: Dover, 1969), pp. 128–129.

6. Randolph Bourne, "War Is the Health of the State," 1918. Available online at http://struggle.ws/hist_texts/warhealthstate1918.html.

7. G. M. Gilbert, *Nuremberg Diary* (New York: Farrar, Straus & Co., 1947), pp. 278–279.

8. Goldman, "Patriotism," pp. 142–143.

9. Leo Tolstoy, "Patriotism and Government." Available online at http://dwardmac.pitzer.edu/Anarchist_Archives/bright/tolstoy/patriotismandgovt.html.

10. http://bari.iww.org/iu120/local/Scribner12.html.

Chapter 8

1. Nina Berman, *Purple Hearts: Back from Iraq* (New York: Trolley, 2004).

2. Kathy Dobie, "AWOL in America," *Harper's*, March 2005, p. 35.

3. David Goodman, "Recruiting the Class of 2005," *Mother Jones*, January/February 2002, pp. 1–8. All information in this paragraph comes from Goodman.

4. ibid., p. 1.

5. Jennifer Wedekind, "The Children's Crusade," *In These Times*, 20 June 2005, pp. 6–7.

6. Goodman, p. 3.

7. Cheryl L. Reed, "Military Finally Gives Hispanic War Dead Proper Recognition," *Chicago Sun Times*, 3 July 2005, pp. A-18–A-19.

8. Bob Herbert, "Uncle Sam Really Wants You," *New York Times*, 16 June 2005, p. A-29.

9. Dobie, p. 40.

10. All quotes in this paragraph are from Dobie, pp. 34, 35.

11. Michael Kilian and Deborah Horan, "Enlistment Drought Spurs New Strategies," *Chicago Tribune*, 31 March 2005, p. 1.

12. Damien Cave, "Growing Problem for Military Recruiters: Parents," *New York Times*, 3 June 2005, p. B-6.

13. ibid., p. A-1.

14. Herbert, op. cit.

15. Sylvia Ashton-Warner, *Teacher* (New York: Simon & Schuster, 1963), p. 100.

16. Herbert, op. cit.

17. Chris Hedges, *What Every Person Should Know About War* (New York: Free Press, 2003), pp. 1, 7, 3, 115.

18. David R. Slavitt, ed., *Seneca: The Tragedies, Volume I* (Baltimore: Johns Hopkins University Press, 1992), p. 17.

19. Hedges, p. 8.

20. Bill Bigelow, "The Recruitment Minefield," *Rethinking Schools*, Spring 2005, p. 46.

Héctor Calderón Point of View

1. *Wild Style,* directed by Charlie Ahearn (New York: First Run Features, 1983).

2. From siadapp.dior.whs.mil/personnel/MILITARY/history/hst1205.pdf (accessed June 2, 2006).

3. From "Hispanics in the Military," a Pew Hispanic Center Fact Sheet, March 27, 2003. Available at pewhispanic.org/files/reports/17.pdf

4. Cited in Bill Berkowitz, "Latinos on the Front Lines: U.S. Military Targets Latinos for Iraq and Future Wars," *Working for Change,* 10 October 2003. Avalable at: www.workingforchange.com/ article.cfm?ItemID=15792

5. Prof. Mariscal cited a recent report called "Strategic Partnership Plan for 2002–2007" in which the U.S. Army Recruiting Command recognized that since "the Hispanic population is the fastest growing demographic in the United States and is projected to become 25% of the U.S. population by the year 2025," it has become a "priority area" for recruitment. The report is available at: www.workingforchange.com/article.cfm?ItemID=15792

6. According to the September 2002 Interim Report of the President's Advisory Commission on Educational Excellence for Hispanic Americans, as reported in Joge Mariscal, "The Future for Latinos in an Era of War and Occupation," *CounterPunch,* 18 April 2003. Available at www.counterpunch.org/mariscal04182003.html

7. Rakesh Kochhar, (2005). *Latino Labor Report, 2004: More Jobs for New Immigrants but at Lower Wages.* Washington, D.C.: Pew Hispanic Center.

8. Center for Naval Analyses, "Non-Citizen in Today's Military." Distributed by Defense Technical Information Center, April 2005. Available at:
stinet.dtic.mil/oai/oai?&verb=getRecord&metadataPrefix=html&identifier=ADA441444

9. Valerie Alvord, "Non-citizens Fight and Die for Adopted Country," *USA Today,* 8 April 2003. Available at: www.usatoday.com/news/world/iraq/2003-04-08-noncitizen-usat_x.htm

10. United States Senate Select Committee on Intelligence, Report of the Select Committee on Intelligence on the U.S. Intelligence Community's Prewar Intelligence Assessments on Iraq together with Additional Views (S. Report 108-301), 9 July 2004. Available at: intelligence.senate.gov/108301.pdf

11. Jorge Mariscal, "The Future for Latinos in an Era of War and Occupation," *Counterpunch,* 18 April 2003. Available at www.counterpunch.org/mariscal04182003.html

Chapter 9

1. Chester E. Finn, Jr., "Teaching Patriotism: An Educational Resource for Americans," *National Review Online,* 6 December 2001. Available at www.nationalreview.com/comment/comment-finnprint120601.html.

2. Chester E. Finn, "Patriotism Revisited," *Center for Education Reform,* 1 October 2001. Available at: edreform.com/index.cfm?fuseAction=document& documentID=208 &sectionID=69NEWSYEAR=2001.

3. William Damon, "What Schools Should Do to Prepare Students for Democracy," paper presented at a meeting on "Youth and Civic Engagement," sponsored by the Center for Information and Research on Learning and Citizenship, Washington, D.C., March 2005.

4. Michael Apple, "Patriotism, Pedagogy, and Freedom: On the Educational Meanings of September 11th," *Teachers College Record,* December 2002, pp. 1760–72; Chris Coryn, James Beale, and Krista Myers, "Response to September 11: Anxiety, Patriotism, and Prejudice in the Aftermath of Terror," *Current Research in Social Psychology,* March 2004, pp. 1–23; and M. Samuel Haque, "Patriotism Versus Imperialism," *Peace Review,* 15, 2003, pp. 451–56.

5. Patrick G. Coy, Gregory M. Maney, and Lynne M. Woehrle, "Contesting Patriotism," *Peace Review,* 15, 2003, pp. 463–70; and Martha Nussbaum and Joshua Cohen, eds., *For Love of Country: Debating the Limits of Patriotism* (Boston: Beacon, 1996).

6. John Dewey, *Democracy and Education* (New York: Free Press, 1916), pp. 83, 87.

7. Igor Primoratz, *Patriotism* (Amherst, NY: Humanity Books, 2002).

8. Stephen Nathanson, "In Defense of 'Moderate Patriotism,'" *Ethics, 99,* 1989, p. 535.

9. Benjamin W. Barber, "Constitutional Faith," in Nussbaum and Cohen, p. 32.

10. R. Freeman Butts, *Civitas: A Framework for Civic Education* (Calabasas, CA: Center for Civic Education, 1991), p. 31.

11. Robert T. Schatz, Ervin Staub, and Howard Lavine, "On the Varieties of National Attachment: Blind Versus Constitutional Patriotism," *Political Psychology*, March 1999, pp. 151–74.

12. Seymour Feshbach, "Attachment Processes in Political Ideology: Patriotism and Nationalism," in Jacob Gerwitz and William Kurtines, eds., *Intersections with Attachment* (Hillsdale, NJ: Lawrence Erlbaum, 1991), pp. 207–26.

13. Schatz, Staub, and Lavine, p. 153.

14. Ervin Staub, *The Roots of Evil: The Origins of Genocide and Other Group Violence* (New York: Cambridge University Press, 1989).

15. Harwood Institute, *Post-September 11th Patriotism, Civic Involvement and Expectations for the 2002 Election Season* (Bethesda, MD: Harwood Institute for Public Innovation, 2002).

16. For information on the campaign, see www.cms-ca.org/index.html. For a report summarizing findings from our broader study, see www.cms-ca.org/civic_survey_final.pdf

17. Participating schools were selected from various geographic areas to provide a portrait of current conditions representing a range of factors including student race, ethnicity, and academic performance levels. The indicator of general patriotism was adapted from items used in the civic education study by the International Association for the Evaluation of Educational Achievement. (Information on the study is available at www.wam.umd.edu/~jtpurta/studentQ.htm.) The measures of blind and constructive patriotism were modified from Schatz, Staub, and Lavine, op. cit. The indicator of active patriotism was developed by the Harwood Institute (www.theharwoodinstitute.org). All items within the scales for constructive patriotism, blind patriotism, active patriotism, and general patriotism were entered into a factor analysis and emerged as four distinct scales. Please contact the authors at jkahne@mills.edu for more details on the measures used in this study.

18. There are numerous ways to deepen the knowledge base in this area. We are currently undertaking a study, for example, that looks at the ways particular classroom contexts and opportunities influence patriotic commitments.

19. Students, we should point out, were not uniformly positive. Only 28% agreed, for example, that "people in government care about what people like me and my family need."

20. Consistent with this finding, 30% of students in a national study reported that the most common theme in their U.S. history and social studies classes had been "great American heroes and the virtues of the American system of government," while only 11% said the most common theme was "problems facing the country today." See Peter Levine and Mark H. Lopez, *Themes Emphasized in Social Studies and Civics Classes: New Evidence* (Washington, D.C.: Center for Information and Research on Civic Learning and Engagement, 2004).

21. Stephen Macedo et al., *Democracy at Risk: How Political Choices Undermine Citizen Participation, and What We Can Do About It* (Washington, D.C.: Brookings Institution, 2005).

22. We judged an individual to be endorsing committed patriotism and constructive patriotism if his or her average response on the items measuring those criteria was greater than 3 and if his or her average response on the items measuring uncritical patriotism was less than 3 (on a 5-point scale on which 3 represented neutral). Only one item measured an individual's commitment to active patriotism, so in that instance, a 4, which signified agreement, was required to be considered an endorsement. Had we used 4 as our standard for endorsing all given forms of patriotism, the percentage of students endorsing a democratic vision of patriotism would have been even lower.

23. Macedo et al., op. cit.

24. Cynthia Gibson and Peter Levine, *The Civic Mission of Schools* (New York: Carnegie Corporation of New York and the Center for Information and Research on Civic Learning, 2003).

25. Margaret Nash, "How to Be Thankful for Being Free: Searching for a Convergence of Discourses on Teaching Patriotism, Citizenship, and United States History," *Teachers College Record, 107,* 2005, pp. 214–40.

26. Jennifer Piscatelli, "Pledge of Allegiance," *Education Commission of the States,* 2003. Available at: www.ecs.org/clearinghouse/47/20/4720.htm

27. Samuel Ichiye Hayakawa in quotegarden.com/patriotism.html

28. See Walter Parker's essay in this book.

Chapter 10

The research reported in this paper was funded by the Center for Information and Research in Civic Learning and Engagement, the Carnegie Corporation of New York, and Brown University. The views expressed are the authors alone.

1. Walter Parker, "Public Schools Are Hotbeds of Democracy," *Seattle Post Intelligencer,* 2006, p. B7.

2. J. Hibbing & E. Theiss-Morse, *Stealth Democracy: Americans' Beliefs About How Government Should Work.* (New York: Cambridge University Press, 2002).

3. ibid.

karen emily suurtamm Point of View

1. "ACLU of Virginia Seeks Guarantee of Student Free Speech in Prince William Schools." Press release (4/24/2006).

2. *Pickering v. Board of Education,* 391 U.S. 563, 568 (1968).

3. ibid.

4. *Russo v. Central School District No. 1,* 469 F.2d 623 (2d Cir. 1972).

5. *James v. Board of Education,* 461 F.2d 566 (2d cir. 1972).

6. *Rankin v. McPherson* 1987.

7. *Melzer v. Board of Education of the city of New York,* No. 02-7338 (2d Cir. July 16, 2003).

8. *Tinker v. Des Moines Community School District,* 383 U.S. 503 (1969).

9. *Bethel v. Fraser,* 478 U.S. 675 (1986).

10. *Tinker v. Des Moines Community School District,* 383 U.S. 503 (1969).

11. *Nixon v. Northern Local School district board of Education,* 2005 WL 2000706 (S.D. Ohio Aug. 18, 2005).

12. *Guzick v. Drebus,* 431 F.2d 594 (6th Cir. 1970).

13. *Nixon v. Northern Local School district board of Education,* 2005 WL 2000706 (S.D. Ohio Aug. 18, 2005).

Chapter 11

1. Molson Canadian advertisement, first aired in April 2000; actor: Jeff Douglas, Canadian; director: Kevin Donovan, American. Available at: www.canadianaconnection. net/iam.html.

2. See for example, John Ralston Saul, *Voltaire's Bastards: The Dictatorship of Reason in the West* (Toronto: Viking, 1992).

3. John Ralston Saul, *Reflections of a Siamese Twin: Canada at the End of the Twentieth Century* (Toronto: Penguin, 1998).

4. Elspeth Deir and John Fielding, *Canada: The Story of a Developing Nation* (Toronto: McGraw-Hill Ryerson, 2000), pp. 336–37.

5. Ministry of Education for Alberta Curriculum Guideline, *Social Studies* (Elementary), 1990, Grade 3, p. 23.

6. *Ontario School Geography, Authorized by the Minister of Education for Use in Forms IV and V of the Public Schools and in the Continuation and High Schools* (Toronto: Educational Book Company Limited, 1910), p. 83.

7. Ministry of Education Curriculum Guidelines, British Columbia, Social Studies K to 7, 1998.

8. Government of the Northwest Territories, "Education, Culture, and Employment Curriculum Guideline, Junior Secondary Social Studies," 2002, n.p.

9. George F. Tomkins, *A Common Countenance: Stability and Change in the Canadian Curriculum* (Scarborough, Ont.: Prentice-Hall, 1986), p. 226.

10. Ontario Department of Education, Grades IX and X Social Studies, History Curriculum Guidelines, 1952, pp. 9–10.

11. Ministry of Education, Ontario Curriculum, Grades 9 and 10, Canadian and World Studies, Civics, pp. 65–69.

Chapter 12

1. Quotes from primary sources are footnoted but, unless otherwise noted, references to the history of patriotism are drawn from Cecilia Elizabeth O'Leary, *To Die For: The Paradox of American Patriotism* (Princeton, NJ: Princeton University Press, 1999); references to homeland security and contemporary right-wing patriotism are drawn from Tony Platt and Cecilia O'Leary, "Patriot Acts," *Social Justice*, *30*(1), 2003; references to instituting rituals of patriotism in the schools following September 11 are drawn from Cecilia O'Leary and Tony Platt, "Pledging Allegiance Does Not a Patriot Make," *Los Angeles Times*, 25 November 2001, editorial page.

2. Frederick Douglass, "January First, 1863," *Douglass' Monthly*, January 1863, 769–70.

3. Joseph W. Morton Jr., ed., *Sparks from the Campfire; or Tales of the Old Veterans* (Philadelphia: Keystone, 1895), n.p.

4. Amos Webber, quoted in Nick Salvatore, *We All Got History: The Memory Books of Amos Webber* (New York: Times Books, 1996), 159–60.

5. Woman's Relief Corps (WRC), *Proceedings of the Third National Convention*, 1885, 57.

6. Woman's Relief Corps (WRC), *Journal of the Thirty-Second National Convention* (Boston: Griffith-Stilling, 1914), 69.

7. *Public Opinion*, 3 March 1888, 510.

8. "The Relief Corps: News and Gossip of the Great Auxiliary," *National Tribune*, 5 August 1897.

9. Francis Bellamy, "Story of the Pledge of Allegiance," 37.

10. Woodrow Wilson, *A History of the American People* (New York: Harper & Brothers, 1902), 4:271, 312, and 5:46, 60, 115–16.

11. W.E.B. Du Bois, *Black Reconstruction in American: An Essay Toward a History of the Part Which Black Folk Played in the Attempt to Reconstruct Democracy in American, 1860–1880* (1935; reprint, New York: Atheneum, 1970), 714.

12. "Hubert Eaves Refuses to Salute the U.S. Flag," *Chicago Defender*, 25 March 1916, reel 5,Tuskegee Clipping File, Howard University, Washington, D.C.

13. "Pledge by Foreign Born," *New York Times*, 5 July 1918, 2.

14. Larry Witham, "If It Says 'God,' So Be It," *Washington Times*, 28 June 2002. Available at: http://www.washtimes.com/national/

Chapter 13

I would like to thank the Social Sciences and Humanities Research Council of Canada, the Center for Information and Research on Civic Learning and Engagement, and the University of Ottawa Research Chair program for funding the research and writing of this essay. All opinions expressed are the author's own. I am also grateful to karen suurtamm and Alessandra Iozzo-Duval for research assistance and Barbara Leckie, Joseph Kahne, Bruce Smith, and Risë Koben for feedback on earlier drafts.

1. Nebraska State Board of Education, "Board Minutes," 1–2 November 2001 (revised following 7 December 2001 meeting).

2. Jennifer Piscatelli, "Pledge of Allegiance," *State Notes: Character and Civic Education*, Education Commission of the States, August 2003.

3. "President Introduces History and Civic Education Initiatives," remarks of the President on Teaching American History and Civic Education Initiative, 17 September 2002. Available at: www.whitehouse.gov.

4. Martha Nussbaum, *For Love of Country: Debating the Limits of Patriotism* (Cambridge, MA: Beacon, 2002), p. 29.

5. C. Douglas Lummis, *Radical Democracy* (Ithaca, NY: Cornell University Press, 1996), p. 37.

6. Henry Steele Commager, *Freedom and Order: A Commentary on the American Political Scene* (New York: George Braziller, 1966), p. 117.

7. See also, Michael Parenti, *Superpatriotism: How Hype, Fear, and Mindless Flag-waving Are Supplanting Informed Debate, Commitment to Democracy, and Real Patriotism* (San Francisco: City Lights, 2004).

8. Brumberg, Stephan F. "New York city Schools March Off to War: The Nature and Extent of Participation of the City Schools in the Great War—April 1917–June 1918," *Urban Education, 24*(4), 1990, 440–475.

9. New York City Board of Education, *Journal of the Board of Education of the City of New York, 1917* (Vols. I, II) (New York: Anchor, 1917) p. 540. Cited in Brumberg, 1990, p. 446.

10. For an interesting take on the significance of post-9/11 expressions of patriotism, including the proliferation of flags across the country, see David Foster Wallace, "The View from Mrs. Thompson's," in *Consider the Lobster: And Other Essays*. (New York: Little, Brown, 2005).

11. See archive.columbiatribune.com/2005/feb/20050201news003.asp.

12. National Public Radio, "Citizen Student: Teaching Patriotism in Time of War," 6 February 2003.

13. Cited in Nat Hentoff, "The Patriotism Enforcers: Miseducating the Young on Freedom," *Village Voice*, 2–8 January 2002.

14. U.S. House of Representatives, Committee on Un-American Activities, Investigation of Communist Activities, New York Area (Entertainment): Hearings, 84th Congress, 18 August 1955. Available at historymatters.gmu.edu/d/6457.

15. U.S. House of Representatives, Committee on Un-American Activities, Investigation of the Unauthorized Use of U.S. Passports, 84th Congress, Part 3, 12 June 1956, in Eric Bentley, ed., *Thirty Years of Treason: Excerpts from Hearings Before the House Committee on Un-American Activities, 1938–1968* (New York: Viking, 1971), p. 770.

16. William Sloane Coffin, *Credo* (London: John Knox, 2005).

17. Many of the examples cited here can be found in Peter Dreier and Dick Flacks, "Patriotism and Progressivism," *Peace Review*, December 2003, p. 399.

18. Carroll, James, "What We Love About America," *The Boston Globe*, 3 July 2006, 17.

19. See www.loc.gov/today/pr/2003/03-095.html.

20. ACLU, *Freedom Under Fire: Dissent in Post-9/11 America* (New York: American Civil Liberties Union, 2003); and Kathleen Kennedy Manzo, "Teachers Grapple with Wartime Role," *Education Week*, 20 March 2003, p. 27.

21. "W. Va. Student Suspended for Starting Anti-War Club: School Says Fliers Disrupted Educational Environment," *Student Press Law Center Report*, Winter 2002, p. 7.

22. Chris Frates, "High School Junior Suspended After Posting Anti-War Fliers," *Denver Post*, 28 February 2003.

23. National Coalition for History, "Senator Alexander's 'American History and Civics Education' Bill Passes Senate," *Washington Update*, 27 June 2003.

24. "Senator Alexander's American History and Civics Bill Passes Senate Unanimously," press release, Sen. Alexander's office, 20 June 2003.

25. Hofstadter is quoted by Sen. Alexander in "Remarks of Senator Lamar Alexander on the Introduction of His Bill: The American History and Civics Education Act," 4 March 2003.

26. "Beware Leftists in Our Schools!!!," anonymous parent posting, Southern Maryland Online chat forum, 2003, http://forums.somd.com.

27. See, for example, Bree Picower's curriculum, "An Unnatural Disaster," which asks students to consider the many interlocking causes of the extensive damage of Katrina and its aftermath, especially for the African American population of New Orleans (www.nycore.org); and "Washin' Away," Ian McFeat's mock-trial activity for Rethinking Schools (www.rethinkingschools.org) that asks students to explore the roles various people and contexts played in the Katrina tragedy. For contrast, see the MindOH Foundation's Hurricane Katrina resources that include, for example, "Thinking It Through: Why Do Bad Things Happen to Good People?" This activity opens with "Life is not always fair. Bad things happen to good people. . . . We may be able to make educated guesses about Mother Nature's weather patterns, but . . ." (www.mindohfoundation.org/hurricanekatrina.htm).

28. Harry C. Boyte, "A Different Kind of Politics: John Dewey and the Meaning of Citizenship in the 21st Century," Dewey Lecture, University of Michigan, Ann Arbor, 1 November 2002, p. 11.

29. Some resources for getting started in seeking such programs include Rethinking Schools (www.rethinkingschools.org); Educators for Social Responsibility (www.esrnational.org); New York Times lessons (www.nytimes.com/learning); American Social History Project: Center for Media and Learning (www.historymatters.gmu.edu); and Teaching for Change (www.teachingforchange.org).

30. Karen Suurtamm, project director for Democratic Dialogue, did the lion's share of research for and writing of the descriptions of El Puente Academy and La Escuela Fratney Elementary School.

31. Catherine Capellaro, "When Small Is Beautiful: An Interview with Héctor Calderón," Rethinking Schools, Summer 2005.

32. Calderón, Héctor. (2006). Personal communication.

33. Bill Carter and Felicity Barringer, "In Patriotic Time, Dissent Is Muted," New York Times, 28 September 2001.

34. Nel Noddings, "What Have We Learned," in Educating Citizens for Global Awareness (New York: Teachers College Press, 2005) pp. 122–135.

35. Stephen Thornton, Incorporating Internationalism in the Social Studies Curriculum, in Noddings, Nel, ed., 2005, pp. 81–92. See also, Stephen Thornton, Teaching Social Studies That Matters: Curriculum for Active Learning (New York: Teachers College Press, 2005).

36. See for example, Robert Stevens, "A Thoughtful Patriotism," from the collection of 9/11 curriculum on the website of the National Council for Social Studies (www.socialstudies.org). Educators for Social Responsibility has a number of excellent curriculum examples under the umbrella title "Reflecting on 9/11" on their New York City chapter website: www.esrmetro.org/reflectingon911.html. See also, Facing History and Ourselves: www.facinghistory.org; Rethinking Schools: www.rethinkingschools.org, especially lesson plans by Bill Bigelow; National Education Association: www.neahin.org. Links to other curricula and classroom materials can be found at www.democraticdialogue.com/patriotism.

37. Dennis Gilbert, "Hamilton College Patriotism Poll: Eleven Key Findings," 20 March 2003, Question 17, Appendix, p. 7. Available at: www.hamilton.edu/levitt/surveys/patriotism/patriotismreport.pdf.

About the Editor and Contributors

William Ayers <bayers@uic.edu> is a distinguished professor of education and senior university scholar at the University of Illinois at Chicago and author of *Teaching Toward Freedom: Moral Commitment and Ethical Action in the Classroom* (Beacon, 2004) and *Teaching the Personal and the Political* (Teachers College Press, 2004).

Michael J. Bader <DrBader@aol.com> is a psychologist and psychoanalyst with over twenty-five years experience, currently practicing in San Francisco. He has been on the progressive edge of his field, publishing a series of important articles that attempt to humanize psychotherapy and make it more practically effective without sacrificing depth. In addition, Dr. Bader has published a series of groundbreaking essays in *Tikkun* magazine and the online journal *Alternet.org,* that analyze the intersection of psychology and politics. Dr. Bader is one of the founders of the Institute for Change, a leadership development program currently associated with the Service Employees International labor union (SEIU).

Bill Bigelow <bbpdx@aol.com> is an editor of *Rethinking Schools* magazine. His latest book is *The Line Between Us: Teaching About the Border and Mexican Immigration* (Rethinking Schools, 2006).

Héctor Calderón <www.elpuente.us> is an educator, activist, and one of the developing members of El Puente Academy for Peace and Justice in the Williamsburg neighborhood of Brooklyn, New York, where he currently serves as principal. He is the recipient of the New Leaders for New Schools Fellowship, a nationally recognized principal's training program. He was awarded the Alex E. Morrisey Award for Excellence in Journalism and has been featured in *Dollars and Sense,* the *Village Voice, The Source,* and *Human Rights and Wrongs* on PBS. Calderón lives in Bushwick, Brooklyn with his wife, Jennifer, and their sons, Gabriel and Camilo.

Robby Cohen <rpc6@nyu.edu> is a historian and is the chair of NYU's Department of Teaching and Learning. He is the author of *When the Old Left Was Young: Student Radicals and America's First Mass Student Movement, 1929–1941,* editor of *Dear Mrs. Roosevelt: Letters from Children of the Great Depression,* and co-editor (with Reginald E. Zelnik) of *The Free Speech Movement: Reflections on Berkeley in the 1960s.* He is currently writing a biography of Mario Savio.

Sharon Anne Cook <scook@uottawa.ca> is Professor at the University of Ottawa with a joint appointment to the Faculty of Education and Department of History. Her research interests include the teaching of History, Civics and Democratic engagement, peace education, the history of moral regulation in formal and informal education, and the gendered and classed meanings of forbidden acts such as smoking and drinking. Among her recent publications is *Framing Our Past: Canadian Women's History* *in the Twentieth Century,* which she edited with Lorna R. McLean and Kate O'Rourke (McGill-Queen's University Press, 2001).

Edwin C. Darden is an attorney and Director of Education Policy for Appleseed, a network of non-profit, public interest law firms in 16 states and Mexico. His career includes serving as senior staff attorney at the National School Boards Association, Director of the Center for Urban Schools Program at the New York State School Boards Association, and most recently as Managing Partner of his own K–12 education law and policy firm, called EdAdvocacy. Mr. Darden is also author of the School Law column for *American School Board Journal* magazine. He holds a law degree from Georgetown University Law Center and serves on the Board of Directors of the Education Law Association.

Peter Dreier <dreier@oxy.edu> is E.P. Clapp Distinguished Professor of Politics and director of the Urban and Environmental Policy Program at Occidental College. He contributes regularly to *The Nation, The American Prospect,* and the *Los Angeles Times* about political issues and is coauthor of *The Next Los Angeles: The Struggle for a Livable City* (University of California Press), *Place Matters: Metropolitics for the 21st Century* (University Press of Kansas), and *Regions That Work* (University of Minnesota Press). He teaches courses on community organizing, social movements, urban politics, and work and labor, and works closely with many community organizations, labor unions, and nonprofit organizations.

Delaine Eastin joined the Mills faculty in fall of 2004 as a Distinguished Visiting Professor of Educational Leadership. Prior to joining the Mills College faculty, Professor Eastin served for eight years as the California State Superintendent of Public Instruction (SPI), the first and only woman in history to hold that position. As SPI, she managed more than 30% of the state of California's budget and oversaw the education of 6.1 million children. As SPI, Eastin championed state standards and assessments aligned to standards, reduced class size in kindergarten through third grade, and strengthened arts education and hands-on science. She fought to rebuild California's school libraries and to wire schools for technology. She was the architect of the innovative Net Days, copied nationally in more than forty states and internationally in more than forty countries. Professor Eastin has been an advocate for substantial increases in school construction funding, improved school nutrition, universal preschool, and greater civic engagement of students. Prior to serving as SPI, she served 8 years in the California State Assembly and chaired the Assembly Education Committee.

Chester E. Finn Jr. is a senior fellow at the Hoover Institution and president and trustee of the Thomas B. Fordham Foundation. Finn serves as a member of the advisory boards for many groups, including the National Association of Scholars, Center of the American Experiment, and Centre for Policy Studies. Formerly, he was a senior fellow of the Hudson Institute (1995 through 1998); founding partner and senior scholar with the Edison Project (1992 through 1994); and assistant secretary for research and improvement and counselor to the secretary of the U.S. Department of Education (1985 to 1988). He is the author of 14 books, including *Leaving No Child Behind: Options for Kids in Failing Schools,* co-edited with Frederick M. Hess; *Charter Schools in Action: Renewing Public Education,* co-authored with Bruno V. Manno and Gregg Vanourek; *The Educated Child: A Parent's Guide from Pre-School Through Eighth Grade,* co-authored with William J. Bennett and John Cribb; and *What Do Our 17-Year-Olds Know?* written with Diane Ravitch. Finn has written more than 350 articles for such publications as the *Weekly Standard,* the *Christian Science Monitor,* the *Wall Street Journal, Commentary,* the *Public Interest,* the *Washington Post,* the *Chronicle of Higher Education, Harvard Business Review,* the *American Spectator,* the *Boston Globe,* and the *New York Times.*

Dick Flacks <rflacks@igc.org> is professor of sociology at the University of California, Santa Barbara. He has written widely on the left in American politics and culture, including Making History: The American Left and the American Mind (1989). His weekly radio program in Santa Barbara, "Culture of Protest," explores the intertwining of music, politics, and protest; it has been on the air for nearly twenty-five years. He is working on a book, Playing for Change, which deals with these themes.

Louis Ganzler <lmganzler@wisc.edu> is a doctoral student in Curriculum and Education at the University of Wisconsin–Madison. He is the primary research associate for a longitudinal study about how deliberating controversial issues in high school courses influences civic learning and participation. The study is housed at the Wisconsin Center for Education Research. Previously, he was a social studies high school teacher in California.

Gerald Graff <ggraff@uic.edu> Professor of English and Education at the University of Illinois at Chicago, is the author of *Professing Literature: An Institutional History* (1987), *Clueless in Academe: How Schooling Obscures the Life of the Mind* (2003), and (with Cathy Birkenstein-Graff) *"They Say/I Say": The Moves That Matter in Academic Writing* (2006). He has been elected President of the Modern Language Association of America for 2008.

Maxine Greene <ogreen@nyc.rr.com> is Professor of Philosophy and Education, Emeritus, at Teachers College; Philosopher-in-Residence at the Lincoln Center Institute; past-President of the American Educational Research Association; and author of *The Dialectic of Freedom* and other books that focus on the social imagination. Maxine is one of those who remembers what it was like to be patriotic in the March on Washington and (later) when protesting the war in Vietnam.

Diana Hess <dhess@education.wisc.edu> is an Associate Professor in the Department of Curriculum and Instruction at the University of Wisconsin-Madison. She is the principal investigator for a longitudinal study about how deliberating controversial issues in high school courses influences civic learning and participation. The study is housed at the Wisconsin Center for Education Research.

Robert Jensen <rjensen@uts.cc.utexas.edu> is a journalism professor at the University of Texas at Austin and board member of the Third Coast Activist Resource Center (http://thirdcoastactivist.org). He is the author of *The Heart of Whiteness: Race, Racism, and White Privilege, Citizens of the Empire: The Struggle to Claim Our Humanity* (both from City Lights Books), and *Writing Dissent: Taking Radical Ideas from the Margins to the Mainstream* (Peter Lang).

Joseph Kahne <jkahne@mills.edu> is the Abbie Valley Professor of Education and is Dean of the School of Education at Mills College. He publishes regularly on the democratic purposes of education and on urban school reform. He is currently conducting a statewide study of the civic/democratic commitments, capacities, and activities of high school students in California and of the distribution and impact of school-based opportunities that aim to develop citizens for democratic citizenship. He is also conducting a longitudinal study of the civic implications of young people's engagement with the internet and other forms of digital media. Professor Kahne serves in an advisory capacity to several school districts, civic education organizations, and foundations.

Joan Kent Kvitka has taught global citizens in Portland, Oregon, and led student ambassadors to China. She remains loyal to democratic ideals while assisting on documentaries about Mikhail Gorbachev and Václav Havel. She recently transitioned from the classroom to become the Cultural Education Director of the Portland Classical Chinese Garden.

Gloria Ladson-Billings is the Kellner Family Professor of Urban Education in the Department of Curriculum & Instruction and Faculty Affiliate in the Department of Educational Policy Studies at the University of Wisconsin-Madison. She is the immediate past president of the American Educational Research Association. Ladson-Billings's research examines the pedagogical practices of teachers who are successful with African American students. She also investigates Critical Race Theory applications to education. She is the author of the critically acclaimed books, *The Dreamkeepers: Successful Teachers of African American Children, Crossing Over to Canaan: The Journey of New Teachers in Diverse Classrooms,* and *Beyond the Big House: African American Educators on Teacher Education,* as well as more than fifty journal articles and book chapters. She is the former editor of the *American Educational Research Journal* and a member of several editorial boards. Her work has won numerous scholarly awards including the H. I. Romnes Faculty Fellowship, The Spencer Post-Doctoral Fellowship, and the Palmer O. Johnson outstanding research award. In 2002, she was awarded an honorary doctorate for Umeå University in Umeå, Sweden. During the 2003–2004 academic year she was a fellow at the Center for Advanced Study in the Behavioral Sciences in Stanford, California. In fall of 2004 she received the George and Louise Spindler Award from the Council on Anthropology and Education for significant and ongoing contributions to the field of educational anthropology. In the spring of 2005 she was elected to the National Academy of Education and the National Society for the Study of Education.

James W. Loewen <jloewen@zoo.uvm.edu>. His book, *Lies My Teacher Told Me: Everything Your American History Textbook Got Wrong* (1994), is perhaps the best-selling book by a living sociologist. It was followed in 1999 by *Lies Across America: What Our Historic Sites Get Wrong.* In 2005, the New Press published *Sundown Towns,* which shows that thousands of communities across the United States kept out people of color for decades, and that some still do. Loewen has given scores of workshops to teacher groups across the United States, promoting a more honest view of our past.

Deborah Meier <dmeier@taconic.net> is currently a senior scholar at New York University. Beginning in the mid-1960s as an early childhood teacher, Meier has been involved for more than forty years inside public K–12 schools in Chicago, New York, and Boston. She is the author of many books, including *Leave No Child Behind, In Schools We Trust,* and *The Power of Their Ideas* (all from Beacon Press). She is a recipient of a MacArthur Award for her work in schools–particularly for the Central Park East schools in East Harlem. She is known as an advocate for public school choice, small schools, and performance-based assessment as means toward creating a more equitable and democratic society. At present she is working on connecting democratic ideas and K–12 schooling, as well as preserving the concept of play; fantasy; and hands-on, child-initiated craftsmanship to the agenda of early childhood education, which is increasingly endangered by the standardization movement.

Ellen Middaugh <emiddaugh@gmail.com> is currently a doctoral student in Human Development at the University of California at Berkeley's Graduate School of Education and is a Researcher in the Institute for Civic Leadership at Mills College. For several years now, she has been conducting both qualitative and quantitative studies of civic education and law-related education programs, specifically, and of civic and political socialization more generally. Her research interests focus on cultural and social contextual influences on development of youth civic identity. She has published recently in *Phi Delta Kappan* and the *Journal of Curriculum and Supervision.*

Pedro Noguera <pedro.noguera@nyu.edu> is Professor in NYU's Steinhardt School of Education and Director of the Center for Research on Urban Schools and Globalization. An urban sociologist, Noguera's scholarship and research focuses on the ways in which schools are influenced by social and economic conditions in the urban environment. Noguera has published over one hundred research articles, monographs, and research reports on topics such as urban school reform, conditions that promote student achievement, youth violence, the potential impact of school choice and vouchers on urban public schools, and race and ethnic relations in American society. His work has appeared in several major research journals and many are available online at inmotionmagazine.com. He is the author of *The Imperatives of Power: Political Change and the Social Basis of Regime Support in Grenada* (Peter Lang, 1997), *City Schools and the American Dream* (Teachers College Press, 2003), *Beyond Resistance* (Routledge, 2006), and his most recent book *Unfinished Business: Closing the Achievement Gap in Our Nation's Schools* (Josey Bass, 2006).

Cecilia O'Leary <cecilia_oleary@csumb.edu> is a professor of history at California State University Monterey Bay (CSUMB). She is the author of *To Die For: The Paradox of American Patriotism* (Princeton University Press, 1999). O'Leary has been interviewed by numerous newspapers and radio programs, has appeared on public television, and has authored several articles on the history of patriotism. She was a Landmarks Scholar at the National Museum of American History, a Smithsonian Institution, and continues to consult on exhibitions. Over the last five years she has been the campus leader of the Visible Knowledge Project (VKP) at CSUMB. VKP is a $4 million project aimed at improving the quality of college and university teaching through a focus on both student learning and faculty development in technology-enhanced environments. Additionally, O'Leary is on the editorial board of the journal *Social Justice* and edited a special issue of the journal, "Pedagogies for Social Change" (vol. 29, no. 4, Winter 2002). Most recently she was a co-researcher with Anthony M. Platt for *Bloodlines: Recovering Hitler's Nuremberg Laws, From Patton's Trophy to Public Memorial* (Paradigm Publishers, 2006).

Walter C. Parker is professor of education and adjunct professor of political science at the University of Washington. His research specializations are the civic development of youth and social studies curriculum and instruction K–12. Parker is the research and practice editor for the journal *Social Education*, and he currently is investigating the new international education movement in schools. His books include *Educating the Democratic Mind* (1996), *Education for Democracy: Curricula, Contexts, Assessments* (2002), *Teaching Democracy: Unity and Diversity in Public Life* (2003), and *Social Studies in Elementary Education* (2005).

Charles M. Payne teaches African American studies, history, and sociology at Duke University, where he holds the Sally Dalton Robinson chair. His areas of research interest include urban education, social inequality, social change, and modern African American history. He is the author of *Getting What We Ask For: The Ambiguity of Success and Failure in Urban Education* (1984), the prize-winning *I've Got the Light of Freedom: The Organizing Tradition in the Mississippi Civil Rights Movement* (1995), and the forthcoming *So Much Reform, So Little Change: The Persistence of Failure in Urban School Systems* (2006). He is co-editor of two anthologies, *Time Longer Than Rope: A Century of African American Activism, 1850–1950* (2003) and the forthcoming *Teach Freedom: The African American Tradition of Education for Liberation* (2006).

Diane Ravitch <dr19@nyu.edu> is Research Professor of Education at New York University. She is a historian of education who has written many books, including *The Great School Wars: New York City, 1805–1973; The Troubled Crusade: American Education, 1945–1980; The Revisionists Revised: A Critique of the Radical Attack on the Schools; The Schools We Deserve; Left Back: A Century of Battles Over School Reform;* and *The Language Police: How Pressure Groups Restrict What Students Learn.* She served as Assistant Secretary of Education from 1991–1993. She was appointed to the National Assessment Governing Board from 1997–2004. She is a senior fellow at the Brookings Institution and the Hoover Institution.

Cindy Sheehan, a founding member of Gold Star Families for Peace, gained international attention in August 2005 when she camped outside President George W. Bush's Texas ranch for five weeks. Sheehan's son, Army Spc. Casey A. Sheehan, was killed in Sadr City, Baghdad, on April 4, 2004.

karen emily suurtamm <kesuurtamm@hotmail.com> served for one year as project director for Democratic Dialogue in the Faculty of Education at the University of Ottawa after completing her M.A. in English Literature from Concordia University. She is currently pursuing a Masters in Archival Studies from the University of Toronto and continues to be actively engaged in community organizing, focusing especially on prisoner justice issues.

Studs Terkel is the author of eleven books of oral history, including *Working* (New Press, 1997), the Pulitzer Prize-winning *The Good War: An Oral History of World War II* (New Press, 1997), and *Hope Dies Last: Keeping the Faith in Difficult Times* (New Press, 1997). He is also the host of the long-running radio program "The Studs Terkel Show." Terkel has won numerous awards, including the Presidential National Humanities Medal, the National Book Foundation Medal for Distinguished Contribution to American Letters, and the George Polk Career Award.

Denise Walsh is an assistant professor of politics and studies in women and gender at the University of Virginia, Charlottesville. She received her M.A. from Columbia University and her Ph.D. from the New School for Social Research. Her dissertation, "Just Debate: Culture and Gender Justice in the New South Africa" examines whether popular support for gender justice increases as deliberation becomes more open and inclusive. She co-edited and contributed to the March 2006 special edition of the *Journal of Southern African Studies*, titled "Women and the Politics of Gender in Southern Africa." Her research interests include deliberative theory, multiculturalism, and gender politics in Southern Africa.

Joel Westheimer <joelw@uottawa.ca> is University Research Chair in Democracy and Education, professor of the social foundations of education, and co-director of Democratic Dialogue: Inquiry into Democracy, Education, and Society at the University of Ottawa. He is also John Glenn Scholar for Service Learning and Social Justice in Education at the John Glenn Institute for Public Service and Public Policy. Westheimer teaches and writes on democracy, social justice, youth activism, and community service learning. He is the author of *Among Schoolteachers* (Teachers College Press) and is currently writing a book on the commercialization of higher education. Much of his work is available online at www.DemocraticDialogue.com. Westheimer is a former musician and teacher in the New York City public schools. He lives in Ottawa, Ontario where in Winter he ice-skates to and from work.

Howard Zinn is a historian, playwright, and social activist. He was a shipyard worker and Air Force bombardier before he went to college under the GI Bill and received his Ph.D. from Columbia University. He has taught at Spelman College and Boston University, and has been a visiting professor at the University of Paris and the University of Bologna. Zinn is the author of the best-selling *A People's History of the United States: 1492–present* (HarperCollins, 2003) and many other books, including *The Zinn Reader* (Seven Stories Press 2000), *Artists in the Time of War* (Seven Stories Press, 2003), *Terrorism and War* (Seven Stories Press, 2002), and his memoir, *You Can't Be Neutral on a Moving Train* (Beacon Press, 2002). He has received the Thomas Merton Award, the Eugene V. Debs Award, the Upton Sinclair Award, and the Lannan Literary Award. He lives in Auburndale, Massachusetts.

Index